The Archetypal Pan in America

The Archetypal Pan in America examines the complex moral and ethical dilemmas that Americans have had to face over the last few decades, including the motivations for the Vietnam War; who was in control of women's productive rights; how to extend civil rights to all; protests for the historically unapologetic narrative of the genocide of Native Americans; and the growing number of school shootings since the Columbine massacre. Fontelieu suggests that the emotional pain these issues created has not resolved and that it continues to surface, in the guise of new issues, but with a similar dysfunctional pattern.

The book argues that this pattern acts in the culture in the same manner as a psychological defense system: stimulating fight, flight, or freeze reactions; requiring great stores of energy when activated; and deflecting attention from other areas. Relying on Jung's theory of the applicability of myth to psychological problems and the post-Jungian theory of cultural complexes, the myths of the Greek god Pan are used to scaffold a metaphor that informs this pattern. Fontelieu proposes that, rather than looking inward as a culture for how to accept its changing role in a global world, this pattern reinforces dysfunctional emotional responses to the reoccurring traumas of modernity, responses such as an increase in the magnetic appeal of hypermasculinity, or choosing to remain naively self-absorbed.

The Archetypal Pan in America will be of great interest to Jungian analysts and scholars of depth psychology, as well as academics and postgraduate students studying psychology, foreign studies, literary criticism, politics, and cultural studies.

Sukey Fontelieu, PhD attended the University of Essex and Pacifica Graduate Institute and is currently a professor in the Jungian and Archetypal Studies Program at Pacifica.

Research in Analytical Psychology and Jungian Studies

Series Advisor: Andrew Samuels, Professor of Analytical Psychology, Essex University, UK.

The *Research in Analytical Psychology and Jungian Studies* series features research-focused volumes involving qualitative and quantitative research, historical/archival research, theoretical developments, heuristic research, grounded theory, narrative approaches, collaborative research, practitioner-led research, and self-study. The series also includes focused works by clinical practitioners, and provides new research informed explorations of the work of C. G Jung that will appeal to researchers, academics, and scholars alike.

Books in this series:

A Japanese Jungian Perspective on Mental Health and Culture Wandering Madness
Iwao Akita
Translated by Waka Shibata and Kittredge Stephenson

Jung and Kierkegaard
Researching a Kindred Spirit in the Shadows
Amy Cook

Consciousness in Jung and Patañjali
Leanne Whitney

Shame and the Making of Art
A Depth Psychological Perspective
Deborah E. Cluff

Modern Myths and Medical Consumerism
The Asclepius Complex
Antonio Karim Lanfranchi

The Archetypal Pan in America
Hypermasculinity and Terror
Sukey Fontelieu

For more information about this series please visit: www.routledge.com/Research-in-Analytical-Psychology-and-Jungian-Studies/book-series/JUNGIANSTUDIES.

The Archetypal Pan in America

Hypermasculinity and Terror

Sukey Fontelieu

Routledge
Taylor & Francis Group
LONDON AND NEW YORK

First published 2018 by Routledge

2 Park Square, Milton Park, Abingdon, Oxfordshire OX14 4RN
52 Vanderbilt Avenue, New York, NY 10017

Routledge is an imprint of the Taylor & Francis Group, an informa business

First issued in paperback 2019

British Library Cataloguing-in-Publication Data
A catalogue record for this book is available from the British Library

Library of Congress Cataloging-in-Publication Data
A catalog record for this book has been requested

ISBN: 978-1-138-69124-7 (hbk)
ISBN: 978-0-367-46640-4 (pbk)

Typeset in Sabon
by Apex CoVantage, LLC

To my mother and father

Contents

Foreword

I had the great pleasure of working with Sukey Fontelieu on her Pan project several years ago when she was advancing toward her PhD. Now, I have the privilege of seeing her entire work, revised, expanded, and enriched by a depth psychological imagination and superb research that enriches our understanding of the Greek god Pan in *The Archetypal Pan in America: Hypermasculinity and Terror*.

First, a word or two about myths, which serve as the backdrop of her entire oeuvre. I am not alone in finding it astonishing that in twelve years of public and most private education, there does not exist one course on mythology. Emphasis continues to be on math and science, two cultural constructs that themselves grow directly from a mythic foundation. The arts, and even psychology courses, if they exist at all, are given little space in the curriculum, often excised from the school budget, or given very brief air time in students' course work. I mention this fact at the front end because, by contrast, Sukey's study of culture in many of its most salient facets, testifies that a mythic, or mytho-poetic approach, with emphasis on the cultural complexes that drive the shared values of an individual or a nation, is fiercely critical to our understanding of a rapidly shifting contemporary world, less through explanations and more by way of psycho-mythic realities that often remain unconscious whenever discussions arise regarding "solutions" to and "why" causations of critical events.

I have written elsewhere concerning myth and archetype, two of the pillars of Sukey's study, that myths "are patterned presences and expose the imprint of the archetypes, which are energy fields in themselves" (Slattery, 2012, p. 12). Moreover, as C.G. Jung reminds us, "an archetypal content expresses itself first and foremost, in metaphors" (Jung 1971, CW 9,1: par. 267). The brilliance of this study of Pan is that it develops the mythic and metaphorical force field with such depth and diversity, that Pan, in essence, is remythologized in Sukey's exploration. Her study reveals, with a poetic eye, the way in which Pan is both a myth and a metaphor. She uses his rich figural presence to explore, for instance, acts of violence in American culture, but indeed throughout the world as well as to expose a field of influences that an ego-directed, cause-effect assortment of explanations cannot hope to fathom. Her study is, then, one in which we learn how myths are birthed and formed, and how they develop, peak, and recede, making way for new myths to gain cultural traction or older myths to be resuscitated or overhauled to help us make sense of current phenomena that have universal roots in the human psyche. She performs this feat most effectively in her exploration of hypermasculinity and its accompanying terror that seems to dominate America's violent culture; hypermasculinity as both a mindset and a mythic method is used far too exclusively by the culture's commentators to understand and solve some of our intractable crises; however, such a narrow lens is doomed to fail because it avoids *unconscious forces* that shape thought patterns, behaviors, and public policy that often do little to stem the violence.

Myths aid us immeasurably in allowing a strengthening of our abilities to make and shape meaning. Agendas block such interests while myths encourage them. But only if myths themselves and in the present study, the figures that populate them, are reimagined; otherwise they will be cast into the dust heap of history as irrelevant to the postmodern world. In his own study of "Mythic Figures," James Hillman introduces the idea that no gods or goddesses, heroes or heroines may be taken on the literal level of concrete enactment, but have an invisible Hillman meaning for the soul in terms of its underworld psychic life (2007, p. 21). Such is certainly the case with the central image of this rich study of Pan's presence today.

Sukey's description in her first chapter, which outlines the entire work, offers in "Pan stalks America" an observation which resonates with Hillman's observation. She writes: "Perhaps a depth psychological perspective can better help us understand what underlies the modern era's inability to stem the anxiety over everyday problems that are on the increase in the US" (2018, p.14). Her methodology, or to use a word I favor, "mythodology," is the field of cultural complexes that C. G. Jung pioneered and that Sukey's study advances eloquently by concentrating on a single deity whose complexity and whose complexes are deeply rooted in the American psyche from the founding of our nation. Beginning from this vantage point, she reveals through a mythic imagination insights into our hunger for violence. But the author is careful to explore the two sides of Pan, as is true of the nature of any archetype: Pan as the violent, warring, raping, violator through acts of violence, but also the Pan who, she writes, "charmed the Olympians with his laughter (Athanassakis, 1976), played the pipes for the nymphs' nightlong, labyrinthine dances (Philostratus, 1931/1960), and provided sustenance from the herds and charmed his lonely hunts; . . . (Pausanias, 1935/1961). (2018, p.22)). (2018, p. 134). Pan was a leader and protector when he allied with others; "he is associated with powers that create terror and the subsequent echoes of traumatic reactions" (2018, pp. 22, 23).

When violent encounters erupt not just in a distant battle that involves our military, but closer to home, in our schools' classrooms and lunchrooms, in our churches, movie theaters, and sites of entertainment like Las Vegas, or in the privacy of our homes and neighborhoods, with greater intensity and acceleration, we have a much better chance to understand their deep psychic roots through Sukey's exploration of the god in our midst.

On the morning of Sunday, November 5, 2017 during a church service in Sutherland Springs, Texas, less than 45 miles from my home in New Braunfels, Texas, Devin Patrick Kelley walked into the First Baptist Church at 11:30 a.m. and opened fire on the congregation, killing 26 and wounding many more. He was soon shot by a neighbor of the church, tried to escape, and died shortly thereafter when he crashed his car a few miles from the site of the carnage. I visited the church less than a week later. Something mysterious, mythic, and beyond all explanations had seized me. In the now white-washed space where the congregation was terrorized and where so many died, I felt the horror of Pan's presence along with the love and grace of church parishioners mingling in the same place. I write now, 11 weeks after the shooting, with a much deeper grasp of what left us all stunned by its "senselessness," because of reading *The Archetypal Pan in America*. To a question she poses early on – can the myths and rites of Pan's cult help us understand how America can relinquish some of its self-absorption? – I would answer: without any doubt.

My own and others' proximity to Pan's rage that left us outraged, confused, and in a state of panic in its wake, certified for me the power of such a god's presence that Sukey's study has revisioned to offer another way of understanding the volatility of violence and its possibility of rearing up anywhere under any circumstances. She also underscores the ubiquity in both time and space of the gods' presences around us and that only if they are allowed to enter into our conversations wearing contemporary clothing will they remain actively present in our imaginations to assist us in plumbing what reason alone cannot but fail to apprehend. Her explorations of violence could not be more timely.

Dennis Patrick Slattery, author of *Riting Myth, Mythic Writing: Plotting Your Personal Story*. Emeritus faculty, Mythological Studies Program, Pacifica Graduate Institute, Carpinteria, California.

Dennis Patrick Slattery

Acknowledgements

There are always too many people to thank. This work was a long time in the making and began with a dream of Pan. Don Sloggy helped me see into that dream and subsequent dreams of the chthonic. That's really where it all began. Thank you, Don, for helping me sense that the gossamer thread linking me to a vast chthonic force deeply buried in the unconscious could be strengthened by my focus upon it. I researched Pan for years at the University of Lancaster with the help of Trevor Curnow and Helen Leathard, and I am grateful for their belief in me. Here in Santa Barbara, Dennis Slattery helped me stay close to the ancients in my imagination and with my research into every nook and cranny of extant text on Pan through the ages. Thank you, Dennis, for our long, winding talks and joyful discoveries together. I brought this research to Andrew Samuels at the University of Essex, and I entered a modern day forge of Hephaistos heating and pounding the research into form and meaning. Thank you, Andrew, for your brilliant intuitive insights and your insistence on the best. All the while, my Hestian friend, Janis Jennings, quietly read my endless drafts and urged me on. Thank you, Janis, for all your kind words and honest feedback. And then, of course, there is my family who has lifted me every time I was ready to let it all go, get back to reading novels on the beach and other important things, and kept me down in the basement banging on the forge until finally the very last tap of the hammer had been tapped and the last polish of the cloth had been swiped. Thank you, Justin and Mary, for helping me remember why.

Chapter 1

Pan stalks America

> O what are heroes, prophets, men
> But pipes through which the breath of Pan doth blow
> A momentary music?
>
> (Emerson, 2018)

In the US, since the turn of the millennium, violent attacks perpetrated by homegrown shooters, radical Jihadists, and rapists have increased in tandem with a rise in a type of hypermasculine leadership, a neoconservative undercurrent in the country that resurfaced as the Tea Party and is now in full display under the current President of the United States, Donald Trump. During the same time period, the amount of reported serious mental disorders have also increased (Weissman, Russell, Jay, Beasley, Malaspina, & Pegus, 2017). The relationship between these three provinces is the theme of this writing. The responses by Americans to iconic events that typify the violence are investigated and are all too often found to have led to fear-based reactions. In many US citizens, panic and/or apathy are found to be creating a stagnating psychic condition, which I am suggesting has led to the current bankruptcy of creative ideas to help find ways out of the problems.

The specific events this study focuses on are the increasing incidence of random shootings, terrorist actions, and rape in the US military, and the ways the country has, since the turn of the millennium, responded to them. In April of 1999 two high school students, Eric Harris and Dylan Klebold, walked into their local high school in Colorado and attempted to blow it up. The media coverage and community responses will be examined to expose a pattern of initial anxieties followed by a general apathy. Why have random shootings not diminished and instead are increasing at alarming rates worldwide, but especially in the US (Gladwell, 2015)? Why is there is no organized response, based on a sense of community responsibility, to the increase in isolation and desperation in disenfranchised youth, especially young men? Why is there no rational response to gun control reform in a nation where gun sales increase dramatically with each incidence of violence

(Aisch & Keller, 2016)? Why have random shootings not diminished and instead are increasing at alarming rates worldwide, but especially in the US (Gladwell, 2015)?

Then, two years later, the 9/11 terrorist attacks initiated the same pattern of anxiety followed by apathy in the US as reflected in the well-documented rise in anxiety over terrorism and safety in general in the United States. That level of anxiety has not returned to pre-9/11 levels (Holman & Silver, 2011). A fear-based citizenry has allowed the Bush, Obama, and Trump's administrations retaliatory and militant responses to Jihadist terrorists. This has led to the government's participation in a constant ongoing multi-theater war against "terrorism."

Apathetic reactions have also allowed violence to go unchecked in the increasing levels of rape and sexual abuse reported in the military by fellow military persons. The military has, essentially, allowed the raping to continue as long as it is being ignored by the government and the mass media (Kirby, 2012). What is compelling these men to rape their own counterparts?

These three areas indicate high levels of anger in the perpetrators and disregard for the victims, both by the perpetrators and in the public reactions, since the response shows a pattern of outrage and then a paralyzed stalemate. This actually impedes constructive change. Perhaps, rather than a sanctimonious sermon on the values of civilized behavior, it is time to listen to what is making so many Americans so mad and beneath this, so frightened.

The perimeter of examining one country with global influence, the US, has been set in order to maintain an achievable focus, though the problem is not understood to be limited to the US. Clearly many problematic areas worldwide are in states of disruption or impotent stagnation, as witnessed in the aftermath to the Paris shootings of 2015 and the continual unrest in the Middle East. Perhaps a depth psychological perspective can better help us understand what underlies the modern era's inability to stem the anxiety over everyday problems that are on the increase in the US. The foundations for this enquiry will include C. G. Jung's theory of the applications of the archetypal and mythic to increase psychological understandings of human patterns of behavior (1931/1981 [CW 8]), complex theory's insights into how the psyche reacts to trauma (Jung, 1948/1960), and post-Jungian additions that consider cultural complexes to be similar to personal complexes, but are ones held mutually by members of a group (Singer & Kimbles, 2004). These theories posit that there is an archetypal level to the psychological life of humankind. But why bother with an analysis of the way the ancients personified these archetypal forces in human nature? In the words of the poet Wendell Berry, in the depths of the psyche humankind has not changed, "The intimacy with the universe that existed in the late Paleolithic period still exists in the depths of our minds" (1993, p. 18). Sometimes, problems are more easily understood when we get some perspective through distance, and so an excursion through the myths may bring new insights to the surface.

It just so happens that violence, a hypermasculine disregard for the victim, and fear are themes from Greek mythology that were personified in the myths of the goat-god Pan (Athanassakis, 1976). Pan is associated with panic and all its myriad psychological burdens. Panic is with him from the moment of his birth when his mother took one look at him and, as told in the Homeric hymn "sprang up and fled" (p. 63). Pan suffered the loss of his mother because his body was monstrous (even Hephaestus with his broken body could still count on his mother's love), which led to a recurring motif for Pan of unrequited love for the feminine. Paradoxically, Pan was the beloved of the gods. In the Homeric hymn Pan's father, Hermes, wraps him in the pelt of a hare and carries him up to Mt Olympus where he charmed the Olympians with his laughter and was named Pan, which the hymn tells us meant "all"(Athanassakis, 1976). But the themes of panic and self-absorption dogged Pan throughout his myths. His unbridled sexuality created panic in the objects of his desire. The nymphs are chased and when the union is not consummated they are indifferently set aside as "collateral damage," left behind in the myth, forever vegetating as pine trees or river reeds. They freeze and are forgotten. Yet panic is also a tool that Pan skillfully wields in his role in battle, where he found victory without the aid of his keen eyed marksmanship, but rather by instilling fear and confusion in the hearts of the enemies of his friends. Pan embodies the unexpected in battle, surprising and out-tricking his enemies (Herodotus, 1921/1960).

In the rise of serious mental disorders, and in the panicky or apathetic responses in America, is an underlying, repetitious, archetypal pattern that reflects tendencies toward the classic instinctive responses to danger: fight, flight, or freeze. This pattern of instinctive reactions resembles motifs in the Greek god of nature, Pan, and his myths about his hypermasculine relations with the nymphs and his alliances in battle.

The psychological state of hypermasculinity to be considered here has three key components. One is that it emphasizes physical prowess such as a modern self-absorption with male body size, fitness, and the sculpted or armored body look. It is also dependent on dangerous action for excitement, as can be seen in current fascinations with extreme sports, action films, and violent video games. Hypermasculinity has an obsessive side to it and leads to self-absorption in those who have fallen into this pathology (Klein, 2012). Hypermasculinity in a culture, it will be shown, promotes a barely repressed excitement at the prospect of going to war. Finally, hypermasculinity encourages callousness toward those who are different than oneself, seeing them as inferior, and so it encourages xenophobia. This disregard for the fundamental rights of others illustrates how hypermasculinity is a state in which a person is cut off from their feeling function. Cut offs such as these fuel alienation and self-centered behavior and surface in individuals in the defense of a what we will come to understand as a cultural complex that is currently acting like a forgotten anchor left overboard, dragging the ship of state to a slow crawl.

The anxiety and apathy in America can be understood as having given rise to a conservative political movement based on hypermasculinity in those in power at the highest level in the modern day US. Though hypermasculinity is referenced as a defense of personal freedom, it can be better understood as protective armor for the vulnerable fears and anxieties at the wounded core of a cultural complex, which resides within Americans who identify with the inflated idea that America is the greatest nation in the world.

Why is the psychological state of hypermasculinity thriving in today's American culture and spreading around the world? It elevates certain behaviors as superior, and as we will see, even godlike. Actually, it can be understood as a modern expression of values of purity and perfection as promoted by the early Puritans. The seeds of this psychological state can be understood as the beginning of a cultural complex and traced to the Puritan ideals of exceptionalism, which led to Manifest Destiny. These notions took form early in the nation's history and helped develop a cultural sense of identity, a unity, for the melting pot of America. The shadow aspects of these ideals, latent for hundreds of years, are going to be shown to now have burst forth in unwanted and unexpected forms.

This is not to imply that America is somehow caught up in an archetype and if Americans are made aware of this its problems will be over. The implication is rather that terrorist and other acts of violence and hypermasculine reactions are causing the pendulum-like arc of the culture to swing wildly between panic and apathy. The myths of Pan will be analyzed to try to better understand the repetitious nature of these swings and the solipsistic thinking, ideological bubbles, and growing anger that permeates America today. Since America has been, and is still, a leader in the world, its apparent impotence in the face of seemingly irresolvable moral dilemmas is observed by many and has influence worldwide. America's inability to make inroads into the causes and solutions to the increasing levels of mental and physical distress that culminate in violent behavior is of import outside its borders as well as within.

The current political solution to violence in America is to blame and punish the perpetrator, increase protection of possible targets, and attempt to profile who is the most likely to attack in the future. But evidence that these acts of violence are increasing in an epidemic-like pattern suggests that these solutions are inadequate and in some instances are contributing to the problem. For instance, profiling as a means to predict who might become a random shooter, rapist, or terrorist will never be accurate because that profile changes as the threshold for violence lowers. This follows the same pattern as that of an infectious epidemic (Gladwell, 2015; Slutkin, 2012, 2013). Taking the Columbine shootings of 1999 as "patient zero" in random shootings as example, one can see the profiles of Eric Harris and Dylan Klebold are very different from the profile of the more recent shooters in these tragedies, often referred to as either rampage shootings or school shootings. In much the same way as social psychology has evidenced a lowered threshold to looting in riots in otherwise law-abiding citizens (Ross & Nisbett, 2011), the ease to shift from being angry to acting on that anger becomes greater when others have already acted. Thus, the profile of the perpetrator changes over time. Punishing the attacker, if they are alive, is simply inadequate once a problem has become systemic. The underlying causes will not change by punishing the attackers harshly.

Trying to stop the violence by profiling and containing "at-risk" potential violators for shooters, home grown or naturalized terrorists, or rapists is like taking an anti-anxiety pill to quell a panic attack. It may work in the short run, but it has no effect, unless it actually increases the likelihood of further attacks, in the long run. This analogy is apt because anxiety, it will be shown, underlies the motivation in the perpetrators of the violence, the reactions of the American public, and both the media and the government responses to the violence. Anxiety fuels the anger and when a person is in an anxious state of mind, anxiety tends to spread into generalized worry about everything and anything.

This study makes the short leap to apply to groups concepts developed by Jung in his studies of individuals, such as the shadow, "the thing a person has no wish to be" (Jung, 1946/1977b, p. 262 [*CW* 16, para. 470]). To speak of the unconscious shadow in a culture is useful in pinpointing the unconscious destructive values in that culture. One supposition considered here is whether, just as an individual's reactions to danger is to resort to an aspect of the instinctive fight-flight-freeze pattern, societal anxiety triggers cultural reactions of the same sort. There is much evidence to support this. After 9/11, for example, the government, for many reasons, chose to respond antagonistically, to fight, while the American public reacted apathetically, froze, and trusted their leaders to do what was right. They allowed passage of the Patriot Act, have never mounted a backlash to the reduction of civil liberties so hard won centuries earlier, and instead took then President George W. Bush's advice and escaped into consumerism.

A group is made up of individuals, and when enough members of that group have individually all agreed upon behaviors, values, and social customs, it begins to shape itself into a culture (Kroeber & Kluckhohn, 1952). The values themselves are held in the psyches of the individuals and also held by the group in common (Kimbles, 2003). One can speak of group values understanding that they are not necessarily always exactly the same within each member of that group. Cultures are able to adapt and acclimate to new ideas and behaviors and are in a constant state of flux as progressive and regressive forces engage with each other. The dynamics of a culture are seen to resemble a pendulum, as long as the swinging stays in a relative state of balance the culture thrives and grows and its ideals and values change with it over time. Often this happens when the people in the culture begin to see things differently because enough of the people in a group (the tipping point) begin to come to grips with certain shadow aspects of the group (the things no one wishes to be). The pendulum then swings and change then becomes possible and possibly eminent. The value of thinking about a group or cultural shadow is that this serves to unmask the culture's impulses to passivity and inertia, which creates an atmosphere where the population tends toward accommodating to new problems by being manipulated by political forces.

Recognizing the country is in an increasing state of stress and anxiety is only a first step, and a very small one, in finding a path to reduction of that state. But we must determine where we are and then start there; at the moment the underlying anxiety in America is largely unconscious. I am an American clinician, so my approach to these concerns is based on my experience working with psychological distress in individuals and families. A psychodynamic approach to clinical work is to take a family history and to link the patterns of behavior in the past to the current problems. To deepen the analysis further, a Jungian approach is to then see what myth this person is unconsciously living out and what archetypal influences are at play. So this study will begin by looking at the history of the country and link early patterns of behavior to current problems and then consider the archetypal forces activated in America, linking the patterns found in those forces to America's past and present.

Jungian theory: complex, myth, and archetype

Chapter two will outline Jung's (1948/1960) theory of complexes and the post-Jungian theory of cultural complexes (Singer & Kimbles, 2004), based on Jung's seminal theory of complexes in individuals. The chapter explores one view of the underlying archetypes resonate in modern America. Jung (1948/1960) analyzed the origin and nature of personal complexes in his essay "A Review of the Complex Theory." He observed that complexes form out of trauma and continually interpret events to fit a viewpoint the complex holds as non-negotiable. When challenged, anxiety, panic, and avoidant behaviors can be activated and can often lead to violence (Schwartz, Beaver, & Barnes, 2015). Jung described complexes as an expression of a characteristic state of the psyche and suggested complexes arise in all people and that they always serve a function.

Jung proposed that the origin of a complex is usually traumatic, due to an irresolvable moral conflict, and that a complex becomes a splintered off part of the psyche with an inner coherence or wholeness to it. An activated complex has autonomy over the ego and is often recognized by the excessive feelings it stirs up. Complexes are most often discovered when a person is in an intense emotional state and says or does things that she or he later regrets. Upon "coming to one's senses," after being caught up in a complex, they are often dismissed as bad moods or just not being one's self that day. But complexes point to disconnects, schisms within the psyche and as Jung cautioned, "if we are to develop further we have to draw to us and drink down to the very dregs what, because of our complexes, we have held at a distance" (1954/1959a, p. 99 [*CW* 9.I, para. 184]).

In 1964, Joseph Henderson (1984) proposed that in his writings Jung had inferred a blueprint for a cultural unconscious. Henderson (1990) posited a cultural layer in the collective psyche that holds historical memories and "lies between the collective unconscious and the manifest pattern of the culture" (p. 103). Thomas Singer (2004) added to this discussion by suggesting "cultural complexes structure emotional experience and operate in the personal and collective psyche in much the same way as individual complexes, although their content might be quite different" (p. 6). A cultural complex may be active in a large group of people, but it forms within the psyches of the individuals in that group.

Life begins in relationship with, at the very least, a mother. The interrelationships between parents and child, siblings, friends, work mates, and with society as a whole comprise much of the material analyzed in psychotherapy because they are integral to a person's life. In a sense one's life is never wholly one's own and so it is not that surprising that the main defensive posture of a complex is its projection onto outside forces and people. Sorting through these misconceptions in a calming, trustworthy environment is one reason therapy is so successful at helping people to know themselves better and, hence, make better choices and solve their problems themselves. The process of individuation, or for that matter all psychotherapy, is to help individuals to know themselves more truly and this naturally means to be able to be true to who you are within the confines of society.

A concept central to this discourse is the idea that complexes form around wounded core beliefs and develop a protective defense system, a shell, to shield the traumatized core beliefs from further wounding. Cultures as well as individuals have wounded core beliefs about themselves. Samuel Kimbles (2000) emphasized that "the psychology of cultural complexes operates both in the collective psychology of the group and in the individual members of the group" (p. 2). Kimbles and Singer agree that such a struggle itself takes place on an individual basis, within the members of that culture. Kimbles suggested cultural complexes surface within individuals as a part of group functioning and that cultures always have a choice to consciously struggle with its complexes or unconsciously ignore them (2000).

Unconsciously projected emotional states in a culture, such as the seventeenth-century descriptions of Native Americans as savages, can be and are reassessed and found wanting. They then become "politically incorrect." Their causes lie in projection of the parts of ourselves, in this case savagery, that need to become conscious and then contained by the person or culture. Affective states in a cultural complex are seen in defensive over-reactions, apathetic regressions into escapism or depression (economic or otherwise), and xenophobic reactions and fears about those who are deemed as enemies.

In order to weaken the autonomy of a complex, Jungian theory advocates analyzing the intense, affect-laden defensive reactions of a person (or here a culture) that form the shell of the complex, and then investigating those affective states in relationship to protected core beliefs (Jung, 1948/1960). Often these have been shaped by patterns from childhood, whether in a person's childhood or in a culture's early days. The goal in therapy is to stimulate the transformation of the shell by examining the emotions activated by it in relationship to the archetypal core of the complex, which paradoxically aids to transform the core beliefs themselves.

In one sense, a study of a young nation like the United States, with its early formation in the recent past, can serve as an excellent litmus test for the theory of cultural complexes, since there is a massive written record available to consult and a relatively short period of history to consider. The traumatic events of recent history are easily compared to earlier eras and patterns of behaviors and attitudes are traceable with the use of the written record. To reframe the pathological events of that history as mythic enactments generates a different perspective. This new perspective allows for the possibility of making meaning out of what otherwise appears as a chaotic, senseless explosion of emotional responses to the difficulties of life in the twenty-first century.

In the US anxiety disorders numbers are rising (Twenge, 2011). Like prey animals foraging and nervously eyeing the landscape for danger, Americans are nervous. As events in the modern world have caused some parents in America to become both more distracted and more fearful, it is my contention that the number of children who are caught in an unconscious cultural complex are rising. My practice in California brings me into daily contact with children whose acting out stems from a combination of physicality and sensitivity. I began to notice how often children who were in trouble for being "too physical" were using their physicality to protect a sensitive core. Being in therapy, in other words, having their worst fears contained by a compassionate listener, allowed them to reveal a vulnerable, hidden sense of self. Apparently I am not alone in finding an increase in anxious children. Post 9/11, "national universities reported a higher rate of students seeking treatment for anxiety disorders (35%)" (Anxiety Disorders Association of America, 2007).

In these children's cases, neither their parents nor society have found a way to positively relate to the combination of sensitivity and physicality in their children. Some of them are brought to therapy because they are angry and defiant, continue to have temper tantrums in their preadolescent years, or have developed compulsive and violent responses to soothe their internal states. They are brought into therapy because they bully or are bullied at school or bully themselves in their bedrooms, cutting themselves in secret. These children are consequently labeled as disordered. Large numbers of children are diagnosed with and medicated for ADHD, Emotional Disregulation disorder, Depression, Intermittent Explosive disorder, Panic disorder, Oppositional Defiant disorder, or BiPolar disorder (American Psychiatric Association, 2013). Their parents, the education system, and society at large are aiming for symptom reduction and conformity rather than reflecting on a deeper understanding of their maladies. In Pan-like fashion the children who are noisy, startling, and more focused on getting their way than fitting in, cause problems for teachers and parents. And also like Pan, these children cause panic in, and often suffer rejection by, their caretakers and their classmates.

Other symptomatic concerns such as the self-absorption inherent to a capitalist system, the undying theme of racism, and the degradation of the environment are also concerns felt by psychologically-minded Americans, but in order to carefully examine the many sides to the problems named above, these will not be included here and are left for further research. To allow these psychological currents to rage unconsciously is to agree to live in a perilous and anxious state, something no one wants, and yet has become a predominant theme of the new millennium.

The great god Pan is dead

Chapter three explores the legend of the death of Pan in the context of the idea that what is psychological does not die but rather sinks into the unconscious. It investigates its meaning in the context of the first century when it was introduced by Plutarch, and the way it has been reinterpreted through history since that time and up until the present. Pan has left us with a cipher to decode. He was an immortal who is said to have died. As reported by the Greek philosopher Plutarch, that death is historically situated within a decade of the crucifixion of Jesus by the inclusion of the interest of Tiberius Caesar in the legend (Tiberius ruled from 14–37 CE, at the time of the crucifixion). Here it is in full:

> As for death among such beings, I have heard the words of a man who was not a fool nor an imposter. The father of Aemilianus the orator, to whom some of you have listened, was Epitherses, who lived in our town and was my teacher in grammar. He said that once upon a time in making a voyage to Italy he embarked on a ship carrying freight and many passengers. It was already evening when, near the Echinades Islands, the wind dropped, and the ship drifted near Paxi. Almost everybody was awake, and a good many had not finished their after-dinner wine. Suddenly from the island of Paxi was heard the voice of

> someone loudly calling Thamus, so that all were amazed. Thamus was an Egyptian pilot, not known by name even to many on board. Twice he was called, and made no reply, but the third time he answered; and the caller, raising his voice, said, "When you come opposite to Palodes announce that Great Pan is dead." On hearing this, all, said Epitherses, were astounded and reasoned among themselves whether it were better to carry out the order or to refuse to meddle and let the matter go. Under the circumstances Thamus made up his mind that if there should be a breeze, he would sail past and keep quiet, but with no wind and a smooth sea about the place he would announce what he had heard. So, when he came opposite Palodes, and there was neither wind nor wave, Thamus from the stern, looking toward the land, said the words as he had heard them: "Great Pan is dead." Even before he had finished there was a great cry of lamentation, not of one person, but of many, mingled with exclamations of amazement. As many persons were on the vessel, the story was soon spread abroad in Rome, and Thamus was sent for by Tiberius Caesar. Tiberius became so convinced of the truth of the story that he caused an inquiry and investigation to be made about Pan; and the scholars, who were numerous at his court; conjectured that he was the son born of Hermes and Penelope.
>
> (Plutarch, 1936/2003b, pp. 401–403)

The story's content, structure, recurring motifs, and themes have resonated for divergent ideologies as examples of their own varied visions. Pan is a repository for unconscious projections, which echo many sides of nature, of being human, of being whole, and of the Greek psyche that first envisioned Pan's nature. Interest in the cryptic story has managed, paradoxically, to keep the goat-god Pan from dying.

A significant point for consideration is that the death of an immortal is an anomaly in Greek myth (Borgeaud, 1983).

> What is unique about the Greek tradition is the radical and thoroughgoing way in which the opposition between the realm of the gods and the realm of the dead was worked out. The gods are the immortals, *athanatoi;* the epithet becomes a definition. To name a festival the "day of the burial of the divinity", as the Phoenicians do, is impossible in Greek. A god bewailed as dead, such as Adonis, is always felt to be foreign; when the Cretans show a grave of Zeus it only serves to prove they are liars.
>
> (Burkert, 1977/1985, p. 201)

This chapter investigates why Pan died, or psychologically went into the unconscious. What are his attributes that are now unconscious? The psychological symptoms of anxiety and panic, which are characterized as a disorder today, were envisioned by the Greek psyche, perhaps even before the Greeks, as a part of the divine as embodied in Pan. For instance, archeologist Marija Gimbutas' (1989, 1991) interpretations of an image of The Mature Male Holding a Hook and The Sorrowful One from the fifth millennium BCE, hunter and fertility figures that are thematic early forerunners of Pan.

Like the other gods who bring madness, Dionysus and Cybele, with whom Pan is often associated, he takes possession of humans through irrational terror. His weapons are sound, invisibility, a sure eye, swiftness, the ability to leap, aggression, and an astounding appearance. In the Greek myths the presence of the goat-god Pan creates, whether through seduction or panic, an uncanny, numinous atmosphere. These characteristics are analyzed for insights into the moribund state of the modern US.

Mythos of Pan

Arcadian Pan: innocence and isolation

Chapter four amplifies themes associated with the nymphs and with Pan's isolated landscape in Arcadia, where his cult began. Pan's unconscious influence can be thought about in relationship to the West as a whole, but when the most brilliant strands of the dominant American culture are separated out from those of the West in general, more can be seen of Pan in the US. The Wild West, the frontiers of space, vast utilizations of natural resources, and freedom for individuals crown American contributions. Pan's dominion over the natural world and his life as a separate and independent god, his freedom from the restraints of civilization and the sense of space that separates him from others in his own territory, parallel that which, by degree, differentiates the *zeitgeist* of the dominant culture in America from its European forbearers. I would suggest that the best and the worst in Pan meet in America. There is a bit of the rustic in both.

Beyond an interesting comparison of Pan to America, can the myths and rites of Pan's cult help an understanding of how America can move to a less self-absorbed and one sided vision in its future? Perhaps the question is better put, can the United States culture individuate? Using the myths of Pan to "clothe" the archetypal core of the proposed cultural complex may bring some insights.

In Arcadia in his early myths, Pan reflects American grandiosity in how he sees the world as his to use for his purposes. But this one sided inflation brings him to grief, as he never consummated his love and those he pursues are left broken, made voiceless, and pine away (Borgeaud, 1979/1988).

Today Pan is remembered for his insensitivity, violence, attempted rapes, and selfish, self-absorbed behaviors. These are all elements of the habitual nature of Pan as relayed to us through the myths and legends of the early

Greeks and Romans (Borgeaud, 1979/1988). Pan embodied more than these best-remembered qualities. Pan did not instigate wars or fight for his own gain; rather, he was enlisted to come to the defense of Dionysus, Zeus, and the people of Athens, which, to the ancients, signified all of civilized humanity (1994). Such is Pan's paradoxical history and nature.

Athenian Pan: panic and the battlefield

Chapter four also includes a broad viewing of the battle myths of Pan after his cult spread to Athens and consequently throughout the Mediterranean basin. His associations with panic and protection are investigated. In times of unrest Pan emerges as an "avenging protector/persecutor in defense of the collective spirit" (Singer, 2004, p. 23), allying with gods and men against outside aggressors. He was deeply feared. He usually used cacophonous noise and surprise to bring panic to the hearts of the enemies of his friends. Pan's strategy to use echoes to create pandemonium in enemy armies brought him popularity because it was understood to avoid great loss of life for his allies. In the second century BCE, Artemidorus (1975) of Ephesus wrote an *Oneirocritica* (an "interpretation of dreams") illustrating Pan's association with panic and anxiety. He stated Pan "signifies confusion and tumult. He also signifies that the things in which a person takes pride will not remain secure" (p. 118). The battle myths of Pan give examples of his presence creating confusion and tumult in various ways, including organized surprise attacks, instilling fears of going crazy or becoming epileptic, and infecting a group into a dissolution into mob mentality.

Panic, as the Greeks would have it, is not a pathology; it is divine madness (Plato, 1914/1966, p. 467). Pan is associated with powers that create terror and the subsequent echoes of traumatic reactions. The nymph Echo and Pan are intertwined here in relationship to war, but they are associated in many ways in the myths, even as sound is at times harmonious but at others noisy and discordant (Nonnos, 1962a, 1962b, 1962c). Pan's relationship to Echo and to sound as din, invoking fear, madness, terror, and joyful release in music and celebration, is articulated throughout the myths.

Perhaps Pan's compulsive rush into life is a symbolic expression of what was once alive in the bold spirit of the European settlers of America, but has since rusted in paralysis and avoidance of initiative toward contemporary problems. Where the US once unconsciously identified with the most courageous and expansive in the Pan archetype, now the archetype of panic stalks America.

Rites of healing and scapegoating in antiquity: metamorphoses

The fifth chapter examines Pan's myths and rites that involve scapegoating and sacrifice in order to draw parallels between how self-absorption, panic, and apathy were "drunk down to the dregs" and where things stand today. Pan's rites of circle dancing with the nymphs and squilling with the young men of his cult suggest possibilities for greater containment of the anxiety and anger that is rising up in an uncontained manner as America finds itself less and less in a central ruling position on the world stage. The relationships between Pan and the nymphs suggest a door that could lead to a positive outcome. When alone, he overpowered a nymph, but when they approached him in groups, the nymphs knew how to soothe his restless, hypermasculine nature. Ultimately, the containment of the anger and violence and its consequent anxiety, fear, and apathetic escapist tendencies in America are in the hands of each and every modern American, as Singer and Kimbles suggest (2004). Each citizen has a choice to consciously struggle to bring greater awareness to the complexes in a culture or to unconsciously ignore them.

In every complex (Jung, 1948/1960), there is a defense system that is protecting an aspect of the self (here the American culture) that has been seriously threatened, often repeatedly. That authentic sense of self always has an archetypal underpinning. Using the Greek pantheon as template for the archetypal (though one could just as easily use the gods and goddesses of the Native Americans) many would argue America is caught in an Ares-like warrior-nation complex. This would explain the massive walls of the American military defense system, by far the greatest on the planet (Sipri, 2014) and the hypermasculine aggression that underlies panicky moves to defense (build a 2000 mile wall at the border to Mexico, deport 11 million Mexican migrants, hunt to kill Saddam Hussein and Osama bin Laden). But a military nation mentality alone does not address the escapist, apathetic responses by much of the American public (the GNP went up 6% in the months following 9/11).

Besides the battle myths in which Pan figures as second in command to various leaders such as Zeus or Dionysus, the myths of Pan with the nymphs are most remembered for the intensity of his sexual hunts. Inherent to those myths is the theme of escape for the nymphs to a sort of dormancy. They devolved into a less free state, unable to speak or move about. Panic and torpor are part of the emotional landscape of Pan's mythic borderline territories where self-absorbed instincts ignore the disenfranchised. Confusion and escape are dominant themes in Pan's battle myths as well. He is able to overcome the enemy through cunning and surprise.

Pan, as with all the gods and goddesses in the Greek religions, also had many helpful sides. He was the god of fertility and sustenance, the god of herders, as well as one of the chief gods of nature. He brought music, the panpipes, and dancing to the nymphs, leading them in nightlong trance-like circle dances. He did not start wars but was a strong ally to others. Perhaps most importantly in terms of suggested alternate solutions for America, he was able to live in harmony with his own nature, half divine and half beast.

Implicit in the inalienable right to personal freedom, so fundamental to the United States, is the possibility of an active and conscious struggle to become a more aware community, to struggle to become psychological, as Samuels put it. Such a positive social impetus was alive in the founding fathers of this country and is still alive in the polity of the US. It is visible in ethical movements such as the waning of resistance toward gay marriage and the momentum toward greater ecologic sustainability. When enough awareness creates critical mass it can tilt public opinion in a certain direction and then public opinion is an inexorable force, nearly impossible to stop.

The most likely outcome is that America will adjust to the difficulties it faces today and muddle through. Rather than the greatest nation destined to lead all nations, the US could embrace the *earth* as Winthrop's Puritan "shining citee upon a hill" and be at peace with the notion that it is one nation of many with the same desire, to preserve life on Earth. The road to such a future begins by recognizing why, at present, the US has lost its way.

American history reconsidered using cultural complex theory

The Puritan birth of American exceptionalism

Chapter six begins to build the argument for a recently triggered cultural complex in the US with an examination of the origins of exceptionalism and its physical counterpart, Manifest Destiny. It considers the social constructions of influences on contemporary culture based on early American ideals and patterns. Values that were created as the new country struggled to discover its identity and its values (the family history of the culture, so to speak). Jungian analyst Andrew Samuels (1993b) argues for the practicality of applying psychological methods to social and cultural issues, which involves "finding out the history of whatever problem is under scrutiny, including the myth or myths which attach to the problem" (para. 125).

One concept that gathered traction was the notion of the country as exceptional. The discovery of the New World had provided the Puritans with what they perceived as a *tabula rasa* on which to practice the new social order they believed their God desired. They saw this as an opportunity to create an outer life that matched their deepest inner values: a way of life that would reconcile cultural tensions between spirituality and free enterprise. The Puritan notion of their exceptionalism was birthed out of the belief that by adhering to their strict religious beliefs and contributing to the wealth of their community through free enterprise, they would remain a chosen people.

The United States formed just 250 years ago when a small group of patriots overthrew the mighty British monarchy, creating a union based on the consent of the people, and then, perhaps as much a surprise to themselves as the rest of the "civilized" world, rapidly prospered. In a way, America's birth in 1776 and remarkable 74 year ceding of the continental lands all the way to the Pacific Ocean (California became a state in 1850) launched a narrative of a nation that was exceptional. That America was founded on ideals rather than evolving out of feudal land rights *was* exceptional. The notion that the country was exceptional was not, as for most patriotic peoples, only believed by Americans; much of the civilized world has been amazed and even awed by its trajectory through history.

The idea that the Puritans were the elect and the people closest to God was originally protected through the defense of shunning. Puritans would have nothing, or as little as possible, to do with others who did not share their exact beliefs. Puritans brought on, even encouraged the disdain and persecution they suffered for their beliefs; shunning their neighbors led to their being rejected by other Christian sects. For a Puritan, to be hated by "reprobates" was a sign that they were of the elect. Tantamount to a psychological defense system, shunning protected the Pilgrims beliefs by blocking out other belief systems and the necessity of trying to understand why others disagreed with their vision of reality. It isolated them, which they then interpreted as a virtue. At the core of a nascent anxiety complex in America was a fragile belief in exceptionalism that is protected by blocking out the value of other systems.

Like many people who are the target of projections and thus traumatized by scapegoating, the Puritan's motivations contained a fairly transparent revenge fantasy, the fantasy that all those they shunned were destined for everlasting hell. But this increased the pressure to make virtue a non-negotiable element of Puritan life. John Winthrop, governor of the Massachusetts Bay Company, warned if the new Americans did not live up to strictly held Puritanical virtues, "wee shall shame the faces of many of God's worthy servants, and cause theire prayers to be turned into curses upon us till wee be consumed out of the good land whither wee are goeing" (Winthrop, as cited in Greenberg, 2012, p. 44). They *had* to see themselves as destined for greatness, and they relied upon high standards and stoicism in the pursuit of this goal. In psychological thinking, the one-sidedness of their lives and perspectives created a split. Greatness was non-negotiable and so relatedness, compassion, and mercy for others were split off to protect the idea of Puritan greatness.

Regardless of the insensitivity of this insular thinking, exceptionalism and Manifest Destiny successfully drove an ideological narcissism in American culture because these ideals were successful at impeding threats to the society as a whole. The fledgling complex was born in, and kindles, a Puritan hubris and unrealistic assumptions that can allow or simply overlook many behaviors that are actually exceptionally dangerous, rather than a sign of exceptional virtue.

The chapter considers how aspects of the current state of affairs in the US are the result of the same belief, though currently toned down from seventeenth and eighteenth century rhetoric. It applies cultural complex theory to exceptionalism, demonstrating how the structure of a complex encouraged both isolation and the idea of American greatness to become inflated within the vacuum that isolation created. The idea that America is destined to lead the world grew out of this viewpoint as an analysis of the echoes of this belief system in the rhetoric of its leaders demonstrates.

The use of Manifest Destiny in colonial expansion

One aspect of the American ideal of exceptionalism that is still quite prevalent, though its influence is largely dismissed (Nugent, 2007) is the justification for empire building, often termed Manifest Destiny. Manifest Destiny is a phrase that first appeared in print in 1839 in the *United States Magazine and Democratic Review*. The strategy, which justifies taking land away from those already inhabiting it, was in place long before the *Democratic Review* named it Manifest Destiny. The anonymous author, thought to be either its editor, John L. O'Sullivan, or contributing writer, Jane McManus Storm Cazneau, declared "our country is destined to be *the great nation* of futurity . . . who will, what can, set limits to our onward march?" (as cited in Greenberg, 2012, pp. 79) and then in 1845 proclaimed "our manifest destiny to overspread the continent allotted by Providence for the free development of our multiplying millions" (as cited in Greenberg, 2012, pp. 98). Though this is certainly not an exclusively American principle, Manifest Destiny proposed that divine sanction made it an *obligation* for Americans to expand their territory across the entire North American continent, including Canada, Mexico, and the Caribbean. Manifest Destiny makes a virtue of the schoolyard bully's tactic of appropriating another's resources by disregarding and overpowering the freedom and rights of others.

Correlations exist between the ethos of Puritanism and the fears and anxieties many early European settlers felt toward Native Americans during the nineteenth century. The reactions of fear toward, and brutalization of, the Indian tribes by the European settlers and their government are considered. The newspaper's scandalizing influence and the discriminating policies and laws of the government scapegoated the Native American ways of life. This history is exampled in a postcolonial reading of the story of Geronimo, how he was demonized, finally captured, and then before his death in 1909 acclaimed as a hero, even marching in Teddy Roosevelt's inaugural parade.

Geronimo's story is a particularly interesting saga because the power structure of the fledgling nation focused on his capture as paramount for the safety of the country. Until capture, the press and the colonial federal government demonized him. But once corralled he became hugely popular and was soon a symbol of the ferocity of American's insistence on freedom. A victim of colonization he then became a symbol of that power structure. America's militant defense of global democracy will be explored as a similar, but modern application of Manifest Destiny, regardless of whether it is instigated by virtuous concern or by American economic interests protecting their global investments abroad.

With rapid development, exceptionalism and Manifest Destiny evolved into a powerful, but latent or unconscious, complex in the American culture. In the nineteenth century the government under its fifth president, James Monroe, ratified the Monroe Doctrine of 1823, which declared acts of colonization by European nations acts of aggression against the US. In 1879, President Rutherford Hayes endorsed Manifest Destiny as dogma. "The annexation to the United States of the adjacent parts of the continent both north and south, seems to be, according to the phrase of 1844, our 'manifest destiny'" (Hayes, 1879, para. 3). Hayes, in the post-Civil War era, also controlled the means of carrying out this policy using military force against the people who claimed these lands as their own; the genocide of many tribes of Native Americans resulted from this narcissism. Hayes was aided in a cover up of hardships caused for Native Americans by the scandalizing and sensationalist commentaries in the main method for communication at the time – the newspapers. The result was the destruction of Indian ways of life.

In-depth psychological thinking, exceptionalism, and Manifest Destiny separated the early Americans into an ideological bubble, which matured into a complex-tinged viewpoint that interpreted events as evidence that justified a superior attitude. Such a complex simultaneously isolates a group and holds it together. Negative repercussions from these factors, it will be shown, remained latent because of the phenomenal success of the colonies.

In 1849 John Sutter discovered gold in California, and this forever changed the delicate balance on the western frontiers. Over the next four years, the gold rush led to a massive migration by immigrant settlers across the North American continent; over 350,000 settlers followed the Oregon and Santa Fe trails across the western US. This migration effectively began the Indian Wars, waged in what was then the Indian Territory, the Great Plains of the United States. Applying an aggressive use of the notion of a Manifest Destiny, a "scorched earth policy" was used to destroy the demonized Indian nations. This was approved of by citizens relying on the reports in the newspapers and legalized by the government. The brutal nature of this genocide was masked by projections of that brutality onto the Indians and, of course, the projection of brutality onto the Native Americans insulated colonial Americans from any consequent guilt or shame characteristic in such a land grab.

Exceptionalism and Manifest Destiny helped catalyze America's rapid rise as a nation. These convictions also tilled the fields of individualism, autonomy, and self-absorption. Exceptionalism and Manifest Destiny have inevitably led to conflict because these ideals ignore the need for balance between the rights of the individual and the needs of the community. By applying depth psychological theory to these foundational ideals, I am suggesting that American culture is blind to an inflated shadow.

The complex is triggered

Chapter sixth also outlines, after two centuries of success, a gradual decline in American confidence in itself that begins to appear symptomatically in the late 1960's following the moon landing (then came the fall of Vietnam, the oil embargo, Watergate, etc.), and has led to the current state of discontent demonstrated by facts such as 60% of the likely voters think that the country is on the wrong track (RealClearPolitics, 2017). Indications, such as polls showing Americans' lack of confidence in the government, suggest a gradual inclination in Americans to feel that something is wrong and that no political party, *mana* personality, or religious movement knows what to do, no matter how loudly they proclaim that they do.

The chapter suggests the complex has begun to surface as the country faces a series of intractable problems. This is, in psychological thinking, a positive sign, because it is the moment of a *kairos*, a time when change becomes possible, because first, naturally enough, one must realize there is a problem, before one can begin to work out how to solve it. As Samuels (1993a) writes "the characteristic of late modernity to try to make use of knowledge about itself can be recast as a struggle within our culture to become self-conscious; *our culture struggles to become psychological*" (p. 8).

The chapter frames the current discontent within the theory of cultural complexes, demonstrating that the complex remained in a latent state as long as the country was admired and prospering, but that recent events, especially the rapid succession of disparate developments around the turn of the millennium, have triggered the complexes' defense system. What had been a protective shell of isolationism and wealth became a defensive curtain of arms buildup and trade agreements. Core beliefs in American benevolence came into question (Lifton, 2003). Protective thoughts and nationalistic feelings of pride began to morph into troubling concerns as the well-educated baby boomer population came of age and voiced doubts about the heretofore ignored underpinnings upon which all the success of America rests (2003). The suffering caused by the complex-tinged attitudes, it will be demonstrated, had primarily been projected onto America's enemies or those to whom the country was indifferent. The fear, depression, and anxieties, which had been successfully projected onto others, had come home to roost and now began to be felt by Americans themselves. It is actually not surprising that a man of Donald Trump's character and values was elected President in 2016. He is a reflection of the values bottled up in the complex and is a further suggestion that, as this complex surfaces into the light of day, there is an opportunity to awaken the citizens of the US to the cause of the country's problems. Though it is not possible to predict future events using complex theory, by evaluating psychological symptoms such as fear, anxiety, and apathy in a culture, it is possible to predict that a continued pattern of apathy and explosiveness, narcissism, and splitting will end if enough Americans can actually drink, as Jung suggested, this foul tasting complex down to the dregs.

Random shootings: American reactions to the massacre at Columbine

Chapter seven begins the close examination of current anxieties in America. The first area to be explored is the random shootings by disenfranchised (often white) young men. This terrible problem first gripped the nation in a common reaction of fear and disbelief when the Columbine massacre was transmitted live on television. "In its more abstract senses, *Columbine* has become a keyword for a complex set of emotions surrounding youth, risk, fear, and delinquency in early 21st Century United States" (Muschert, 2007, p. 365). The Columbine shootings, perpetrated by Eric Harris and Dylan Klebold, or "Columbine," as the massacre has come to be called, occurred on April 20, 1999. Harris and Klebold entered their high school in Jefferson County, Colorado, and shot to death 12 students and one teacher, while injuring 24 other students. Moments like the Columbine shootings can be turning points for cultures, with the responses to disaster often more significant than the catastrophe itself.

The school shootings left a reverberating question mark for Americans. How could those boys have done it? The narrative constructions advanced in media and popular print, such as alienated youth influenced by films, music, and video games (a so-called Trench Coat Mafia), narcissistic parenting and the community's "benign neglect," or psychopathic (natural born) killers (Frymer, 2009), never put the traumatized reactions to rest. Nor have efforts to punish those responsible for school shootings stopped them from recurring.

Rather, it will be argued, the discourses themselves projected imagined simulacra onto the perpetrators. Manic leaps were generated by the media coverage as it followed the real time action and an overnight metamorphosis froze the two shooters into monsters (Cullen, 2009). The viewing public accepted an oversimplification of the factors that drove Eric Harris and Dylan Klebold to homicide/suicide. This attitude has not been influenced by the methodical study of the actual events in the years that followed – though much of what was first thought to be fact was later found to be erroneous (Cullen, 2009). The reportage was compelling to a horrified and fascinated public, driving the profit-driven news industry to demonize the perpetrators, exploit the victims, and create instant heroes (Moore, 2002). Eric Harris and Dylan Klebold were immediately split off from the community. They were banished as aberrations of nightmarish proportions and viewed as symbolic of evil in a modern passion play in which the slain students became the martyred heroes (Spencer & Muschert, 2009).

Actually, Eric and Dylan were not contained by their family, school, or community while alive and believed their future was hopeless. No one was paying attention as they meticulously planned and tested out their attack. Their uncontained anxiety and fears were violently projected. As will be shown, they targeted the entire American culture (Harris, 1998–1999; Klebold, 1997–1999). Even more worrisome is that these types of plots continue to be enacted onto the "enemy" by alienated children in the American public school system (Larkin, 2007).

Efforts to fix blame and create lockdown systems are an inadequate solution because they do not address the cycle of anger, fear, and despair the shooters felt (as seen in the journals and films they left behind), which is also the cycle the school shootings provoke in the community (Barak, 2005). From a depth psychological perspective, this suggests that an unconscious layer encompassing the entire culture drives the recurring horror of school rampages. This is the price for a complex being allowed to remain unconsciously projected out onto others, in this case back and forth between disenfranchised youth and the larger community.

The fear of another outbreak and the need to feel protected from danger, it is theorized here, began to trigger a latent cultural complex. The isolationist tendencies and superior attitude seen in early US history match Dylan's and Eric's internal states and both reflect a number of motifs in the myths of Pan. Pan was a hypermasculine aggressor and a lonely isolate; Pan's animal nature buttressed his virility, survival skills, and self-absorption, but his divinity denotes his sensitivity; Pan was quick to violence to get what he wanted, and he did not honor the sexual rights of the feminine figures in his myths, even as Eric wrote disrespectfully about women's sexual choices. At times in myth Pan shared their role as a bully, and at other times he shared their role as a scapegoat. These characteristic motifs of the sad story of Eric Harris and Dylan Klebold and Pan's role in the Greek Pantheon reflect modern America's confusion about its identity and the self-destructive tendencies that confusion spawns.

When Pan was scapegoated his cult performed a ritual to contain the anxiety this provoked (Borgeaud, 1979/1988), whereas Eric and Dylan were not contained by their family, school, or community while alive and believed their future was hopeless. So they planned and executed a violent revenge. Their uncontained anxiety and fears were violently projected. As will be shown, they targeted the entire American culture (Harris, 1998–1999; Klebold, 1997–1999).

The tragedy came to be narrated as a hero myth, which, like Goethe's *The Sorcerer's Apprentice*, is multiplying into chaos and is presented as one example of hypermasculinity and defensive splitting in the US culture. A lack of containment of anxiety in modern American society is causing repetitive dramas involving innocent fatalities, which could eventually lead to chaos.

American reactions to 9/11: panic and naiveté

Overly inflated attitudes in the United States, chapter eight suggests, are creating unconscious compensations that affect Americans and other cultures. American reactions to 9/11 will be used as a prototype for this pattern. Columbine was barely in the rearview mirror before the millennial Y2K scare stirred up anxiety. 9/11 followed just one year later, causing shock and panic that retriggered anxiety in the country. The traumatic reactions to 9/11 altered both laws and attitudes in America and put the country on an emotional high alert for that has, at this writing, never subsided. A fear-based apocalyptic vision began to dominant the culture as perceptions of America's safety and stability came into doubt. Laws were swiftly passed curtailing freedoms. A frightened and docile public accepted the rapid changes, as the majority of Americans chose to allow the "experts" to decide what was best, which included waging multiple simultaneous wars in the oil-rich Middle East.

Following the trauma of the terrorist attacks mainstream American reactions rapidly solidified into two attitudes: panicked compulsive action and states of torpor. The first was promoted by a swift call to action, an attempt to "shock and awe" the perpetrators fueled by then President George W. Bush's rhetorical "crusade" (Maddox, 2003). This was followed by a sluggish avoidance to relate to the painful experience at all, which reflects a basic naïveté in the culture. Bush's public recommendations encouraged a return to consumerism and to passively leave the terrorists to the professionals (Pyszczynski, Solomon, & Greenberg, 2003).

A projection of panic and subsequent torpor followed the attacks. "The intolerable affects of the terrorists are projected into the recipients of terror. . . . The victims experience a transformation of their subjectivity, as they are now possessed by terror. They now feel powerlessness, frustration, grief and terror previously carried by the terrorist" (Perlman, 2002, p. 32). Panic, derived from the Greek *panikos*, means "literally, of Pan" (*Webster's Unabridged Dictionary*, 1983, p. 1293). A recurring motif in Pan's myths reflects his tendency toward self-absorption and how his uncontained sexual arousal prompts him to chase young, innocent nymphs. This forces the nymphs, overwhelmed by panic, to make their escape, as did many Americans, through metamorphoses into torpid, vegetative states. They escaped by devolving (Larson, 2001).

In other myths, where Pan is a general in one or another army, he used panic strategically in a similar way to the US and radical Islamists; by hurting the few it is possible to frighten the many. Al-Qaeda's admitted strategy to surprise and create panic was remarkably effective given the US military advantage. The Bush administration opportunistically retaliated by becoming the aggressor, using a pandean "shock and awe" campaign slogan against Saddam Hussein's Iraq (Clarke, 2004). The cultures mirror each other (Adams, 1996). Both sides appear driven to use aggression rather than communication to protect themselves. Both are in denial about these similarities and the unconscious projections onto each other.

Panicky anxieties and apathetic retreats into escapism are understandable temporary reactions to Columbine and 9/11 (Pyszczynski et al., 2003). Cultural complex theory can help understand these choices as unhealthy knee-jerk reactions that could be transformed into more reasoned and compassionate responses (Kimbles, 2003).

American apathy toward sexual violence: rape in the military

Panic and torpor are part of the emotional landscape of Pan's borderline territories where self-absorbed instincts ignore the disenfranchised. Chapter nine introduces the alarming notion that these emotional states are generated in the US by an open secret in the military. Rather than protecting the citizens who choose to serve in the military of the US, the military hierarchy and its Congressional overseers are protecting their own unquestioned authority. A symptomatic ethos that has given rise to leniency for rape and sexual assault in the military has been shaped by three attitudes. These are the unquestioned assumption of integrity in the US military leaders' chain of command, a belief that justice is best served by the traditional approaches the concern in the general public about justice for the victims.

Women in the US military who are sexually assaulted by their fellow servicemen comprise an estimated 23% of their totals (Hankin, Skinner, Sullivan, Miller, Frayne, & Tripp, 1999). The numbers of sexual assaults and rapes are rising (Steinhauer, 2013, p. A1). The Department of Defense (DoD) acknowledges the problem, yet it remains resistant to changing the methods for prosecuting rape charges. The reactions to the problem by the general public are apathetic. Is an overly inflated attitude in the psyche of the American soldier, "The Few, The Proud . . . The Marines" (usmilitary.about.com) shaping an ethos that allows sexual assault to go nearly unnoticed?

A closed system like the military provides a prime, target-rich environment for sexual predation. In the Pentagon's 2012 annual report, 6.1% of the military's women and men came forward in a confidential survey and detailed their experience of sexual assault. In contrast only 0.2% of civilian Americans reported sexual assault in the same year (Steinhauer, 2013, pp. A1, A14). The annual report stated "In FY12, there were 3,374 reports of sexual assault involving Service members" (p. 3), which raises the estimated number of annual assaults to 26,000. The discrepancy between estimated number of assaults and the reported numbers exists because it is accepted (even by the DoD) that victims do not speak up for fear of the damage to their reputation, rank, and even survival in the military. The chain of command consistently fails to contain epidemic levels of soldiers raping their fellow soldiers. Instead, the command structure forms a persecutory element within the massive wall of military defense that is intended to protect its people.

The best and the worst in soldiering is amplified in the Greek god Pan. Pan went to battle with many armies (Kerenyi, 1998; Lucian, 1913/1961, p. 53 [Dionysus. 4]; Pausanias, 1959, p. 149 [xxviii.4]), and he also hunted down nymphs to satisfy his own lustings. The panic the soldiers inject in their victims and the apathy in the American public reflect the same pattern as the reactions to Columbine and 9/11 and is considered a prototype of another type of eruption from within an anxiety-based cultural complex.

Panic stalks America

The final chapter draws conclusions on the theme that a hypermasculine culture that prefers to ignore the needs of the disenfranchised as much as possible has eventually led to an anxious civilization that keeps splitting the chaotic population into states of panic and apathy. Further, hypermasculinity promotes a lack of sensitivity, which causes collisions between different cultures and social groups, and this in turn has led to terrorism. Perhaps the compensatory archetype for the hypermasculine does not fight, nurtures rather than wounds, and naturally induces the development of beauty and harmony in human life. Perhaps we need to calm the winds and stop the fires. The approach the nymphs used toward the Greek god Pan's hypermasculine traits could prove to be a trail to cultural metamorphosis. Pan's mythic aggression and brutality still exists, present in modernity's agendas though not recognized as such, but where is the archetype of the nymph?

One group of myths has Pan dancing in harmony with the nymphs. A recent find of a tableau of terra-cotta figurines from the mid fifth century BCE at the Corycian cave above Delphi depicts a wheel with spokes: Pan stands at the center about to play the syrinx while nymphs encircle him at equal points on the wheel – all are poised, ready to begin the dance (Pasquier, 1977). The final chapter will develop the themes inherent to the rite of the circle dance and apply them to our theme.

Though one can argue that a hypermasculine inflation of the archetypal protector and provider has become noticeably stronger since 9/11, perhaps this signals that the patriarchy needs greater defense, and so, hopefully, forewarns a weakening, signaled by an unconscious need to defend itself more and more – though this may only be a defense of current patriarchies and not the system itself, since one main adversary, radical Islamists, are even more patriarchal than Western governments; nevertheless, defensive overreactions tend to indicate high levels of insecurity that the defense system is attempting to keep hidden.

This last chapter is a call to action. It is time to assess that we, the citizens of the Earth, are in a profound moment of change, that change will come no matter what we do, but that what we do will affect the outcome of that change. This leads me to look to the universal patterns the Greeks intuitively tapped into, to leave behind a simplistic "good guys and bad guys" worldview, and to adopt a more complex and fluid attitude toward the reshaping of the coming global union in order to circumvent the possibility of a global apocalypse. Perhaps by aiming so high, we will manage to muddle through somewhere between the poles of total reinvention and total destruction.

Chapter 2

Jungian theory

Complex, myth, and archetype

For Jung the "whole of mythology could be taken as a sort of projection of the collective unconscious" (1931/1981, p. 152 [*CW* 8, para. 325]). In Jung's theory, as in Sigmund Freud's, glimpses of the structure of the psyche are made visible using psychological understandings of myth. Archetypal theory depends on understandings of the symbolic meanings of recurring patterns in human behavior. Where anthropologist James Frazer saw the death and rebirth of a vegetative god to be a physical process (2009), Jung saw the same recurring motif but interpreted it "as a return of the ego to the unconscious – a kind of temporary death of the ego – and its reemergence, or rebirth" (Segal, 1998a, p. 4). Jung observed the traumas a person endures are helped to heal when framed within a theory of archetypes. The use of myth to see the archetypal more clearly is a cornerstone of Jungian theory and is used to help us increase psychological understandings of human patterns of behavior. For instance, to understand a person's actions as heroic is to see psychological life as having a mythical dimension and this gives it greater meaning (Segal, 1998a, p. 4).

Jung never ruled out the possibility that any or all gods might not also have a separate existence (Segal, 1998b). But he did conclude that there is an aspect within the unconscious that makes meaning of life. He termed this part of the psyche *the Self* (Jung, 1951/1959e [*CW* 9II]). Jung postulated that it is the Self that is projected onto natural phenomena, such as the cycle of life and death (Segal, 1998b). This projection begins in the minds of humans and, Jung deduced, is in service to psychological growth or rebirth in a person. It enables humans to find value in the detritus of life (1951/1959e [*CW* 9II]). Jung chose the term the Self for the archetype of the God-image in the psyche because it is a neutral, explicitly nonspiritual word and so can express the transcendent regardless of the religion or culture of individuals (Segal, 1998b). It is used to describe an objective or greater aspect of the personality, as opposed to the ego, which is used to define the subjective and conscious personality (Jung, 1951/1959e [*CW* 9II]).

The *collective unconscious*, sometimes referred to as the objective psyche, is Jung's term for "a dimension of the unconscious psyche that is of an *a priori*, general human character, rather than merely the precipitate of personal repressed material" (Whitmont, 1991, p. 41). The "general human character" Jungian analyst Edward Whitmont referred to is specified as "the repository of man's psychic heritage and possibilities" (Samuels et al., 2005, p. 32). Jung stated the contents of the collective unconscious are "mythological associations, the motifs and images that can spring up anew anytime anywhere, independently of historical tradition or migration" (1921/1977a, p. 485 [*CW* 6, para. 842]). He concluded that if the collective unconscious exists, everything that is deposited into it has been translated into its picture-language and so appears in impersonal images (Jung, 1931/1981, p. 150 [*CW* 8, para. 316]). Since it is common to all humankind it "is the true basis of the individual psyche" (p. 152 [*CW* 8, para. 321]).

The application of myth in Jungian theory

Though the collective unconscious is timeless in and of itself, it also can be expected to react with contemporary adaptations of mythological motifs, or archetypes, that are activated by events in modern day (Jung, 1931/1981, p. 152 [*CW* 8, para. 324]). Jung concluded, "we can therefore study the collective unconscious in two ways, either in mythology or in the analysis of the individual" (p. 153 [*CW* 8, para. 325]). He most commonly called the motifs found in the collective unconscious *archetypes*. "Dangerous situations . . . arouse affect-laden fantasies, and, in so far as such situations typically repeat themselves, they give rise to *archetypes*" (p. 155 [*CW* 8, para. 334]). An archetype is a "continually effective and recurrent expression that awakens certain psychic experiences or else formulates them in an appropriate way" (Jung, 1921/1977a, p. 444 [*CW* 6, para. 748]). He theorized that in times of trouble archetypes surface as symbols to support the cohesion of a fragmenting person or a people (Jung, 1961/1965). Archetypal theory considers an archetypal structure to be filled with psychic contents that emerge into consciousness as strongly felt images, or *numina*, either internally or on the world stage (Samuels et al., 2005). Jung wrote in "Answer to Job" an archetype can be an independent and autonomous initiating force (1952/1973a, p. 470 [*CW* 11, para. 758]). Jung (1953/1973b) did not identify historical figures as archetypes, but stated that a historical, mythical, or imaginative figure can be fitted into an archetypal structure. Jung explained, in a letter to Pastor William La Chat discussing metaphysical interpretations of Christ, that he could not identify Christ,

> with the archetype of the Self in the sense that Christ is himself the archetype. I cannot prove the identity of an historical personage with a psychological archetype. That is why I stop after establishing the fact that in the Occident this archetype, or this "God-image," is seen in Christ; in the Orient, in the Buddha.
>
> (p. 267)

For Jung, a myth parallels a physical process in life, but the process does not account for the existence of myth (1951/1959d p. 154 [*CW* 9I, para. 260]). Therefore a historical figure as well as a spiritual being can energize collective identification with an archetype when members of a group project numinous qualities on to him or her. "Gods are metaphors of archetypal behaviours and myths are archetypal enactments" (Samuels et al., 2005, p. 27).

Unlike Durkheim and Harrison, Jung studied the structure of myths to better understand the intrapersonal psyche. He agreed with Freud that mythic structures, such as the Oedipus cycle, would not still engage audiences today if the function and meaning of myth were merely a literal explanation of physical events. For Jung, the function of myth is to a doorway through which to enter into the unconscious (R. Segal, 2003, p. 601, 604).

Jung often spoke in comparative ways about mythology. He wrote about symbols that spontaneously arise in people regardless of cultural heritage. An example Jung often used of the cross-cultural nature of the collective unconscious is the archetype of the wise old man or *senex*. He described this figure as symbolic of "the superior master and teacher, the archetype of the spirit, who symbolizes the pre-existent meaning hidden in the chaos of life" (1954/1959a, p. 35 [*CW* 9I, para. 74]). That this principle is seen as universal is evidenced in examples such as China's legendary Bodhidharma, the wily Odysseus, and the visionary Oglala Sioux Black Elk. Jung posited that the structuring for a numinous symbolic figure such as the wise old man exists in the collective unconscious of humanity and that a group of people will fill that structure with modern iconic figures or images, such as Nelson Mandela, that fit the *zeitgeist* of the times.

Analysis of a specific archetypal image that has emerged in a person's consciousness is often found to be helpful in a time of crisis, whether external or internal. Jung deduced one purpose of archetypes is to help humans understand the significance of certain events in their lives (1951/1959d, p. 155 [*CW* 9I, para. 262–263]). "Archetypal qualities are found in symbols and this accounts in part for their fascination, utility and recurrence" (Samuels et al., 2005, p. 27).

Jung did not say archetypes control or dictate human behavior, though he suspected archetypes might be unconscious images of instincts, which do, in some instances automatically, control behavior. He wrote:

> instincts are not vague and indefinite by nature, but are specifically formed motive forces which, long before there is any consciousness, and in spite of any degree of consciousness later on, pursue their inherent goals. Consequently they form very close analogies to the archetypes, so close, in fact, that there is good reason for supposing that the archetypes are the unconscious images of the instincts themselves, in other words, that they are *patterns of instinctual behaviour*.
>
> (1936–1937/1959b, pp. 43–44 [*CW* 9I, para. 91])

Criticisms of Jung's theory of the application of myth to psychology

Jung and Freud famously disagreed about the existence of a collective unconscious. This was the theoretical position that broke their relationship in 1913, though many other elements, both latent and manifest, contributed and have subsequently been extensively analyzed (Bair, 2003; Shamdasani, 2005). In *Symbols of Transformation* (1912/1956), Jung posited that the collective unconscious is the universal source in humans urging us to see life as meaningful and based this observation on studies done at Burghölzli, the psychiatric hospital of the University of Zürich (1961/1965). An often-quoted example of the evidence upon which Jung based his theory is the story of a schizophrenic patient seen by Johann Honegger, one of Jung's students, who reported "he could see an erect phallus on the sun. When he moved his head from side to side, he said, the sun's phallus moved with it, and *that was where the wind came from*" (Jung, 1912/1956, p. 101 [*CW* 5, para. 151]). Jung found the same image in a Mithraic liturgy: "And likewise the so-called tube, the origin of the ministering wind. For you will see hanging down from the disc of the sun something that looks like a tube" (p. 100 [*CW* 5, para. 149]). The mystery cult of Mithras emerged in what is now Iran during the Hellenistic period, and it rivaled Christianity up until the fourth century. Islam subsequently surpassed Mithraism in the Near East in the seventh century (Campbell, 1972, pp. 255 *ff.*). All agreed there was no conceivable way that this particular patient could have had any knowledge of Mithraic liturgies.

Jung gave other examples and concluded: "it is not a question of a specifically racial heredity, but of a universally human characteristic. Nor is it a question of *inherited ideas*, but of a functional disposition I later called the *archetype*" (1912/1956, p. 102 [*CW* 5, para. 149]). He stated that he understood this disposition to have found expression in religion and myth and that this aspect of the unconscious could be called the phylogenetic unconscious. Eventually he turned to the term the collective unconscious (1912/1956). This position continues to excite criticism and labeling as metaphysical and "unscientific" (Stevens, 1998).

Jung's writing has been criticized because his terminology changed over time. Jung continued to refine his theories for over 60 years and his understanding developed gradually. This caused discrepancies in writings from different periods. Though in this early writing he had not yet termed the impersonal layers of the unconscious the collective unconscious; this was what he was referring to when he stated that when patients are accessing mythological material unknown to them: "we must be dealing with 'autochthonous' revivals independent of all tradition, and, consequently, that 'myth-forming' structural elements must be present in the unconscious psyche" (1951/1959d, p. 152 [*CW* 9.I, para. 259]).

Initially, Freud did not object to Jung's new position. In 1912 in the psychoanalytic journal *Imago* he remarked:

> For everyone involved in the development of psychoanalysis, it was a memorable moment when C. G. Jung, at a private scientific gathering, reported through one of his students that the fantasies of certain mental patients (*dementia praecox*) coincided strikingly with the mythological cosmogonies of ancient peoples of whom these uneducated patients could not possibly have any scholarly knowledge. *Für jeden an der Entwicklung der psychoanalytischen Forschung Beteiligten war es ein denkwürdiger Moment, als C. G. Jung auf einer privaten wissenschaftlichen Zusammenkkunft durch einen siener Schüler mitteilen ließ, daß die Phantasiebildungen gewisser Geisteskranker (Dementia praecox) in auffälligster Weise mit den mythologischen Kosmogenien alter Völker zusammenstimmten, von denen die ungebildeten Kranken eine wissenschaftliche Kunde unmöglich erhalten hatten.*
>
> (Freud, 1912, p. 18)

Most of this essay is now published as a chapter in *Totem and Taboo* (1938), but these sentences were eliminated between the printing in 1912 and the original printing of *Totem and Taboo* in 1913, precisely as the split between Freud and Jung widened into an unsurpassable chasm.

The break between the two took place by letter. Whether the rift was political or actually based on theoretical differences, the tone first set by the breakup of the leader of the psychoanalytic movement and his heir apparent continues to reverberate through the field of depth psychology today (Bair, 2003). The split rapidly turned personal. On March 27, 1913, Freud in letters to Karl Abraham wrote: "his [Jung's] bad theories do not compensate me for his disagreeable character" (as cited in Falzeder, with Trollope, and King, 2002, p. 181) and on June 1, 1913, Freud wrote, "Jung is crazy, but I am not working for a separation, should like to let him reach rock bottom first" (as cited in Falzeder et al., 2002, p. 186).

Jung joined the fracas. On October 29, 1913 he wrote to another "Züricher" (as they were called at that time) Alphonse Maeder: "I shall soon be able to give you news of Deuticke and Freud, if the latter does not deem it beneath his papal dignity to answer me" (Jung 1953/1973b, p. 28). The formal split in October of 1913 was the result of a dispute concerning their joint publication efforts rather than more substantive issues. On July 26, 1914, just as Europe was collapsing into war, and only two days before Austria declared war on Serbia, Freud wrote: "we are rid at last of them, the brutal, sanctimonious Jung and his parrots!" (as cited in Falzeder et al., 2002, p. 264). 16 years later, in 1930, Jung was still referring to the end of relations. On October 16, 1930 he wrote, "An essentially reductive analysis like Freud's and the collectivizing psychology of Adler, which erases all differences, are the most virulent poison imaginable for the attitude of the artist and the creative person in general" (1953/1973b, p. 77).

Samuels pointed out that one, but not the only, reason Jung's work is still unwelcome among post-Freudians is due to the virulent nature of the initial split.

> The secret "committee" set up by Freud and Jones in 1912 to defend the cause of "true" psychoanalysis spent a good deal of time and energy on disparaging Jung. The fall-out from this historical moment has taken a very long time to evaporate, making the reception of Jung's ideas in psychoanalytic circles a rough ride.
>
> (1991, p. viii)

In Jung's theory the inherited potential for archetypal structure exists in the unconscious. "Instead of conceiving [of] the psyche as the product of postulated drives and conflicts, Jung saw it as the richly adaptive consequence of the evolution of the human species" (Stevens, 1998, p. 352). Jung disagreed with "Freud's view of the unconscious precisely because Freud seemingly bridges this divide by deriving the unconscious from consciousness" (R. Segal 1998a, pp. 10–11).

The discordant rift was never resolved between the two men and remains open to vastly different interpretations. For Jung, once he had posited a collective unconscious he was then able to interpret myths as products of it (R. Segal, 1998a, p. 8). Jung was very clearly against any definitive interpretations of myths because myths, derived from the unconscious, can only express themselves in symbols, hence obliquely. Symbols, Jung stated, exist in a state of fluidity that defies attempts to pin them down if one is to still retain access to their numinous quality (Jung, 1951/1959d, p. 179 [*CW* 9I, para. 301]). "Every interpretation necessarily remains an 'as-if.' The ultimate core of meaning may be circumscribed, but not described" (p. 156 [*CW* 9I, para. 265]).

Jung's uses of amplification

Jung applied his comparative studies of mythology to symbolic material and "used any and all materials from world history that had a bearing on mental processes. This method he called 'amplification'" (Stein, 1998, p. 5). He used *amplification* in his own personal analysis and applied it to his client's dreams and hypnogogic material (Main, 2004, p. 23). The unconscious, as Jung understood it, expresses itself through dreams and semi-conscious musings. The unconscious does this without any intention to deceive the conscious mind (1961/1965, pp. 161–162).

Amplification, Jung cautioned, was not a tool he used reductively. He understood amplification to be quite the opposite of a reductive method and was instead employed to "widen the basis on which the construction is to rest" (Jung, 1914/1989b, p. 187 [*CW* 3, para. 413]). Jung stated that by making what was implicit explicit in a symbol dreamers had the opportunity to understand their dreams as both mythical and unique to themselves. This opens a door to the possibility that a life is interconnected with others not only relationally, but on an inaudible, mysterious level, often compared to a common structure in plant life where an underground rhizome sends up shoots from many nodes (Samuels et al., 2005).

A co-inspired analysis of a dream begins by establishing the context of the images for the dreamer (in her or his own words) and continues by working to identify various interconnected personal associations (Main, 2004, p. 23). Jung stated that his method involves amplifying personal, cultural, and mythic metaphors that emerge out of the unconscious (1961/1965, p. 178). He found active imagination a tool that could coax the symbolic meaning to come forward more clearly into consciousness (Main, 2004, p. 23).

Amplification is not without its dangers. Everything can be seen to be related to everything in one way or another and this can lead to inflation (Samuels et al., 2005). Also a person can over-intellectualize through amplification (2005). For example, the fear of falling into a giant dream spider's web could be intellectually inflated into a "profound initiation" into the nature of the cunning Iktomi of the Oglala Sioux, a spider whose web could make one invulnerable (Brown, J. E., 1992, pp. 47–51). But if the actual gut-wrenching fear the dream produced in the dreamer is ignored, the dreamer will miss the chance to understand the affective side of the symbol and this causes the transformative personal value of the dream to be lost.

Archetypes are a fundamental psychic structure in Jung's theories (1961/1965, p. 173) and amplification was crucial to his understanding of both the inner and outer person (p. 345). Jung stated an effort is needed to find,

> a new *interpretation* appropriate to this stage, in order to connect the life of the past that still exists in us with the life of the present, which threatens to slip away from it. If this link-up does not take place, a kind of rootless consciousness comes into being. . . . The most we can do is to *dream the myth onwards* and give it a modern dress.
>
> (1951/1959d, pp. 157–160 [*CW* 9I, paras. 267–271])

Jung pointed out a regressive pull exists within the psyche as well. He called this the price one pays for the acquisition of one pointed consciousness. The ability to focus on "relatively few contents and to raise them to the highest pitch of clarity" (1951/1959d p. 162 [*CW* 9I, para. 276]) requires the exclusion of many other inner threads. This, Jung suggested, results in true progress only when the forward pull of conscious awareness and the regressive pull of unconscious psychic contents are able to co-operate (p. 163 [*CW* 9I, para. 277]). Jung developed these ideas in tandem with his theory of the psychological complex.

Jung's theory of a psychological complex

Jung analyzed the origin and nature of complexes in his essay "A Review of the Complex Theory" (1948/1960 [*CW* 8]). He theorized that wounded and rejected aspects of a person cluster into complexes in the unconscious (1948/1960 [*CW* 8]). When a complex is triggered it surfaces and often causes behaviors that make people feel like they are overreacting or "they just aren't themselves." Complexes can cause panic, anxiety, and repetitious, avoidant behaviors. They tend to isolate a person or a people (1948/1960 [*CW* 8]). Jung posited that suffering through becoming conscious of the splits in oneself and resacralizing the rejected parts of the complexed self is healing because it restores wholeness (1948/1960 [*CW* 8]). This is, essentially, the ongoing work of Jungian-based psychotherapy.

Jung found evidence to confirm the existence of complexes in his word association experiments, conducted from 1904 to 1911 (1948/1960 [*CW* 8]). He used a psycho-galvanometer to clock subjects' reactions to words and concluded that unconscious processes were determining conscious behavior by the varieties in reactions. His subjects had delayed responses or difficulties with responses to words that when later analyzed were found to correlate with their unresolved psychological problems. The word association test eventually became the basis for the lie detector test that is still in common use today.

Jung reasoned that these delays are caused by associations between the stimulus words and hidden, unconscious contents. He called these unconscious contents complexes (1948/1960 [*CW* 8]). Jung concluded other complexes besides the Oedipus complex could form in a person's unconscious. He acknowledged that this thinking was built upon Freud's conception of "the unconscious as consisting essentially of incompatible tendencies which are repressed on account of their immorality" (1948/1960, p. 102 [*CW* 8, para. 212]). But Jung differed with Freud about the specifics of the nature of these forces in the unconscious.

Jung (1948/1960 [*CW* 8]) observed that the origin of a complex was frequently traumatic and due to an irresolvable moral conflict. He argued that originally an emotional shock had caused a disturbance in the unity of the psyche and that the "constellation of a complex postulates a disturbed state of consciousness" (1948/1960, p. 96 [*CW* 8, para. 200]). Jung made five main points about the nature of a complex. He stated that in a personality a complex is a splintered off part of the psyche, has an inner coherence or wholeness, holds some amount of autonomy over the ego-complex, acts as a disruption putting a person under stress and so is accompanied by strong feelings, and finally that a complex is not necessarily negative, but rather is an expression of a characteristic state of the psyche (1948/1960 [*CW* 8]).

When a complex is activated a person is unable to overcome it with will power; it causes compulsive thinking and behaviors to be constellated in ways that are both overreactions and yet predictable (Jung, 1948/1960, p. 94 [*CW* 8, para. 198]). As Jung put it, "The only appropriate term would be the judicial concept of diminished responsibility" (p. 96 [*CW* 8, para. 200]). He observed that people go to great lengths to get rid of a complex and will even try to make it disappear by giving it a different name (p. 99 [*CW* 8, para. 206]). An example of an attempt to make a complex unreal on a cultural level is the euphemistic language used to discuss American wars, such as acts of aggression being renamed "pre-emptive strikes" and the bombing of city streets referred to as "surgical strikes." The language obfuscates the harsh reality of distant battles by "embedded" journalists on the television news and so, using Jung's theory, is an indicator of a hidden, unconscious complex. Jung stated fear and avoidance of complexes steer one away from the unconscious and is a prognosticator of a poor outcome for a person's psychological development (p. 101 [*CW* 8, para. 211]). He also noted that it takes determination to overcome the imprisonment of resistance, fear, and repulsion one feels about one's complexes (p. 101 [*CW* 8, para. 212]).

Complexes cause people to react, Jung argued, as if there is a foreign body inside them. The natural response is to want to expel it through projection or by rationalizing that their problems are nothing but their own invention and all in their heads. But often people simply cannot stop falling into states where they do or say things that seem to them to be out of character and that are causing them problems (1948/1960, p. 99 [*CW* 8, para. 205]). Jung pointed out "more primitive people did not 'psychologize' disturbing complexes as we do, but regarded them as beings in their own right, that is, as demons" (1948/1960, p. 98 [*CW* 8, para. 204]). Later in the same essay, Jung explained that by primitive he means "primordial" and that the term does not "mean to imply any kind of value judgment" (p. 104 [*CW* 8, para. 218]). The choice of the word, since "primitive" implies undifferentiated and crude, reflects the positivism of Jung's era, seeing aboriginal cultures in relation to Eurocentric culture.

Jung took the basic human tendencies to project and to fear one's complexes as markers of the high degree of importance complexes are for individuation. He stated that complexes are the "living units" of the unconscious and studying them makes it possible to understand the constitution of the unconscious. He called the complexes "the architect of dreams and of symptoms" (p. 101 [*CW* 8, para. 210]), implying the complexes design the evolving shape of one's psyche. These energetic fields act as both bunkers and aggressors during a traumatic event. They function to protect the wounded or rejected aspect of the person. The protective nature of the complex triggers autonomous, defensive responses, which result in affect-laden reactions and repetitive thoughts and behaviors (1948/1960 [*CW* 8]). Further, a complex feels to a person as if it has a life of its own (1948/1960 [*CW* 8]). Jung's emphasis on the importance of the complex is because a found complex can also serve as a portal to what is otherwise submerged in the unconscious in a person.

Jung referred to cultural complexes, which he termed "public complexes," and he gave the example of his violent reaction to some of Freud's writings (1948/1960, p. 103 [*CW* 8, para. 216]). He wrote of the necessity to apply "knowledge of cultural patterns through which we glimpse the creative power of the archetypes" (Jung as cited in Henderson, 1990, p. 123) and stated that when symptoms are common in a number of individuals, psychology can begin to examine a mass phenomenon (1946/1978, p. 218 [*CW* 10, para. 445]).

Jung concluded in "A Review of the Complex Theory": "Complexes are not entirely morbid by nature but are *characteristic expressions of the psyche*, irrespective of whether this psyche is differentiated or primitive" (p. 101 [*CW* 8, para. 209]). The importance Jung attaches to complexes is apparent in his consideration of naming his approach to psychology Complex Psychology instead of Analytical Psychology (Samuels et al., 2005). Jung's theory of the complex has stood up for over 100 years with additions made by post-Jungian theorists as more understandings come to light.

Developments in complex theory

Contributions to complex theory are found in the writings of Erich Neumann (1954/1993), Marie-Louise von Franz's ideas presented in lectures in 1958 and 1959 (1972), the writings of Edward Whitmont (1991) first published in 1969, and in John W. Perry (1970). Also included here are writings of James Hillman (1975), Andrew Samuels (1985, 1989), Donald Kalsched (1996), Murray Stein (1998), and Susan Rowland (2002). Many additional authors have discussed Jung's ideas on the value and nature of the complex. However, this review is limited to the writings that have added innovations relevant to this study. These innovations include re-emphasis on the relational dynamics in a complex, the somatic nature of a complex, and the personification of the archetypal core of a complex.

Edward Whitmont (1991) emphasized clinical applications of Jung's complex theory. He defined a complex as having an outer shell as well as an archetypal core. For Whitmont the shell is the intense, affect-laden reactions of a person, usually shaped by patterns from childhood (p. 68). Its purpose is to defend the wounded core beliefs at the heart of the complex. The goal in therapy is to transform the shell by examining it in relationship to the archetypal core, which paradoxically will transform the core of the complex itself. In order to relieve the suffering caused by a complex the symbolic meaning of the client's personal history needs to be analyzed within the context of the archetypal core. Otherwise, the driving power, which is directly related to the meaning for the sufferer, will remain hidden in the unconscious (p. 69). "In transformation *the drive itself* becomes changed and ceases to trouble us, because it has turned its other face, has been made into a constructive and helpful impulse. . . . Transformation indicates a change in the unconscious itself" (p. 67). Interpersonal effects of complexes are helpful areas for clinical focus as complexes "operate not only as sets of inner tendencies and drives but also as expectations, hopes and fears concerning the outward behavior of people and objects" (p. 60).

Samuels (1985) envisioned archetypes "in a cybernetic manner, more as linking agencies containing the possibility of sense" (p. 53) then as discrete underlying structures. He warned against overemphasis on naming the parts of a complex and losing sight of the "feeling-tone" as the new, once-hidden meaning of the complex emerges for an individual. "What is needed is an approach that enables us to have a theory of inner agents affecting our lives without unduly reifying or personifying those agents" (p. 51).

Erich Neumann (1954/1993), an Israeli Jungian analyst and psychologist, wrote extensively about Jung's theories. In *The Origins and History of Consciousness* (1954/1993) he considered the relevance of the body and somatics to a complex. He wrote,

> The more primitive the psychic level, the more it is identical with the bodily events which rule it. Even personal complexes, i.e., semiconscious "split offs" which belong to the upper layers of the personal unconscious and are affectively charged and "feeling-toned," can evoke physical alterations in the circulatory system, in the respiration, blood pressure, and so on.
>
> (pp. 287–288)

The body is often a person's first alert system that a complex is activated. The compulsive nature of the somatic reactions tends to match the obsessive nature of the thoughts and ideas when the ego has been overtaken by a splintered off reaction in the psyche (1954/1993).

Murray Stein (1998), a Jungian analyst, observed that when "disturbances perseverate for shorter lengths of time than they did before" (p. 50) this signals a weakening in the autonomy of a complex. As a quick return to a normal heart rate after an aerobic workout is a sign of good physical health, the decrease in the buildup in the energetic field of a complex can be deduced by observing the length and depth of the overreaction of emotions in a person. Stein also re-iterated the importance of Samuels' point that the feeling-tone is a key issue in a complex (1998).

Jungian analyst Donald Kalsched (1996) suggested that the shell of a complex is a self-defense system that interprets impulses to change as threats. He credited Jungian analyst John W. Perry (1970) with conceiving of "the entire psyche as structured not only in complexes, but in their bipolar systems or arrangements" (para. 38). Kalsched (1996) investigated the dynamic relationship between what he refers to as a *daimonic* shell and the core of a complex.

A *daimon* (or *daemon*) was a personal spirit protector to the early Greeks. In the polytheistic mindset of ancient Greece, the existence of daemons was accepted with many subtle derivations in meaning (Dodds, 1965). These differences were loosely held together within the broad conceptual frame that they were intermediaries between the human realm and the divine. E. R. Dodds (1965), a classical scholar, stated a precise definition of the vague terms *daemon* and *daemonios* was something of a novelty in Plato's day, but by the second century after Christ it was an expression of a truism. Dodds stated virtually everyone, pagan, Jewish, Christian, or Gnostic, believed in the existence of these beings and in their function as mediators, whether they were called daemons or angels or *aions* or simply "spirits" (pp. 37–38). A daemon as a mediator is akin to a Christian guardian angel. They were thought of as the beings "pure souls on occasion can come into contact with [as a] spiritual power, can hear a spiritual, but wordless, voice and be guided accordingly" (Barrow, 1967, p. 90).

Kalsched has revived this term. In Kalsched's view, the daimonic shell of a complex protects an authentic self that has regressed into an archaic and archetypal state at the core of the complex (1996). The shell creates blocks in the energetic field, pathways that do not lead to connections or learning but instead to repetitious thoughts and compulsive behaviors (1996). The ego adopts a false self for the world, while the energetic field behind the daimonic defense system becomes blocked and so fails to grow or evolve (1996).

In 1958 and 1959 Jungian analyst Marie-Louise von Franz delivered a series of lectures that were published as *The Feminine in Fairytales* (1972). Von Franz emphasized the archetypal nature at the core of complexes in her writings. She understood the normal structuring of the psyche itself to have dynamic zones of energy embedded in it, which, she stated, are generally personified by gods and goddesses (1972). She emphasized the value of personification and usually referred to the Greek gods and goddesses when she discussed gods and goddesses. She stated, "if a god is forgotten, it means that some aspects of collective consciousness are so much in the foreground that others are ignored to a great extent" (p. 25). She envisioned every instinctive dynamism as having an archetypal basis and so understood that the "gods are representations of general complexes" (p. 59). Von Franz focused on using the stories of the mythological figures to help unravel the meaning in a particular complex.

In *Re-Visioning Psychology* (1975) Hillman emphasized personification of the archetypal. As a clinical approach to complexes, he stressed Jung's phenomenological ideology that the therapist does well to stick with the images that arise in the client. Jung (1951/1959c) stated, "In view of the enormous complexity of psychic phenomena, a purely phenomenological point of view is, and will be for a long time, the only possible one and the only one with any prospect of success" (p. 182 [*CW* 9.I, para. 308]). Hillman followed a thread from the pathological personal fantasies to a mythic core. He underscored the importance that clinicians do not merely name the core this god or that, but rather attempt to truly understand its relationship to the client. He said "a complex must be laid at the proper altar, because it makes a difference both to our suffering and perhaps to the God who is manifesting" (p. 104). He stated "to study the complex only personally, or to examine only personally the psychodynamics and history of a case is not enough, since the other half of pathology belongs to the Gods" (pp. 104–105).

Neumann (1954/1993) remarked on Jung's choice to personify the split off complexes in the psyche.

> Besides the ego, analytical psychology distinguishes as such authorities the self, . . . the persona, the anima (or animus in women), and the shadow. The fact that these authorities appear as "persons" is consistent with the fundamental teaching of analytical theory that all unconscious contents manifest themselves "like partial personalities." Each of these authorities can, as an autonomous complex, obsess the ego and lead to a state of possession.
>
> (p. 350)

Personification of the many sided nature of the psyche and Jung's metaphorical language (such as "shadow" as the unseen corners in the unconscious) helps make Jung's psychological theories more accessible, but can also lead to concretization. Jung discussed in "The Syzygy: Anima and Animus" (1951/1959g [*CW* 9II]) purposely personifying the archetypes of the personality in metaphorical language. He stated his understanding that this languaging more accurately reflects the face of the unconscious than does concrete, "scientific" wording (1951/1959g p. 13 [*CW* 9II, para. 25]).

Susan Rowland (2002), a feminist and psychologist, stated that in feminist archetypal theory the archetypal images derived from a female psyche (as from a male) produce "culturally contingent images" (p. 85). Thus in and of themselves they express any sort of differences that exist. When the cultural context is elevated to the foreground, a universal "immanent" image is irrelevant. Rowland quoted feminist theorists Estella Lauter and Carol Schreier:

> In the case of feminist theory, if we regard the archetype not as an image whose content is frozen . . . but as a tendency to form and re-form

> images in relation to certain kinds of repeated experience, then the concept could serve to clarify distinctively female concerns that have persisted throughout history.
>
> (as cited in Rowland, 2002, p. 85)

She devalued the importance of universality of the archetypes and encouraged the notion that the collective unconscious and the archetypes can never be fully known. Instead they are constantly in flux. If archetypes are not something concrete or tangible, but instead are dynamic energetic centers in a reciprocal relationship with consciousness, this implies there is not an ideal model into which humans can be expected to fit. Rowland's understanding of the kaleidoscopic fluidity of archetypal images also reflects recent understandings in cognitive psychology's image schema as a dynamic component of the psyche, rather than a fixed structure (Knox, 2004, pp. 9–10).

Rowland noted:

> What most Jungian feminisms will probably have in common is Jung's defining concept of the irreducible and transformative "otherness" of the unconscious. Feminist archetypal theory combines this principle with a successful renunciation of hierarchies amongst women and their archetypes-as-images.
>
> (p. 86)

Rowland observed that establishing any sort of norms or hierarchal positioning for archetypal images is antithetical to feminist theory. "Both archetypal psychology [as inspired by James Hillman] and feminist archetypal theory reject the transcendent archetype for the immanent image" (2002, p. 85).

In *The Plural Psyche* (1989), Samuels argued that the specifically contrasexual images (in particular the *anima* and *animus*) in the psyche can be understood as metaphors rather than as a particular set of gendered characteristics. "On the one hand, the *concepts* of archetypes and archetypal images are grand theory and logocentric. On the other hand, archetypal images are signifiers without fixed, knowable signifieds. They are subject to slippage and denied logocentric fulfillment" (Rowland, 2002, p. 106). Rowland and Samuels agree that only in theory are archetypes fixed, eternal, or universal. In reality, archetypal images are subjective images, which express a personal dynamic. They are symbolic representations that arise spontaneously out of the unconscious. Rather than exploring a metaphysical understanding of archetypes, a feminist critique agrees with Hillman that only by sticking to the image as fact can Jungians avoid the allure of categorizing, labeling, and quantifying archetypes, thus building a structure of an objective psyche with "empirical data" to prove its existence. By avoiding this contemporary red herring, it is possible to stay close to the inherent personal value arising from the collective unconscious in the form of archetypal images (p. 107).

Finally, in the definition of a complex in *A Critical Dictionary of Jungian Analysis*, Jungian analysts A. Samuels, B. Shorter, and F. Plaut (2005) stated:

> The concept [of a complex] enabled Jung to link the personal and archetypal components of an individual's various experiences. . . . Without such a concept, it would be difficult to express just how experience is built up; psychological life would be a series of unconnected incidents.
>
> (p. 34)

To conceptualize the psyche as an energetic body filled with the knotted ganglia of complexes, which are protecting archetypal cores that nevertheless constantly transmit emotional and imagistic messages, brings theory into the consulting room in a practical manner. This theory has aided in the deconstruction of suffering in the system of personal analysis Jung entitled individuation. Jung emphasized the use of metaphor and analogy as the closest way to articulate any sort of structure for the psyche. For instance he wrote, "the way pointed out by the complex is more like a rough and uncommonly devious footpath" (Jung, 1948/1960, p. 101 [*CW* 8, para. 210]). He steadied his focus on the psychological value for the individual sufferer of complexes rather than on their structure.

Jung's task in the first part of the twentieth century involved deconstructing ideas inspired by Enlightenment thinking as well as promoting his own innovative ideas (Rowland, 2002, p. 106). Recently thought has turned toward questions of a cultural unconscious and cultural complexes, building on Jung's theory of personal complexes. Jung offered passing mention of cultural complexes or "public complexes" (1948/1960, p. 103 [*CW* 8, para. 216]), but he never investigated these ideas himself. Cultural complexes are thought by post-Jungians to populate regions of the psyche that are partly conscious and partly unconscious.

Joseph Henderson's theory of the cultural unconscious

In 1964, at the Second International Congress of Analytical Psychology, Jungian analyst Joseph Henderson (1990) suggested the existence of a cultural unconscious within the collective unconscious. Henderson identified a field in the psyche he outlined as "an area of historical memory that lies between the collective unconscious and the manifest pattern of the culture. It may include both these modalities, conscious, and unconscious" (p. 103). He based this on his observations of a cultural component in a "mutual projection of unconscious factors" (1984, p. 11) between the transference in some of his clients and his own countertransference. He understood these to be based on differences in cultural identities.

Henderson presented these ideas as a continuation of Jung's theory of the personal and collective unconscious (1984, 1990). He cited Jung's discussion, in *Dream Analysis: Notes of a Seminar 1928–1930*, of "applied knowledge of cultural patterns through which we glimpse the creative power of the archetypes" (as cited in Henderson, 1990, p. 123). He suggested that a study of unconscious cultural conditioning would help broaden an understanding of the ways people project onto one another (1990). Though Jung inferred a cultural unconscious in his writing, he focused on mapping the terrain in the deeper, archetypal layers of the unconscious. Henderson argued that he had left this work for others.

Henderson did not see his ideas as being in opposition to Jung's. He (1984) identified four aspects to a cultural unconscious: social, religious, aesthetic, and philosophical. His ideas on a social perspective in individuals are those relevant to this discussion. Henderson considered a social orientation in humans to be the part of the psyche that values the maintenance of an ethical code in their culture, whether the code is that of the dominant culture or one in opposition to the dominant culture (p. 17). Post-Jungians Samuel Kimbles, Michael Vannoy Adams, Thomas Singer, and Donald Kalsched have discussed the merit of Henderson's ideas.

Post-Jungian theory of the cultural complex

In an introduction to *The Cultural Complex: Contemporary Jungian Perspectives on Psyche and Society*, Jungian analysts Thomas Singer and Samuel Kimbles (2004) stated:

> In our ripe time or *kairos*, when understanding the uniqueness and commonality of cultures from around the world has become essential for the well-being of the global community . . . it is our hope that the notion of a "cultural complex" will lead to an enhanced capacity to see more objectively the shadow of the group in its cultural complexes.
>
> (pp. 1–4)

They propose that a cultural complex has similar attributes to a personal complex: it has a life of its own, resists being made conscious, tends to be repetitive, and is selective in its observations of experience, tending to focus on what confirms the complexed point of view (p. 6). Singer and Kimbles see an activated complex as most easily distinguished by "intense collective emotion" (p. 6). They understand cultural complexes to have at their core an archetypal pattern, of which the culture is unaware (p. 6). Above all, a cultural complex is an aspect of a culture's shadow.

A cultural complex leads to destructive behaviors in its members when aspects of the group identity are repressed. The distress inherent in a cultural shadow inevitably leads to the disowned parts of the group identity being cast off through projection onto an out-group (Kimbles, 2003, p. 219). When fear emerges as the primary affect that organizes a group, it leads to scapegoating and an apathetic softening toward fundamental rights of humans, whether those of the in-group or the out-groups (p. 227). The safety of the group supersedes other considerations.

The archetype of the Self is activated by a cultural complex and provides a tremendous organizing force, which sets in motion strong feelings of identifying with the threatened group and its history (Kimbles, 2003, p. 231). While caught in an archetypal spell of "intolerable anxiety" (p. 220) animated by a cultural complex, a tendency to devolve into a lynch mob mentality, overtaken by a moral panic, can be interpreted at the time as patriotic action and can override reasoned responses to problems. Though the inherent threat of violence is quite worrisome, Kimbles is not altogether unhopeful about this all too human tendency. He stated, "individual awareness that some of one's complexes are cultural . . . allows for the creation of a narrating third, a space for symbolization, and the possibility of reflection" (p. 232).

Singer (2004) incorporated Henderson's theory of the cultural unconscious and Kalsched's (1996) theory of archetypal defenses into his work and focused his discussion on "a specific type of cultural complex in which archetypal defenses of the group spirit play a primary role" (p. 13). In such a group, Singer hypothesized, a defensive system, a daimon or daimons, protects the group by presenting a false self to the world and repressing attempts at self-reflection concerning its vulnerability and one sidedness. "The rest of the world which is not part of the traumatized group may see only the more hardened '*daimonic*' front men or women and respond to their aggression and impenetrability as if they were the whole group" (p. 19).

Singer (2004) advanced Perry's (1970) idea that complexes tend to be bipolar (para. 38). Perry, like Whitmont, conceived of a complex as consisting of a traumatized core that is protected by a vigilant, protective shell. "When they are activated the group ego becomes identified with one part of the unconscious complex, while the other part is projected out onto the suitable hook of another group" (Singer, 2004, p. 21). The group shadow is then split. It forms into an inner core that feels unseen or misunderstood and an easily triggered defense system. The two work together spinning the projection of the unconscious split onto an outlying group or groups, which are then interpreted as a threat.

In *The Inner World of Trauma*, Kalsched (1996) wrote about the dynamics of the relationship between the daimonic shell and the core of a complex. He understood the shell as a protective spirit defending an authentic self that lies at the core of the complex in a regressed, archaic, and archetypal state. The shell creates blocks in the psychic energetic field in an attempt to defend the weakened internal psychic core. Like highways going nowhere, psychic pathways are blocked. The traumatized core of the complex freezes and is unable to respond insightfully to the feared outer threat. Instead repetitious thoughts and compulsive behaviors ensue (p. 91). The ego adopts a false self for the world, while the energetic field behind the daimonic defense system fails to grow or evolve (p. 95). Kalsched (1996, 2013) discussed the shell of a complex as originally designed to protect the self, but when it fails to stand down, the complex begins to destructively respond to impulses to change as threats.

Singer and Kimbles have applied these principles to groups, since groups are made of individuals. "Individual and environment really cannot be thought of as separate phenomena without triggering the severe epistemological quandary that leads to suspicion about the effectiveness of modern science" (Dunlap, 2011, p. 51). Their impulse is to help understand why a specific group of people tends to identify as a whole and how the need for identity can turn dangerous (Kimbles, 2000). Singer articulated some of the reasoning behind working toward overcoming the tendency in humans to project group shadow.

> The theory of cultural complexes and their archetypal defenses of the group spirit suggest that Jung was not entirely correct when he said, "nowadays particularly, the world hangs by a thin thread, and that thread is the psyche of man" (McGuire and Hull, 1977). An important piece was left out of that otherwise remarkable – one might even say – primal insight. The fate of the world does not in fact hinge on the thread of the individual psyche. Rather, the emergence of a theory of cultural complexes suggests that an understanding of the individual psyche through its consciousness will not be enough. The group itself will need to develop a consciousness of its cultural complexes. Perhaps each injured culture – be it Balkan, American, Black, White, Palestinian, Israeli, Iraqi, Catholic, Jewish, Jungian, Freudian, Men, Women (the list is endless once you begin to think in terms of cultural complexes) – needs to learn how to drink to the dregs its own complexes, as well as those of its neighbors, allies, and enemies. To settle down the archetypal defenses of the group spirit, the collective psyche itself and its often traumatized, sometimes immature or stunted, spirit needs to individuate – and this is not the work of an individual alone or of analysis alone.
>
> (Singer, 2006, p. 211)

Cultural complex theory has been applied in a number of other disciplines. Educator Joanne Gozawa (2009) discussed its value in theories of education. "An enhanced pedagogy, informed by the contemporary Jungian idea of the cultural complex, may help reveal the invisible cultural prohibitions in transformative learning environments" (para. 1). Anthropologist Mark Moritz (2008) applied the theory of cultural complexes to an anthropological study of African pastoral societies and found a link between "the psychological roots of pastoral aggression to the cultural complex of honor" (para. 1). Evolutionary anthropologists Keith Hunley and Jeffrey Long (2005) argued that, "languages are part of a cultural complex" (para. 1).

Psychiatrist Vamik Volkan (2002) introduced a theory wherein unresolved traumas of one generation, such as those victimized during the Nazi holocaust, are transmitted down through the generations. The trauma lodges within the social group as a whole and deforms healthy behavior in future generations. This theory has valuable clinical application to individuals who suffer pain based on multigenerational transmissions. Volkan stated,

> I will not dwell here on the psychological (especially unconscious) explanations of why these signs and symptoms emerge, except to say that at the bottom of it all is the shared attempt to protect, repair, or maintain the large-group identity and separate it from the 'enemie's' identity.
>
> (2002, p. 459)

This theory has been developed using clinical studies and so has empirically-based observations about groups based on studies of individuals within that group. It dovetails with cultural complex theory's understandings of the unconscious elements in groups and brings to the foreground the lack of clinically-based studies of cultural complex theory, an area which deserves further research to help solidify the validity of cultural complex theory.

Criticisms of cultural complex theory

Jungian historian Kevin Lu (2013) has suggested weaknesses in Kimbles's and Singer's theory of cultural complexes. He posits the need for deeper consideration of the theoretical foundations of cultural complex theory and especially its place within the broader sphere of socio-cultural theories. Lu objected to 1) the theory failing to justify why it has utilized theoretical considerations of the psychology of an individual to analyze collective processes; 2) the lack of adherence to methodological boundaries within the discipline of history; 3) Singer's idea that a *mana* personality in a culture may be a way to resolve cultural complexes; and 4) that there is an inherent fatalistic acceptance of hopelessness regarding group projections embedded in the theory (2013).

Lu's (2013) first point is that cultural complex theory fails to justify applying Jung's theory of a complex in an individual to groups of people. In Jungian thinking, as in most psychological theories, the interpersonal or group life of a person is analyzed as well as the intrapersonal life. Life begins in relationship, and the interrelationships between parents and child, siblings, friends, work, other groups, and with society as a whole comprise much of an analysis. Transference, countertransference, and projection would be meaningless terms if the concepts developed about the individual were only applied to the intrapersonal life. The process of individuation, or for that matter all psychotherapy, is to help individuals to know themselves more truly and this naturally means to be able to be true to who you are within the confines of society. So, in a sense, it is debatable whether there is a clear line between group psychology and the psychology of individuals.

In the literature there have been post-Jungian examinations of the practicality of applying individual analytic method to social and cultural issues. Samuels stated:

> No matter what model of the mind is adhered to, analytical method may still be a valid way of approaching political, social and cultural issues – a way of practicing cultural analysis. This is true despite the origin of analytical technique in the clinical situation. The cultural analyst strives to get into a transference-countertransference relationship with the cultural problem. . . . When there is no individual patient, this understanding means finding out the history of whatever problem is under scrutiny, including the myth or myths which attach to the problem. Finally, the cultural analyst tries to raise the level of the culture's consciousness so as to allow the culture to gain a degree of control and knowledge of the problem.
>
> (1993b, "Analytical method and cultural analysis," para. 1)

Post-Jungian thinking on cultural complex theory has evolved out of Jung's original ideas. Though Jung did not specifically apply complex theory to groups in his seminal essay on complex theory (1948/1960), he did discuss the psychopathology of groups in other essays. Jung analyzed collective processes of peoples and applied his complex theory to groups. Jung stated, "The psychopathology of the masses is rooted in the psychology of the individual" (1946/1978, p. 218 [*CW* 10, para. 445]).

Though not widely, Jung did apply complex theory in other essays concerning cultural phenomena, and he certainly thought quite a lot about cultural phenomena (1988/1998, pp. 139–141; Jung, 1910/1989a, p. 393 [*CW* 18, para. 927]; 1946/1978, p. 222 [*CW* 10, para. 453]). One example is his essay on "The Fight with the Shadow" (1946/1978 [*CW* 10]). He stated that when symptoms are common in a number of individuals, psychology can begin to examine a mass phenomenon (p. 218 [*CW* 10, para. 445]). He applied complex theory to the state of the German people (p. 225 [*CW* 10, para. 456]) and to "Western democracies" ([*CW* 10, para. 457]). Here, he argued, "the indescribable events of the last decade lead one to suspect that a peculiar psychological disturbance was a possible cause" (p. 218 [*CW* 10, para. 444]) of the terrible occurrences during the Nazi Reich.

Lu's point that a chronology of Jung's ideas and post-Jungian thought would aid Singer and Kimbles, as well as the need to consider other socio-cultural authors' writings on trauma, group psychology, and historical events, is a useful addition to the discussion. This writing aspires to contribute to the filling of this lacunae.

The field of psychohistory has set a precedent for research into group psychologies. Psycho-historians expanded historical research's traditional questions of who, what, where, and when to include why (Szaluta, 1999). It applied Freud's theory of personality and his theoretical positions on mass psychology to historical events. Further, psycho-historical theory explored "collective mentality" (1999, p. 61) and argued that better understandings of the irrational forces that can seize a group and at times overwhelm rational thinking are available through applying Freud's and post-Freudians' discussions of individual psychology to history (p. 61).

Lu (2013) stated that oftentimes Jungian scholars have improperly applied a historical method to psychological theory, thereby muddying the argument. This is a point well taken. Jungians could learn from Jung himself, who undertook long apprenticeships to the studies of mythology and alchemy and made efforts to contextualize his arguments based on his predecessors' and contemporaries' writings (Jung, 1961/1965). The lack of adherence to scholarly historical method is an unfortunate and unnecessary by-product in the valuable cross-fertilization between these different areas of research.

Lu (2013) urged Jungians to be cautious with applications of historical symbols (p. 11). The use of the historical method, going to primary sources and other extant evidence as the basis of research, while often ignored in post-Jungian studies, is planned as a cornerstone of this work. Examples include reading the journals of Eric Harris to understand the violence of the Columbine massacres and turning to the extant ancient sources to decipher Pan as an archetypal force. The data found in historical sources will be employed to attempt a hermeneutic dialogue between the history of these events and a psychological understanding of anxiety in America.

Singer (2010) suggested that cultural complexes might be mitigated by the appearance on the world stage of mana personalities who can hold the tension of the opposites and help constellate the transcendent function. Lu (2013) questioned these remarks, and I am inclined to agree with Lu. History just does not seem to resolve itself in this way. Depending on one's cultural viewpoint, Mandela, Obama, or Trump may have felt like the second coming to a people, but underlying projections onto other cultures rage on despite their appearance on the world stage. Lu's argument (2013) speaks to the need for depth psychologists to be more attentive to historical methodology if they aspire to find an audience outside the confines of the Jungian community.

Lu's (2013) last point is that there is a fatalism implied in cultural complex theory that stifles change. Though cultural complex theory is not a solution-based psychological theory, it remains true to the idea that raising consciousness and generating ideas and discussion furthers the development of solution-based tools and methods to advance change. There is an abundance of new sociocultural theories attempting to understand the effects of violence on culture (Barak, 2005; Pyszczynski et al., 2003; Cohen, D., 1998). This implies that we are in a time when this issue is overdue for understanding, which can lead to change naturally emerging from within a culture *if* the culture becomes more aware of itself. Change, such as ending racism, can be legislated by political bodies, but the emergence of unbiased attitudes is never created by legislators. These arise through the progression of the culture itself toward a more tolerant and enlightened attitude. Change can be influenced through the advancement and inspiration of theory that leads to greater awareness. This is the ground on which cultural complex theory has been birthed.

Samuel Kimbles weighed in on specific ways that cultural complex theory contributes:

> Bringing self-awareness to collective remembering facilitates our relationship to personal and group memories and hopefully helps us find different ways to relate to them. We may turn ethnos logic into an awareness of cultural complexes and begin the long psychological work of processing and metabolizing their potent venom. When in the grip of archaic identity, our culture would have us affirm that its tenets are incontrovertible facts. Without an awareness of this largely unconscious process, our history becomes nothing more than the manifestation of one more cultural complex. The psyche becomes tied to a specific cultural history of trauma. We miss the opportunity to, as Hillman states, "turn events into experiences" that can be reflected on, potentially digested, and redeemed.
>
> (2006, p. 109)

Finally Samuels expressed his ideas on the value of cultural analysis by depth psychotherapists:

> Generally speaking, political and cultural analysis, as I envision it, would avoid quiet acceptance of things as they are, or meditative emptiness, or an "Eastern" way to cure the madness of "Western" society. But these should not be ruled out. "Sometimes I sits and thinks and sometimes I just sits," was the rural sage's solution. Drawing on professional experience, an analyst can offer the men and women of action – though the

> most brilliant of them know it already – a trained sense of timing: when to interpret and when to keep silent. Reflection is itself a psychological contribution to the resacralization of culture.
>
> (1993b, "Analytical method and cultural analysis," para. 3)

The following chapters explore ways in which the multivalent meanings attributed to the goat-god Pan are also archetypal energetics existing, as Jung suggested, *in potentia* in the psyche (1951/1959d, p. 152 [*CW* 9.I, para. 259]) and so still capable of affecting complexes in modern day humans. In subsequent chapters, a comparison between an unconscious complex that functions as an "architect of dreams and of symptoms" (Jung, 1948/1960, p. 101 [*CW* 8, para. 210]) and the dynamics underlying patterns of anxiety and violent reactions in the prototypical events following the Columbine massacre, 9/11, and rape in the military will be sifted and combed through in the hope that Kimbles's "narrating third, a space for symbolization, and the possibility of reflection" (2003, p. 232) will emerge.

Chapter 3

The great god Pan is dead

With the advantage of hindsight, the timing of the legend of the death of Pan has proved to be a significant indicator of the decline of the Greek tradition of worship of the divine in nature. Over the centuries, different understandings of Pan's significance have developed and faded away, while Pan himself has been projected upon in paradoxical ways. An oracular event announced the death of Pan during the same era during in which Jesus was crucified. In a story recorded by Plutarch in 83 or 84 CE, Pan is said to have died during the reign of Tiberius Caesar (14–37 CE), and Jesus Christ was crucified during Tiberius' short reign as well. He has been equated with the Christian devil and, conversely, with Jesus. More recently, he has been seen as a universal god-image, a misunderstood, romantic figure, a symbol of what humankind lost with the end of antiquity, and, since the Industrial age, a symbol of the loss of connection to the enigmatic mystery of life's vitality that the ancients projected onto the nature gods and goddesses of their time (Boardman, 1997; Merivale, 1969; del Toro, 2006a). "Creatures of a day. What is a someone, what is a no one? Man is the dream of a shade. But when the brightness given by Zeus comes, there is at hand the shining light of men, and the life-force [*aiōn*] gives pleasure" (Pindar, 2017, para. 16).

The legend of the death of Pan

The story of Pan's unresurrected end was sandwiched into a Greek dialogue of Plutarch's, written in 83 or 84 CE, in which he pondered the probability that daemons at oracular sites may be finite rather than immortal, and so could be the cause of the failure of many of these sites in the first century. He concluded that since Pan died, he must be a daemon (Plutarch, 1936/2003b). Pan was a lesser god in the Greek Pantheon, but until Plutarch's recording of this tale he was consistently referred to in the extant literature as a god (Borgeaud, 1983). Even in the tale itself, Pan is named a god, and a "Great God" at that (1936/2003b). Never the less, Plutarch used Pan's death to argue his point in "On the Obsolescence of the Oracles" that although a daemon may die, this did not constitute the end of conduits for communication with the gods (1936/2003b, pp. 401–403 [419B-D]). Within its own context, the report of Pan's death served this purpose only.

The dating of the text can be approximated by events Plutarch mentioned in his opening paragraphs. Plutarch introduced the debate about oracles, which he described as taking place "a short time before the Pythian games, which were held when Callistratus was in office in our day" (1936/2003b, p. 351). That places the gathering of the men in 83 or 84 CE.

Here is the legend in full:

> As for death among such beings, I have heard the words of a man who was not a fool nor an imposter. The father of Aemilianus the orator, to whom some of you have listened, was Epitherses, who lived in our town and was my teacher in grammar. He said that once upon a time in making a voyage to Italy he embarked on a ship carrying freight and many passengers. It was already evening when, near the Echinades Islands, the wind dropped, and the ship drifted near Paxi. Almost everybody was awake, and a good many had not finished their after-dinner wine. Suddenly from the island of Paxi was heard the voice of someone loudly calling Thamus, so that all were amazed. Thamus was an Egyptian pilot, not known by name even to many on board. Twice he was called, and made no reply, but the third time he answered; and the caller, raising his voice, said, "When you come opposite to Palodes announce that Great Pan is dead." On hearing this, all, said Epitherses, were astounded and reasoned among themselves whether it were better to carry out the order or to refuse to meddle and let the matter go. Under the circumstances Thamus made up his mind that if there should be a breeze, he would sail past and keep quiet, but with no wind and a smooth sea about the place he would announce what he had heard. So, when he came opposite Palodes, and there was neither wind nor wave, Thamus from the stern, looking toward the land, said the words as he had heard them: "Great Pan is dead." Even before he had finished there was a great cry of lamentation, not of one person, but of many, mingled with exclamations of amazement. As many persons were on the vessel, the story was soon spread abroad in Rome, and Thamus was sent for by Tiberius Caesar. Tiberius became so convinced of the truth of the story that he caused an inquiry and investigation to be made about Pan; and the scholars, who were numerous at his court; conjectured that he was the son born of Hermes and Penelope.
>
> (Plutarch, 1936/2003b, p. 403 [419D])

Over the course of time this curious tale has been investigated and interpreted again and again. The story's final words, "he was the son born of Hermes and Penelope" (Plutarch, 1936/2003b, p. 403 [419D]), began the conjecturing. Tiberius Caesar (42 BCE- 17CE) ordered an investigation because he was fearful of what such an omen might mean for himself and for his empire (Cramer, 1996). His scholars determined that the Pan who died was the son of Hermes and not the same Pan as the son of Zeus, who figured in Roman creation myths. Concerns that the story might be a bad omen for the Caesers were allayed. The significance of the story lay elsewhere.

The death of an immortal

The Greek gods were immortal, and a significant point to consider is that the death of Pan, an immortal, is an anomaly in the Greek myths (Borgeaud, 1983, p. 255):

> What is unique about the Greek tradition is the radical and thoroughgoing way in which the opposition between the realm of the gods and the realm of the dead was worked out. The gods are the immortals, *athanatoi;* the epithet becomes a definition. To name a festival the "day of the burial of the divinity," as the Phoenicians do, is impossible in Greek. A god bewailed as dead, such as Adonis, is always felt to be foreign.
>
> (Burkert, 1977/1985, p. 201)

If an immortal is thought of psychologically as a god-image that lives within the psyche, then death occurs when a god or goddesses followers forget him or her. But Pan's cult continued in Arcadia, as evidenced by Pausanias's eyewitness accounts from the second century (1935/1961). He described temples dedicated to Pan (1935/1961, p. 29 [VIII. xxvi, 2]), mountains sacred to him (p. 15 [VIII, xxiv, 4]), altars with his image (p. 53 [VIII. xxx. 3]), and statues of Pan (p. 53 [VIII. xxx. 6]). As he traveled through Arcadia Pausanias observed, "Mount Maenalus is held to be especially sacred to Pan, so that those who dwell around it say that they can actually hear him playing on his pipes" (p. 83 [VIII, xxxvi, 10]). Though Pausanias is known at times to have relied on previous sources, his observations have been validated by archeological finds (Alcock, 1993).

Also in the second century, the Roman Neo-Platonic philosopher Apuleius, in his novel *The Golden Ass* (1915/1958; von Franz, 1980), colored Pan with a late antiquity hue as a kindly guide to Psyche. He counseled her to remain true to love rather than to choose death when she teetered on the edge of suicide after Eros had left her. There can be little doubt that Pan was still actively worshipped at least into the sixth century (Alcock, 1994). So the legend is not a reflection of his death in the hearts and minds of his followers.

There are no extant records of outcries or even commentaries from the philosophers or cult worshippers at the time concerning this strange tale. The legend has proved itself to be paradoxical. His cult had not forgotten him and now the story itself ensured he was not forgotten when most of the Greek gods and goddesses of his stature have been (Boardman, 1997). The lack of a historical record indicates it is most likely that the legend was not of interest to many at the time and appears to have gained in value with hindsight.

The historical record indicates the legend was used to advance Christianity by suppressing the worship of the divine in nature and replacing the myths with Christian beliefs in the fourth century by Eusebius (c. 265–c. 340), a bishop of Caesarea, to help establish the Nicine Creed. The desire to convert everyone to one way of conceiving of the divine was enforced with a heavy hand at that time by Justinian I. He became the Roman emperor in 528 and established laws reflecting the imperial position presupposing a unity of faith in the empire. In 529, "legislation forbidding pagans to teach effectively put an end to the existence of the Academy at Athens" (Cameron, 2000, p. 69). Until then, the classics were still being taught from the Greek, now considered pagan, points of view. Pagan from the Latin, *paganus*, meaning rural or belonging to a village, is the Christian name for what they believed to be heretical cults (Simpson, 1968, p. 420).

The scholars were given the opportunity to become Christians but refused. Agathias (c. 532–c. 579), a young man at the time, later recorded, in his *The Histories:*

> the philosophers of our age, had come to the conclusion, since the official religion of the Roman empire was not to their liking, that the Persian state was much superior . . . they were forbidden by law to take part in public life with impunity owing to the fact that they did not conform to the established religion.
>
> (1975, p. 65 [II. 30, 3–4])

Justinian's *Codex* suppressed the Greek cults as living traditions (Cameron, 2000) and the Nicine Creed began a long history of Christian leaders denouncing Pan as a demon and certainly not immortal. The year 529 is considered by many to date of the end of antiquity.

A reciprocal oracle

The dual nature of Pan's body reflects a reciprocal link that was understood by the ancients to exist on a much greater scale: between nature and divinity. The choice of Pan, whose body contained these opposing forces, as the god who must die, suggests that at the time of the story the concept of the divine residing in nature was dying rather than evolving. The animated world of Greek myth, as reflected in its poetry and art, would seem to be threatened by this prospect. The story is about a unique style of communication between the human and the divine worlds. The communication is direct and emphasized a synchronous linking of the two worlds as seen in the supernatural reactions to his death.

In the story itself the divine world needs Thamus, a man and the pilot of the ship, to announce the sad news in Palodes. The pilot (the navigator who follows the captain's orders and is responsible to chart a course and bring a ship into port) acted as a go-between, piloting the course the invisible's loud voice had uncannily called out. The message is passed from the isolation of an island (Paxi) to an area of the mainland to suggest exactly what happens: the news spreads because of this occurrence.

The ship's course is identifiable. A ship heading north from Paxi toward Palodes is on a course still followed by steamships and ferries today to travel the shortest distance of open water from Greece to Italy, the destination designated in the tale. Paxi is in the Ionian Sea just south of Corfu and over 12 miles from the mainland. It was a haven for pirates and otherwise uninhabited during early Roman times (Grunewald, 1999/2004, p. 23). Palodes (Pelodes) harbor was part of the Roman protectorate of Buthrotum and was given to soldiers as payment in the defeat of Marc Antony at Actium in 31 BCE. It was a bustling outer hub of the empire (Bescoby, Cawley, & Chroston, 2004, p. 189). Thamus was instructed to take a message heard in the wilderness to the closest outpost of the civilized world.

The nature and delivery of the message of Pan's death fails to fall into any common pattern of Greek oracles, prophecies, or supernatural messages. In divination, an oracular voice usually answers questions about the ordinary "day" world; it is consulted because it responds to questions mortals bring concerning themselves (Aune, 1983). A person would approach the divine through an oracle, usually for personal advice or to settle questions concerning ritual protocols. That the unseen voice instructed Thamus was remarkable in itself because traditionally oracles were heard only in response to a person's or a nation's requests (Cicero, 1950, p. 343 [1.6.24]).

This in part explains why the ship's passengers were "astounded" and nervous about how to respond to this direct command. Thamus made a wise choice and put himself in accord with the supernatural occurrence. He did not try to interpret or to pass judgement on its validity. Instead, he followed along, and when the wind died near Palodes he took this as confirmation from the unseen source.

No one is reported to be visible when Thamus called out and yet a multitude responded. That the ship's pilot, Thamus, is asked to echo back to the eternal realm what the voice told him also deviates from the ancient historical norms (Aune, 1983, pp. 247–248). The proclamation of Pan's death is from an unseen and inhuman (in psychological terms, the unconscious) source, to humans (or consciousness), and then from the human world, back to invisible voices, "not of one person, but of many" (Plutarch, 1936/2003b, p. 403 [419D]). The structure of the legend is that an invisible voice enters the human realm and asks the mortals to become the echo of the voice. The lamentations and amazement at this also comes from unseen beings. There is a reciprocal structure to the tale, which implies that direct communication between the two worlds is desired or needed by the divine.

The notion that the divine is in a reciprocal relationship with humanity is radical. Is the divine evolving or is it fixed? Is the archetypal structure of the collective unconscious fluid or is it that the contents within the structure change while the structure remains the same? In the story, the supernatural realm receives information it did not have from the human realm. The gods have gained from human intervention, suggesting that the divine is not fixed but evolving and this evolution involves humans. This intimates that Epicurus was wrong when he said the gods have no interest in humans (Epicurus, 1964, p. 53) and that Socrates was right when he intuited that the gods do not need material offerings from humans (Plato, 1914/1966). Rather than material offerings, the divine, in this story, ask for more direct communication with the human world. Perhaps as the god dies who carried for his cult the interwoven nature of the divine and nature, a new and more conscious human/divine communication or intermingling was born.

Thamus piloted north to Palodes, and when the wind was light and the ocean becalmed, he called out the message. Before he finished, "a great cry of lamentation, not of one person, but of many, mingled with exclamations of amazement" was released. The cries and the voyager's reactions are reminiscent of Pan's associations with noise, fear, and panic. The empty landscape of Paxi and the rough border town denote his isolation and wildness. In the Greek myths the presence of the goat-god Pan, whether through seduction or panic, created an uncanny, numinous atmosphere (Borgeaud, 1979/1988). Here the emotional landscape reflects Pan's own nature.

> But solitude, being wisdom's training-ground, is a good character-builder, and moulds and reforms men's souls. . . . Here the mind turns to diviner sorts of learning and sees with a clearer vision. This, surely, is the reason why it was in solitary spots that man founded all those shrines of the gods that have been long established from ancient times, above all those of the Muses, [and] of Pan and the Nymphs.
>
> (Plutarch, 1969, p. 269 [XV. Fr. 143])

Pan, like all the Greek gods, had oracular power: "It is said in the days of old this god gave oracles" and "Pan, equally with the most powerful gods, can bring men's prayers to accomplishment" (Pausanias, 1961, p. 91 [VIII. xxxvii, 11]). Here, unasked, an oracle astounds the humans and dismays the invisibles.

Plutarch's problem

Plutarch's problem and the driving force in "On the Obsolesence of the Oracles" (1936/2003b) is what value is an oracle if prophecy does not work anymore? His purpose was to determine whether his gods were still in communication with humankind. At the time, belief in the Greek oracles was fading. As a priest at Delphi, Plutarch's interest in this subject was not academic. The Roman orator Cicero (106–43 BCE) had commented on the decline in his *On Divination*.

> The Delphic oracle would never have been so famous, so crowded with throngs of people, so rich in gifts of kings and commoners from the very ends of the earth, if the passing centuries had not thoroughly tested its predictions and pronounced them veracious. For some time this has not been true. Therefore, as its former glory has now faded because its utterances are no longer to be implicitly trusted, so in the old days it would not have enjoyed such high honor if it had not been infallible.
>
> (1950, p. 356 [I. 19.26])

Strabo recorded that "among the ancients both divination in general and oracles were held in greater honour, but now great neglect of them prevails" (1932/1949, p. 115 [XVII.1.43]).

As described by the narrator in "On the Obsolesence of the Oracles" (1936/2003b), Plutarch portrayed daemons as the protectors of oracular sites. He was not alone in this understanding. In *Timaeus* (1965/1971), Plato stated:

> We should think of the most authoritative part of our soul as a guardian spirit given by god, living in the summit of the body, which can properly be said to lift us from the earth towards our home in heaven . . . a man who has given his heart to learning and true wisdom and exercised that part of himself is surely bound if he attains to truth, to have immortal and divine thoughts, and cannot fail to achieve immortality as fully as is permitted to human nature; and because he has always looked after the divine element in himself and kept his guardian spirit in good order he must be happy above all men.
>
> (p. 119 [90])

Plato's translator, H. D. P. Lee, added in a footnote, "'Looked after': the word can bear a religious significance in Greek, to 'serve' a god." (p. 119). A daemon at times refers to an individual's guiding spirit: "A daemon was an intermediary between the human realm and the divine" (Dodds, 1965, p. 37). It was the explanation for when "pure souls on occasion can come into contact with spiritual power, can hear a spiritual, but wordless, voice and be guided accordingly" (Barrow, 1967, p. 90). A daemon protected by intervening in human affairs and guided through divination. Plutarch concluded that daemons are mortal, though incredibly long-lived, and stated that Pan must have been a daemon rather than a god and that this is why he died (1936/2003b).

Plutarch used Pan's death to argue his point that although a daemon may die, this did not constitute the end of communication with the gods (1936/2003b, pp. 401–403 [419B-D]). In context, this may have had more to do with the waning cultural influence of Greek culture in the Mediterranean than with Pan (Alcock, 1993).

Is Plutarch a worthy source of information? It would appear so. He was a patriotic Greek and throughout his life remained true to his philosophy that it was everyman's (Plutarch, in accordance with the traditions of his time, directed his thoughts to men and about men. Women were not considered men's equals. The term "men" here is not meant to imply humanity) duty to serve his country and his gods to his utmost capacity. Rather uncharacteristically for his time, Plutarch counseled that kindness and sympathy were hallmarks of a good man. He outlined, or more accurately meandered gracefully through, his beliefs in both his *Parallel Lives* and *Moralia*, which due to their popularity, even through the Middle Ages, have been handed down to the present in much greater parts than works of many ancient writers. He conceptualized the universe as dualistic and believed that an ongoing tension existed between good and evil. In this, he, a Middle Platonist, differed with Plotinus and the Neoplatonists who followed Plato's idea that evil exists only within humans.

Plutarch was born on or around 46 CE in the Boeotian town of Chaeronea to a wealthy, aristocratic family and attended the Academy of Plato in Athens beginning in 67 CE. He was probably in Athens when Nero gave Greece its short-lived freedom in November of 67 CE (Jones, 1971). The arrogant retraction by the Emperor Vespasian only years later had economic as well as philosophic repercussions for all the people of Greece. Greek efforts in the first century were by necessity keenly devoted to survival and subsistence (Pausanias, 1959, p. 231 [7.17.1]; Strabo, 1932/1949, p. 319 [IX.2.25]). The golden day of Socrates had passed; instead, Greece woke up every day under the darkening shadow of Rome's *Pax Romana* (Alcock, 1993, pp. 38–39). What the Greeks could and did cherish was their cultural heritage (Goodman with Sherwood, 2002, p. 229).

Greece, Rome's superior in philosophy, arts, and letters, was her captive (Bowie, 1970, p. 18). The economics of the *Pax Romana* and the persistent drain through tributes (including her art treasures) to Rome (Alcock, 1993), severe declines in population (Sallares, 1991, p. 106), and the loss of her dominion as a world power probably galled even the most sagacious. During the Second Sophistic period, the memory of the past heroes and questions of co-mingling with the gods would have been a welcome relief from the reality of Greece's fall to backwater status.

Plutarch's dialogue about the death of an immortal would only stand as a historical oddity if there were not so many subsequent interpretations of the story beginning with Eusebius in the fourth century. Over time, the content, structure, recurring motifs, and themes of the legend have resonated for disparate ideologies as examples of their particular vision. The cryptic story has, paradoxically, kept the goat-god Pan from dying in the imagination of subsequent generations. Shifts in the imagination of who Pan was, or is, demonstrate how he functions as a fluid repository for unconscious psychological projections. Pan still echoes divergent sides of being human, wholeness, and distantly, the Greek psyche that first envisioned his nature.

Daemon to Demon

James S. Grotstein, a psychoanalyst, described the devil's "medieval portraiture – as a demon with horns, tail, and cloven feet. From one point of view we can behold a latter-day transformation of the Dionysian goat-god, Pan" (1997, para. 40). This transformation can be traced to the writings of Eusebius (2011) (c. 275–339), a prominent voice in the creation of the Nicene Creed. The purpose of the Nicene Creed, written in 325 was to establish a conformity of belief among Christians and to establish what beliefs deviated from the orthodox and so were heretical (Wackernage & Vale, 1999). Eusebius (2011) wrote his *Praeparatio Evangelica* at the beginning of the fourth century.

Eusebius is credited with first interpreting the legend of the death of Pan as proof of Jesus Christ's power over the pagan gods. He wrote that this was evidenced by Christ's many exorcisms in the New Testament (Barnes, 2009; Eusebius, 2011, [V, VXII]). Eusebius reinterpreted Pan as one of the demons cast out by Jesus.

Here he addresses Plutarch's question concerning why the oracles were in decline:

> It is important to observe the time at which he [Plutarch] says that the death of the daemon took place. For it was the time of Tiberius, in which our Saviour, making His sojourn among men, is recorded to have been ridding human life from daemons of every kind: so that there were some of them now kneeling before Him and beseeching Him not to deliver them over to the Tartarus that awaited them. You have therefore the date of the overthrow of the daemons, of which there was no record at any other time.
>
> (Eusebius, 2011, [V, XVII])

Eusebius used Plutarch's argument in "On the Obsolescence of the Oracles" (1936/2003b) that if Pan died he must be a daemon, but he reconceived of Pan as a demon or an unclean spirit. The daemons of Greek religion became the demons of the New Testament, and Pan "was dubbed the devil by Christianity" (Halford, 1993, p. 58). Pan, with his lusty, scary, smelly nature (Boer, 1970), has been reduced to only the negative sides of the archetype: a force that is feared by Christians today as Satan, a living, breathing being with power over humankind. In the current fundamentalist revival, the influence of the devil in the biblical scriptures is interpreted literally (Davis, W. A., 2006). To many, the devil is not only a subjective reality, but an actual living, breathing being.

The fallen angel referred to in the Old Testament as Satan or Lucifer or an angel, is just that, an angel who is in opposition (a satan) to God. The number of times Satan is mentioned in the Old Testament is usually thought to be four (Num. 22.22–35; Job 1–2; Zech. 3.1–7; and 1 Chron. 21.1–22.1) (Brown, D., 2011, p. 203). It is important to "resist reading back into these texts a later notion of a theologically developed figure of Satan since these OT passages don't necessarily assume the existence of such a figure" (p. 203). In the few references to Satan in the Old Testament none are described with any of Pan's features (Tate, 1992).

The voices of the earlier polytheistic religions advocating for the plurality of the psyche, were overpowered by the Christian myth of one god and one devil, especially in the New Testament. "The Gospels of the NT contain the most concentrated amount of references to Satan among the biblical literature" (Brown, D., 2011, p. 209).

When Satan, or the Devil, appeared in opposition to Jesus in the New Testament, he needed to be identifiable and was clothed in the physical attributes of Pan. By the Middle Ages, the Catholic Church had adopted the belief that Pan's image and qualities were the principal symbols of the Devil (Martin, J., 1880; Grotstein, 1997). The physical identity of the Devil of Christianity owed a great deal to him. "The Devil acquired the features of Pan by medieval monks" (Martin, J., 1880). In the *Dictionary of Medieval Latin from British Sources* (Howlett, 2005), Pan is defined as meaning an Arcadian pastoral god and an "evil spirit, incubus" (p. 404). The characteristics most identified with the Devil: horns, tail, cloven hoofs, repulsive odor, and ugly countenance are all shared with Pan (Hillman, 1988; Halford, 1993; Mulyran, 1980). "Pan elements in the iconography of the Devil were rather inconsistently applied, but his reputation and behavior were thought good qualifications for his service as a model" (Boardman, 1997, p. 24). Perhaps art historian Ad de Vries's *Dictionary of Symbols and Images* (1984) puts it the most succinctly: "Pan (god) Nature, represented as a semi-goat: (later) Satan" (p. 357). Pan was demonized, scapegoated, and rejected. But if the psychological maxim that what is remembered is not dead is applied, he did not die.

The all

Conversely, Pan also survived past the end of antiquity as a source of inspiration (Merivale, 1969; Russell, 1993). Building on the mythic motif in the *Homeric Hymn to Pan* where Hermes takes his new-born son to Olympus, he is understood by the Olympians, as a god of nature, to be a god named All, one that includes the sum total of all things (Athanassakis, 1976). The Olympians found his differences endearing and "called him Pan because he cheered the hearts of all" (p. 63). Socrates took up the point that Pan is all in Plato's *Cratylus* (1917). The All is a quintessential symbolling of a central theme in life, the innate drive toward wholeness and acceptance of oneself, flaws and all.

In Greek *Pá¯n* means all, while *pãn* means herder (Kerenyi, 1998). In antiquity Pan was understood as both the goat herder *and* the all. The etymology of Pan's name as meaning "all" has been disputed. Lewis Farnell, a classical scholar, interpreted his name as "the 'feeder' or 'grazier' [herder] this etymology is supported by a dedication in his temple on Mount Lykaion" (1909/1971, p. 431). Walter Burkert, scholar of Greek mythology and cult, accepted early understandings of Pan as both. "Speculations concerning a universal god were later attached to his name" (1977/1985, p. 172). As a symbol of universal Nature, Pan became for some the "Supreme Governor or 'soul' of the World" (Merivale, 1969, p. 9).

By the fifteenth century, for some Pan and Jesus had become indicators of the same archetypal energy for some. Paulus Marsus, an Italian humanist and poet (1440–1484), wrote:

> The holiest men declare that this voice was heard from Paxis that night . . . in the nineteenth year of Tiberius' reign: at which time indeed Christ died: who, with a voice miraculously issuing forth from the solitude of the deserted rocks, was announcing that the Lord . . . was dead. Now what does Pan mean, if not all. Thus the lord of all and of universal nature had died. . . . Truly we are dealing with the Pan of whom better [is said] of Theodosius [Macrobius] when he says not the lord of the woods, but the ruler of the material substance of the universe. . . . The strength of whose nature forms the essence of universal bodies whether they are divine or earthly.
>
> (as cited in Merivale, 1969, p. 13)

Pan and Jesus were both referred to as "all," represented as shepherds, and understood as having taken on the suffering of their worshippers. This construction resurfaced in the written record in a popular book from the Renaissance, written in 1542, by the Spaniard Pedro Mexia, entitled *Silva di varia lecció* (as cited in Russell, 1993). It outlined the notion that Pan was named "all" by the Olympians in the same sense that Jesus is "all" to a Christian (1993). Soon he was joined in his ideas by Cardinal du Bellay as recorded in his *Christianae Philosophiae Praeludium*, published in Toulouse in 1549 (as cited in Russell, 1993), and in 1552 by Cardinal du Bellay's faithful secretary and doctor, Francois Rabelais (1955) in *Pantagruel*. In

Rabelais a chapter entitled, "Pantagruel's Pitiable story about the Death of Heroes," told the story of the death of Pan and then went on to say:

> I should interpret this anecdote, nevertheless, to refer to that great Savior of the Faithful, who was shamefully put to death in Judaea through the envy and wickedness of the pontiffs, doctors, priests, and monks of the Mosaic Law, and I do not consider my reading of the story far-fetched. For he can rightfully be called, in the Greek tongue, Pan; seeing that he is our All. All that we are, all that we live by, all that we have, all that we hope for is from him, in him, of him, and by him. He is the good Pan, the great shepherd. . . . At his death there were wailings, sighs, fears, and lamentations throughout the whole mechanical universe, throughout the heavens, the earth, the sea, and hell beneath. The date agrees with this interpretation of mine. For that most good and mighty Pan, our Saviour, died outside Jerusalem in the reign of Tiberius Caesar.
>
> (pp. 511–512)

Later, Francis Bacon's (1561–1626) *De Sapientia Veterum* (*The Wisdom of the Ancients*) took up the theme of Pan as all, a universal god, and used his attributes "as a kind of memory system or frame of reference for an exposition of his theory of the universe, with the different facts pegged on to the different physical and historical characteristics of Pan" (Mulyran, 1980, p. 216). For some, Pan represented archetypal wholeness. If he seems repulsive, that is because repulsiveness is part of the "all." These were people who appear to have had faith in Pan's ability to conjoin disparate facets in human nature as a path toward healing and redemption for the psyche.

A melancholy spirit

During the Renaissance, Pan was sometimes portrayed as a melancholy musician. Italian painter Luca Signorelli created *The Court of Pan* (also known as *The School of Pan*) in about 1484. Unfortunately, it was destroyed during World War II. In it Pan is a dignified and melancholy figure. With his horns a crescent moon and his goaty legs reduced to below the knee, his animal nature is overshadowed, or sublimated, by his artistry (Boardman, 1997).

In the early nineteenth century during the Romantic era, poetic and pictorial representations reflected on the loss for all when Pan was forgotten and left for dead (Russell, 1993). He was reinterpreted with a renewed emphasis on his pastoral, rustic, and melancholy qualities. During this period Pan lost the brutal, frightening side of the dark chthonic realms but maintained his hidden, sad, and mysterious qualities (Merivale, 1969). The poems of Elizabeth Barrett Browning (1900), Robert Browning (Davies, 2006), William Wordsworth (1982), John Keats (1935), as well as the art of Arnold

Böcklin (1856–1857) and Aubrey Beardsley (1898) emphasize the melancholy, kinder, and more approachable side of Pan's nature. He is rarely on the move, whereas in the ancient texts he overflowed with energy, chasing after his prey. His power to create sudden change diminished. He was often imagined alone or with one woman, especially with Psyche, playing his pipes.

Browning wrote eloquently of Pan as the harbinger of loss in the poem "The Dead Pan" (first published in 1844):

> And that dismal cry rose slowly
> And sank slowly through the air,
> Full of spirit's melancholy
> And eternity's despair!
> And they heard the words it said –
> – GREAT PAN IS DEAD –
> PAN, PAN IS DEAD. (1900)

A prevailing sense of a loss for all with the diminishment of Pan's power took hold as a symbol of the Romantics' protest of the new Industrial age. The domination of nature by humankind, and more specifically by the technological advances of the white Eurocentric culture, inspired creative thinkers of that time to express their loss and to mourn for the ancient god of nature.

The torpor of Pan in modernity

D. H. Lawrence's essay *Pan in America* (1936), first written in 1924 (McDonald, 1936, p. xii), theorized that modern American life had lost the Pan power, or Pan mystery, as he called it. He regretted this loss. On the heels of New Mexico receiving statehood, Lawrence lived on a ranch in the still wild land. From there he observed the desacrilization of nature as the vast resources of America were turned to monetary profits. He envisioned Pan as the carrier of a vanishing archetypal field and imagined the rustic god Pan at home in the great sweep of the American wilderness as he once was in the bucolic landscapes of Arcadia. Lawrence expressed the pain he felt as he watched the new Americans' apathy toward their remarkable land and wrote this attitude was erasing a direct link to the divine in nature.

Lawrence (1936) saw Pan as a "lurking rustic god. . . . A sort of fugitive, hidden among leaves . . . a dark body within the darkness" (p. 22). As the industrialized nations moved to the cities, "Pan became old and grey-bearded and goat-legged, and his passion was degraded with the lust of senility" (p. 23). The mechanistic view of the world is what Lawrence determined really killed the benevolent force in the Pan power. The loss of an understanding of the universe as animated left Pan a murderer and rapist (Borgeaud, 1979/1988). The unexamined expansionist aggressions, the "rape" of nature, were projected onto Pan. As he put it, "The old Allness was severed and can never be ideally restored. Great Pan is dead" (Lawrence, 1936, p. 29).

Contemporary writing, such as T. C. Boyle's *Drop City* (2003) and Tom Robbins' *Jitterbug Perfume* (1984), bring an abdicated Pan to life in the modern American urban wilderness. Boyles' Pan is a Peter Pan, Robbie, who refused to adapt and so dies. Robbins' Pan was a god slowly losing his powers as Christianity took over the hearts and minds of Americans. It is set in New Orleans, an American city dedicated to unrestrained enjoyments. As they say, "*Laissez les bons temps rouler*" ("let the good times roll"). New Orleans is a city closely associated to Pan's nature through music, dance, revelry, sexuality, violence, and Mardi Gras. In a sense, New Orleans, with homes built as much as eight feet below sea level, has its existence in the chthonic. *Jitterbug Perfume* is particularly poignant, nearly prophetic, given the near death experience in 2005 the city of New Orleans suffered following the flooding related to Hurricane Katrina.

Perhaps Robert Frost (1933), American poet (1874–1963), best captured the hopelessness and impending doom engendered when Pan is not felt as a quickening presence. His poem, "Pan with Us," published in his first book of poems in 1913, spoke wistfully of Pan's depressing torpor as twentieth-century America slashed away at the vanishing wilderness of the "new world." An old gray-haired Pan comes out of the woods, takes a look around, and cannot be bothered to play the pipes. His fearsome countenance not scaring even the young milkmaid he chances upon. Frost has juxtaposed the end of the American frontier with the end of antiquity. A world-weary, listless Pan is alone in his woods, with no nymphs to enjoy his pipes. He knows the world has moved on. These writers allude to the flatness and torpor in a life without Pan.

In a recent story of Pan, the film *Pan's Labyrinth* (del Toro, 2006a) saw Pan as a fascinating, sexual, solitary, and sinister figure. A dominant theme rippling through the film is that humankind lost *something* when we lost Pan. Exactly what we have lost is indicated by the figure of Pan as both a problem that is frightening to approach but also essential for a rebirth of the endangered adult world in the film.

Pan, or the Faun (the Roman name for Pan), as he is imagined by director Guillermo del Toro, envisions an underworld figure without any of the romantic emphasis sometimes projected onto Pan. As the film begins we are told this all took place long ago in an underworld. This was a place where everyone was honest and no one suffered pain. In that realm lived a young princess who dreamt dreams about the world of humans. This is heard as one sees a young girl lying in the dark on stone, surrounded by roots and earth. From her hand and nose blood is dripping down into an abyss (even as blood was poured into the earth to summon the dead in Greek chthonic ritual). But the film is going in reverse. The viewer is shocked to realize the blood is flowing into her. The underworld is filling her with her life-blood (del Toro, 2006a).

As the story unwinds, the girl learns that she must be disobedient in both the real and the fantasy worlds and, at times, do what she believes is right rather than what she is told. The key, the film tells us, is learning when to disobey. This is how she is revitalized and the underworld is redeemed. Her name is Ofelia (del Toro, 2006a) and one can hardly ignore the reference to Hamlet's doomed, misunderstood lover. The outstanding trait with which Ofelia begins her descent into this underworld fairy tale is that, in both worlds, she sees the truth even when she cannot do anything about it. Then she learns how to be brave even when she is afraid. She journeys alone into the unkempt underworld, down the stairs of the steep labyrinth, and when she reaches an ancient standing stone her presence awakens the Faun. He is an enigma, is he helpful or dangerous, pedophile or savior? He tells the brave, but frightened young Ofelia he has had many names over uncounted centuries, some of which can only be known to the natural world, and now he is now the Faun (del Toro, 2006a). The movie frightens, not by a numbing bombardment of violence, but because the violence is sudden, visceral, and ugly. In short, so pandean.

Pan's Labyrinth (del Toro, 2006a) cast Pan in the role of an intermediate functionary to a greater power deep in the chthonic underworld. The vast riches that reside there, which in the film are aspects of the inner world of the imagination, equal the danger of approaching that terrain. The film never attempts to concretize the world of the imagination by taking a stand on whether it is real or not, but it does attempt to show how rapidly human life devolves into factionalism, selfishness, and violence when the imaginative world is forgotten. The film also suggests that the future survival of the real world is dependent on the revival of a relationship with the underworld of imagination. In the adult world the rebellious but loving forces overwhelmed the sadistic invaders and in the underworld Ofelia's risky entrance restored the balance and she, now honored as a princess, is welcomed home.

For the Greek cults the chthonic forces contained vast wealth, even while the underworld was also the land of the dead (Fontelieu, 2013). In *Pan's Labyrinth* (2006a), Pan stood at a crossroads between death and the wealth of the imagination. He is the transforming agent. As a reflection of some of the same motifs that were alive for the Arcadians beginning in at least the eighth century BCE, this latest, modern Pan brings both revitalization and the reminder to be vigilant of the great danger in forgetting that it is through the use of the imagination that it is possible to contain aggression and violence in human nature as well as to find new answers to old, stuck problems. The nymph-like innocence of Ofelia is able to contain the towering might of Pan, even as the nymphs could soothe the aggressions of Pan.

Del Toro stated that he made this film as a sequel to *The Devil's Backbone* (2001), which also explored the themes of innocence and violence. He wanted to connect the films to the explosion of a naïve sense of safety that had cocooned the US for centuries, but was forever changed after 9/11 (del Toro, 2006b). *The Devil's Backbone* (2001) came out the year the World Trade Center (WTC) fell and the premiere of *Pan's Labyrinth* was five years later. *The Devil's Backbone* was set in 1939 and so del Toro set *Pan's Labyrinth* in 1944 to link the two films imaginatively to reality (2006b).

Perhaps, following del Toro's lead, it is all for the best that a naïve confidence in the invulnerability of America has exploded into selfishness, factionalism, and a penchant for brutal violence. The opportunity to abandon the hypermasculine goal of being "number one" is imploding but in its death throws it is clutching to power more aggressively than ever. Just as the time has come to consider the consequences of actions by Americans for all humankind, rather than only for US citizens, the regressive pull of the beliefs, passionate emotions, and overreactions of a cultural complex attempt to strengthen US defenses, build walls, keep out all but the most pure. It is as if America is in a dark labyrinth with unseen twists and turns and no easy answers. It is a time ripe for discoveries if we can follow Ofelia's lead and not freeze in fear and awe at the Faun's unseen source of strength.

Singer and Kimbles maintain that envisioning cultures as having group complexes will "lead to an enhanced capacity to see more objectively the shadow of the group" (2004, p. 4). In ancient Greece scapegoat rituals, such as squilling, offered an imaginative solution for containing the cult's unchecked aggressions. Today del Toro (2006a, 2006b) has sent us a nightmare of a message that is actually quite hopeful. He concluded that it is possible to be brave enough to make peace with Pan, or in other words, find modern versions for containment of aggression and restore some balance between the divine and the instinctive sides of human nature.

When did America lose touch with the Pan Power? Lawrence targeted the industrial revolution, Frost the destruction of the natural world, Robbins and Boyle the loss of chthonic and orgiastic renewals of life, and del Toro the escalating lack of balance between reality and the imaginal in the modern day, not just in America, but in the world.

Perhaps it began even sooner. The expansionist doctrine of Manifest Destiny made it a god-given right to create a continental United States. Exceptionalism continues to preserve a regressive drive to consider the source of integrity to lie in making one's in-group wealthy and powerful. As Lifton pointed out following the attack on 9/11, "American forces claimed to be restrained and reasonable but were no less visionary in their projection of a cleansing war-making and military power [than the radical Jihadists]" (2003, p. 1), and that in all complexes of cultural superiority, "As in fundamentalist thought in general, the purification sought is modeled on a past of perfect harmony, that never was" (2003, p. 78). If the current trends are not to end in total destruction, coming to terms with the problems of living in harmony with the diversity of ways of relating to the divine becomes a priority. This underlies exceptionalism and Manifest Destiny and so is fundamental to American political beliefs. Perhaps it is not too late, and America, like Ofelia, can adapt and learn from the Pan force to become one of many enjoying the pleasures of "the brightness given by Zeus" (Pindar, 2017, para. 16). The problem involves finding a way to weave the diverse attitudes about what America means to its own citizenry, just as the ancients did by envisioning the complexity of a god that conjoins the animal and the spiritual. Then perhaps America will be ready to turn and join hands on an equal basis with the other nations of this great planet.

Chapter 4

Mythos of Pan

Isolation, innocence, panic, and the battlefield

> Heard melodies are sweet, but those unheard
> Are sweeter: therefore, ye soft pipes, play on.
>
> (Keats, 1935, p. 353 [II.12])

Arcadian Pan: innocence and isolation

Pan was revered as a god to his cult, yet came to be understood as a daemon, or demi-god, as the Greek religions lost numinosity (Plutarch, 1936/2003b) and Christianity's message of one god swept through the Mediterranean basin. Eventually Pan was demonized, and by the Middle Ages his countenance had morphed into the attributes of the Christian antichrist, Satan (Boardman, 1997). But Pan began as a nature god in Arcadia, the land of acorn eaters, on the Greek Peloponnesian peninsula. His origins are relevant to the mythic themes associated with him (Borgeaud, 1979/1988). Pan's rustic nature is exampled in his associations with the hardships of life in Arcadia, its reliance on herding for sustenance, the rapid fluctuations in nature between peace and danger, and the isolation of the wilderness (1979/1988).

Mythos of isolation

Arcadia

Classical scholar Susan Cole (2004) considered the relationship between the divine and the Greek cults to be a communal one. She focuses attention on the assumption the ancients held that the Earth was shared within three landscapes: the natural, the human, and the gods. These three landscapes were intertwined and created a worldview where Pan's sphere of influence was in the wilderness and on the edges of the human world, but never in the cities or towns. "Although shrines were sometimes built to him in cities, his sanctuaries were more often to be found in wild and isolated places, on mountainsides, in grottos and in caves" (Schofield, 2005, pp. 9–10). Others came into his territory, but a careful examination of his myths indicates he never left that landscape, rather that his territory grew over time (Borgeaud, 1979/1988). Caves, grottos, oak and pine groves, and mountaintops were considered sacred to him. Though some temples were built for him, such as the apse shaped "Temple of Pan and the Goats" at Caesarea Philippi in modern day Israel (Berlin, 1999, p. 29), for the most part his cult worshipped him at natural sites. He represented the dark, isolated areas of the natural world (but not the Greek underworld), places that are far from the centers of civilization. Though agriculture was the pursuit of a small proportion of the Arcadian population, for the most part Arcadians lived by pasturing goats and sheep for milk and wool and were sustained by hunting (Jost, 1994, p. 221). The people of Phigaleia were described by early historians as living like the god Pan, who stayed near Bassai as a shepherd "in a hut made of fallen branches" (Palatine Anthology [6. 253]) and also like Pan went "hunting now on one mountain and now on another" (Pausanias, 2017 [8. 42.3]).

From the most common story of his birth, the Homeric hymn to Pan, his myths place him in a rustic world far from the contemporaneous sphere of the more civilized Athenians (Boer, 1970). Pan's father, Hermes, successfully won the love of King Dryops's daughter, who gave birth to Pan while tending a flock of goats for the king, who was the master of Mount Kyllene in northeastern Arcadia (1970). Known today as Mt Kyllini, it is nearly 8,000 feet and forested to 6,500 feet, above which it is rocky and barren. Mountains, elevated above the natural habitats of humans, were, due to their sheer mass, steep slopes, and general inaccessibility, understood by the ancients to be created as homes for the gods. "Barrenness, vastness, impenetrability, and isolation: these name only the most conspicuous features composing the desolate look (and feel) of wild land" (Casey, 1993, pp. 196–197).

For subsistence populations, mountains also form natural barriers, hemming them in safety. In the imagination of his cult, Pan freely roamed these protective mountains untamed by civilizing rules. Pan was a mythic extension of the mountain's natural protective barrier, separating the Arcadians from other peoples.

Strabo, a geographer and historian in the first century, recorded an earlier history of the region.

> The Arcadian tribes . . . are reputed to be the most ancient tribes of the Greeks. But on account of the complete devastation of the country it would be inappropriate to speak at length about these tribes; for the cities, which in earlier times had become famous, were wiped out by the continuous wars, and the tillers of the soil have been disappearing even since the times when most of the cities were united into what was called the "Great City."
>
> (Strabo, 1932/1949, pp. 227–229 [VIII. 8. 1])

The mountainous area around Megalopolis on the Pellopenese peninsula, where the "Great City" thrived, is where Pan had a cult following that predates recorded history (Borgeaud, 1979/1988).

Locales

Following Pan's introduction to Athens after the battle of Marathon, his celebrity rapidly spread throughout the Mediterranean basin (Borgeaud, 1979/1988). Pan was worshipped as far west as the modern day Iberian Peninsula, in northern Africa, the Middle East, in Turkey, and Iran, and possibly in India.

Recent and ongoing excavations have produced abundant remains marking Pan's worship in the Middle East at Caesarea Phillipi (in the present day Golan Heights) while under Roman domination. "From the third century BC through the fifth century A. D. a sanctuary to the Greek god Pan existed at the mouth of the Jordan River" (Berlin, 1999, p. 270). The sanctuary was built in a rural area about six kilometers from the town (1999) and King Herod dedicated a temple at this site to Augustus in 19 BCE. Inscriptions at the site indicate that Romans worshipped here alongside the local population. People of diverse cultures and races worshiped Pan. His reputation is reflected in "the fact that the city retained its original name of Paneas or Panias, besides its official name Caesarea . . . [and this] can be considered proof that Pan was the real patron-god of the place and the city" (Tzaferis, 1992, p. 195).

Herodotus, c. 484 BCE – 425 BCE, a Greek historian, mentioned Pan's worship in Egypt and stated that he and Mendes were interchangeable. "The Mendesians reckon Pan among the eight gods. . . . In the Egyptian language Mendes is the name both for the he-goat and for Pan" (Herodotus, 1921/1960, p. 333 [II. 46]). Strabo corroborated this: "Mendes, at which place they worship Pan and, among animals, a he-goat; and as Pindar says, the he-goats have intercourse with women there" (1932/1949, p. 69 [XVII.1.19]). An ancient cross-cultural link between Mendes, Pan, and goats is established here connecting fertility and wild bursts of tabooed behaviors elevated to divine acts. Later damned as pagan devil worship by the early church, Clement of Alexandria, a Christian convert (c. 150 CE), wrote of "little fixtures of Pan, naked girls, drunken satyrs; and obscene emblems, plainly exhibited in pictures, and self-condemned by their indecency" (1919/1960, p. 137).

From Pliny's explanation it would appear that Pan's following in Spain pre-dated the Roman conquest. He wrote that "Marcus Varro records that the whole of Spain was penetrated by invasions" including the region called "Lusitania, and that Pan was the governor of the whole of it" (1942/1961, p. 11). The Mount Milë Pan bronze statuette discovered in Southern Albania in 1981 (at an as yet unexcavated sanctuary) placed his cult in this region. The statue was found on an isolated hill overlooking the area known as Palodes in Plutarch's day (Schofield, 2005). This is where in the legend of the death of Pan the ship's pilot called out for all to hear that "The Great God Pan is dead" (Plutarch, 1936/2003b, p. 403 [419D]). Unfortunately, the dating of this statue is still undetermined, so whether it predates Plutarch's writing is unclear (Schofield, 2005). It does, however, firmly link Pan as a cult deity to this region.

Though no extant corroborative materials exist, Lucian, an Assyrian-Roman writer and rhetorician, (120 CE–c. 180 CE) recorded:

> Among the Machlean Indians who feed their flocks on the left banks of the Indus river as you look down stream, and who reach clear to the Ocean – in their country there is a grove in an enclosed place of no great size; it is completely sheltered, however, for rank ivy and grapevines overshadow it quite. In it there are three springs of fair, clear water: one belongs to the Satyrs, another to Pan, the third to Silenus.
>
> (1913/1961, p. 57 [*Dionysus*, 6])

So, if Lucian is to be believed, Pan was worshipped as far from Arcadia as western India. As his cult expanded, he was still known as a protector and a nature god in these diverse cultures (Borgeaud, 1979/1988).

Wilderness

Charles Segal, a classical scholar, wrote:

> Since Wordsworth, it has been a commonplace to observe that for modern man nature has lost her mystery. But for the ancients dense forests, rushing rivers, ever-flowing springs, and desolate mountains could still be felt as the haunts of divine powers.
>
> (1969, p. 5)

Though Pan was often associated with brutality and selfish behaviors in these wild places, paradoxically, the wilderness was, and has continued to be, a source of mythic intoxication and inspiration. Pan's cult worshipped him in the areas where the wild intermingles with the domesticated; the regions used for hunting and herding (Borgeaud, 1979/1988) and was revered for providing sustenance as well as protection. In the wilderness he also encouraged wildness and release through music and nightlong, labyrinthine dances with the nymphs (1979/1988).

The borderline regions that were known as Pan's territory are today called "ecotones" by ecologists because they are transitional areas between different ecological zones (Traut, 2005, p. 279). An ecotone tolerates flora and fauna from adjacent ecozones, such as meadows and forests. They harbor life that is not sustainable elsewhere. Like ecotones, Pan's body, with his split nature, both animal and divine, represents the diversity of the many as all parts of one whole.

Pan's locations also reflect a recurring theme of isolation. His territory was understood to include a variety of landscapes, but he was worshipped in the hidden, dank caves and on lonely mountain sides. His cult epithets reflect the diversity coexisting in the union of the divine and the animal: Pan *Nomios*, "Of the Pastures;" *Agrotas*, "Giver of Pasture;" *Agreus*, "Of the Hunt;" *Skoleitas*, "Winding or Crooked;" *Haliplanktos*, "Sea Roaming;" *Lyterius*, "the Releaser;" and *Phorbas*, "Terrifying One" (Pan Cult, 2013). Isolation left the innocence of the nymphs available for Pan to care for or to take advantage of, both of which are reflected in repeating mythic themes.

The use of landscape as metaphor is well established in Greek and Roman literature. "From Homer on, nature in classical poetry proves a large, ultimately moral frame for human action" (Segal, C. P., 1969, p. 1). As a metaphor for an internal landscape, the epithets Pan *Phorbus* and Pan *Lyterius* suggest areas where unmitigated passions can bubble up. Pan's archetypal locations suggest there is an area for negotiations with the unknown and the unexpected in oneself. These are, psychologically, the edges where the unconscious can become conscious. Pan's locality in part of the wilderness near the borders of civilization symbolically represents lurking fears, excitements, and possibilities of losing self-control when near the shadowy borderland of the unconscious. As reflected in his locales, Pan represented both fertility and the chthonic sides of the natural world.

Chthonic dimensions of reality

The Greek worship of the chthonic was born from recognition of the capacity for wholeness in nature. Chthonic is from the Greek, *khthonios*, meaning "of the earth" and is used in reference to that which is beneath the surface of the Earth, or the underworld and its state of darkness. The chthonic is not to be confused with the visible layer of the soil, where Demeter reigned as the goddess of the harvest or with Gaia, the earth mother who bore and united with Ouranus and is a primal life force (Farnell, 1909/1971). Chthonic implies lower, abundance, darkness, and death. The chthonic was worshipped as the land of the dead and the place of great wealth. The chthonic meant much more to the Greeks then the aspects of it which Pan embodied. Hades, Persephone, Dionysus, Hecate, Haephestus, and Hermes carried different shades of the chthonic spirit, which the polytheistic Greeks saw as parts of the many-sided mysteries of the divine.

The chthonic, then, is the carrier of the projection of human nature's instinctive drives and dark, rejected propensities, and yet it is also a fertile source of abundance. The irrational sides of human nature are not thought of as "bad," but as the darker sides of being human. Aspects of human nature that were wisely discerned by the ancient Greeks with caution and recognized as potentially dangerous in humans were nonetheless honored in their gods. Through ritual, the Greeks participated with the projected darker parts of their own nature. Devotion to this principle has fallen into disuse and, today, might even be called devil worship.

Today in mainstream psychology and in religion rather than a reverential attitude toward the awesome power of the chthonic force, much of this drive is the target for a lifelong battle to contain, banish, or defeat it in oneself and in society. The corralling of impulses that lead to harmful behaviors has met with limited success. Today darkness is not worshipped, it is feared. Denial of the dark side of the soul, and by dark I do not mean evil, I mean an insufficiency of illumination, inevitably creates projection and out of this projection are spawned the murky societal problems that lack easy answers, but ignored, build up and, often but not always embodied by young men, explode into violence, whether as violent criminal behaviors or war.

Caves

Caves consecrated to Pan were widespread and many have been excavated revealing reliefs and dedications to him (Alcock, 1994). Caves were dedicated to him in all the regions in which he was worshipped. Caves were also used in Greek dramas as places for clandestine affairs (1994). On the northwestern slope of the Acropolis in Athens, a cave dedicated to Pan, Long Cliffs, was found and excavated in 1896–1897 when a relief of Pan playing his pipes for the nymphs, now known as the Rock of Pan, was discovered cut into a rock. This cave was immortalized by Euripides in *Ion* in a scene where Apollo raped the maid, Kreusa, who consequently bore him Ion (1999). In Aristophanes' antiwar comedy, *Lysistrata* (2000), the aborted seduction of Myrhhine by Kinesias took place at Long Cliffs as well. The poets regarded Pan's sacred caves to be exempt from the standards of sexual purity afforded to the sanctuaries of the other gods and goddesses of their day. The proximity of Long Cliffs, below the Parthenon, offered a convenient location for these instinctive but boundary transgressing acts (even though Myrhhine is Kinesias' wife, she, and the rest of the Athenian women, had agreed to withhold sex until the men ended the war). Through comedic and dramatic expression, Pan *Lyterius*, the loosener, was an outlet for the Athenians' imagination.

Caves were thought by the ancients to sometimes be openings to the underworld (Homer, 1996). The dark nature of caves reflects both Pan's chthonic and his rustic nature. A cave can be a shelter, a hiding place, or, alternatively, a trap. The Roman poet Ovid (43 BCE–17/18 CE) often used caves to reflect a suspension of everyday reality (Segal, C. P., 1969). Ironically, caves suggest both safety and sudden, unexpected dangers. Both of these themes are associated with Pan, especially in his ongoing affairs with the nymphs.

Mythos of innocence

Nymphs

The etymology of the word nymph is helpful in providing a contextual understanding of what they represented to the ancients. "The very name belongs to the human and family relations, the original meaning being probably 'bride' or 'young woman'" (Farnell, 1909, p. 424). This understanding of the Greek is corroborated by the classicist Walter Burkert in *Greek Religion* (1977/1985) and in the *Dictionary of Symbols and Imagery* (de Vries, 1984).

Pan had ongoing involvements with specific nymphs and is also often described in the company of unnamed ones. For the Greeks, the nymphs were found everywhere in nature, usually in places of great beauty. Their role as a mediator between the humans and the gods is symbolically represented by their attachment to places, such as to specific trees or springs (Clay, 2006, p. 195). Unlike Pan who was worshipped over wide areas in ancient times, most nymphs remained attached to a specific place.

Nymphs were feminine, productive, local nature spirits of mountains, trees, caves, and especially of bodies of fresh water such as streams, springs, and glades. Cults to the copious numbers of nymphs were widespread. For instance, the Titan god Oceanus was said to have 3,000 "light stepping daughters," all of who were nymphs (Hesiod, 2002, p. 144 [364]). The numbers and types of nymphs are significant because they reflect the diverse and animated landscape in which the Greeks lived. Great expanses of the natural world were thus understood to be divine and ensouled.

The classifications of nymphs make for long lists: the Neireides of the sea, the Dryades of the trees and forests, the Oreiades of the mountains, the Aurai of the cooling breezes to name a few. For example, every spring had its youthful, graceful nymph (a Naiade) who dwelled there. They lived as long as their spring ran free, just as a Dryade would live as long as her tree grew. The nymphs who followed Artemis were virginal, such as the Hyperboreiai who were her handmaidens from the land beyond the north wind (Larson, 2001), while the Bakkhai danced to Dionysus' beat and quite freely loved whom they wished (2001). The nymphs were often involved in the care of others and were understood to bring pleasure, healing, and beauty into life (Philostratus, 1931/1960).

Nymphs had the power to transform themselves into natural objects and contact with them could transform people in the same way. The metamorphoses the nymphs brought about often were to more restricted forms of life. Ovid tells the story of Venelus, a shepherd who paid dearly for insulting the nymphs by:

> imitating their dance with his clownish steps, adding to this boorish insults and vulgar words. Nor did he cease speaking until the rising wood covered his mouth. For now he is a tree. You could tell its kind from the savour of its fruit; for the wild olive bears the traces of his tongue in its bitter berries. The sharpness of his words has passed to them.
>
> (1916/1976, p. 337 [XIV. 512–526])

Nymphs were said to have themselves birthed the autochthonic (born from the earth) race of heroes. This was the race from which all "true" Greek citizens were descended (Rosivach, 1987). Nymphs thus brought about the original metamorphoses of the creation of people; humans are thus descendants of the divine. "Early Athenians expressed this belief in mythological terms, as relatively primitive people do, by saying that their nation was, literally, sprung from the soil of its native land" (p. 294).

As primordial figures, they were loved and sacrificed to from at least as far back as the time of the Homeric epics. "The picture [of the nymphs] that we find in Homer proves to be remarkably stable through time" (Larson, 2001, p. 29). For example in *The Odyssey* (Homer, 1996), after Athena lifts the mists and reveals Ithaca, Odysseus at last feels the thrill of standing on his homeland's soil. In his first moments home, he kissed "the good green earth and raised his hands to the nymphs and prayed at once" (p. 298 [XIII. 403–404]). Athena shows him the harbor's head with "the welcome cave nearby it, dank with sea-mist, sacred to nymphs of the springs we call the Naiads. Here, under its arching vault, time and again you'd offer the nymphs a generous sacrifice to bring you success!" (p. 297 [XIII. 395–399]). It appears that a highly respectful attitude toward the lands in which they lived informed the early Greek's choices. The view that beautiful deities, nymphs, inhabited the most beautiful places on Earth suggests they represented the harmony and balance in the order of the natural world.

The nymphs were capable of cooling Pan's hypermasculine heat. They soothed him and helped him relax (Philostratus, 1931/1960). When Pan was not on the hunt the nymphs are safe with him, he was their protector and they were his "dear nymphs" (Aristophanes, 2000, p. 579 [978–981]), able to get away with playing tricks on him. He led them in dance, playing his panpipes (Boer, 1970). As a group, the nymphs were able to ensnare and subdue Pan's lusty and overly aggressive nature, but when alone the nymphs were less equipped to match Pan's power and resorted to self-destructive measures to escape him. Though they were not immortal, they were much more long-lived than humans or animals, and so really, "for practical purposes, they were immortal" (Larson, 2001, p. 4).

The ancient Greeks recognized that aggression in sexuality as well as in war produces panic. Though Pan had happy love affairs with nymphs and goddesses, when he lost control of his desire he was never victorious. The most common outcome for his nymph victims was a metamorphosis to a devolved state of being, while Pan was left unfulfilled and on his own (Borgeaud, 1979/1988). Pan's conquests were only successful when the desire was mutual.

Echo

Echo is present in the earliest extant telling of Pan's stories, the Homeric hymn to Pan:

> And the mountain nymphs
> with clear voices
> go along with him
> their feet excited,
> they sing too,
> by the springs of dark water –
> Echo wailing
> on the mountain-top. (Boer, 1970, p. 65)

Alone Echo wailed, in another translation she "moans" (Athanassakis, 1976). Meanwhile, by a spring, Pan cavorted with other nymphs. The recurring motifs of innocence, isolation, and pain are Echo's story. Here Pan ignored Echo, but in another myth Echo rejected Pan as her lover (Longus, 1916/1978, p. 168 [III. 23]). In that story after she had spurned him, he heard her beautiful singing and became so infuriated he destroyed what he desired (1916/1978). Echo's freedom disintegrated in his rage. He "sends a madness among the shepherds and goatherds, and they in a desperate fury, like so many dogs and wolves, tore her all to pieces and flung about them all over the earth her yet singing limbs" (p. 163 [III. 23]). This story is similar to the more familiar myth of Echo and Narcissus (Ovid, 1916/1977, p. 151 [III, 374–375]).

Echo's stories with Narcissus and Pan are filled with obsessive attraction neutralized by a deadening pull of indifference, either by her or for her. She is alone and in pieces, fragmented, a disembodied voice in both versions (Longus, 1916/1978). The pursuer, Pan, is left with his dogs to sniff out new prey, trapped in frustrated isolation. The themes of isolation and sadness, expressed in sound, receive strong emphasis here. Sound as music attracts Pan to Echo and then endures even after she is disembodied, both in her "singing limbs" and as echoes. Like the swing of a metronome, cacophony and music, chaos and harmony, both echo and make a balance in Pan's myths.

The self-absorbed protector became the persecutor, and the innocent became the prey. Echo was ripped to pieces and condemned to repeat others, and like the women in the #metoo movement never able to say what she meant, in the powerless position of one who has no voice of her own. The self-involved, compulsive, and hypermasculine aspects of Pan rendered her ineffectual. As the extant writings from antiquity demonstrate, Pan's unmitigated aggression leaves him angry and frustrated as he dangerously faded back into the shadowed landscape, itching to retaliate. Pan's actions overwhelmed and caused panic, but his motivation was not to murder or out of hatred. Though his desire was to join the nymphs in love, his aggressive approaches end in failures (Ovid, 1916/1977, p. 151 [III, 374–375]; Tatius, 1917/1969, pp. 405–407 [VIII. 6, 7–12]; Nonnos, 1940/1962b, p. 27 [XVI. 330–334]).

Pitys

There are two versions of the story of Pan and Pitys. Pitys was classified as an Oreiades, a Dryade nymph of mountain pines and in the first version Pitys was changed into a pine. In the adaptation recorded in the *Geoponica* (a collection compiled in the tenth century), "Pan loved the girl, Boreas (the North Wind) competed with him in his love for her . . . [but] she rather inclined to Pan" (as cited in Borgeaud, 1979/1988, p. 78). Boreas was one of the four *Anemoi*, the directional winds. Purple-winged, he brought the winter winds with his glacial breath and ice-spiked hair (Bulfinch, 1855). Boreas became jealous and flung Pitys off the side of the cliff. She died but Gaia took pity on her and transformed her into a pine tree whose branches are used to crown Pan – in ritual he wears sprays of pine needles in his hair (Longus, 1916/1955). As a "pine, beloved of Arcady's god" (Propertius, 1912, p. 49 [I. XVIII, 20]) she is left alone in the mountains to moan when the north wind blows through her needles.

In the version set down by Nonnos, Gaia is now seen as being at fault rather than compassionate and Boreas is not personified. The windy element survives, but as an aspect of the nymph herself.

> Pitys who hated marriage, who fled fast as the wind over the mountains to escape the unlawful wooing of Pan . . . disappeared into the soil itself; put the blame on the Earth! Then she may perhaps lament the sorrows and the fate of the wailing nymph.
>
> (Nonnos, 1940/1962c, pp. 245–247 [XLII. 255–261])

In both versions, Pitys is trapped in a state of mourning, alone on the mountain, singing her sad song and crying "the honey sweet tears of the sorrowing maid" (Nonnos, 1940/1962c, p. 247 [XLII. 262]). In the surviving variations of this myth, one has a triangular love motif, but in both the result is the same, Pan goes away frustrated and Pitys (piteous) is transformed by Gaia into a pine tree or hidden in the earth, an isolated victim, pining away.

Syrinx

The story goes that Pan, craving Syrinx's attention, burst into the peace of the piney banks of Arcadia's Ladon river (Ovid, 1955/1986). She ran from him, "scorning his prayers" (p. 47 [I. 689]). As told in the *Metamorphoses* (1916/1977) of Ovid, Syrinx prayed to her sisters of the stream to change her form so just as Pan thought he had caught her, instead he held marsh reeds. "He sighed in disappointment, the soft air stirring in the reeds gave forth a low and complaining sound. Touched by this wonder and charmed by the sweet tones, the god exclaimed: 'This converse, at least, shall I have with thee' " (p. 53 [I.705–712]), and he broke the reeds in unequal pieces to create the panpipes. In the original tellings of the Syrinx myth the various versions all emphasize Pan's sadness, rather than anger, at his loss (Ovid, 1916/1977; Tatius, 1917/1969; Nonnos, 1940/1962b).

Pursued and cornered by Pan, Syrinx chose metamorphosis rather than to surrender to him (Tatius, 1917/1969). For Syrinx this myth is an unhappy tale of an abrupt, traumatic, life changing moment, while for Pan it is another story of unrequited desire. It also exemplified the pattern of Pan's single-minded pursuit of his desires without concern for the consequences for others. In these stories, Pan destroyed innocence. The mythic motif in the story of Pan and Echo is repeated; innocence requires protection to exist, and when left unprotected it devolves into a lesser state of consciousness.

Neither Syrinx nor Pan got what they wanted, but out of this tension and frustration a new element was born. The Greek writer Achilles Tatius (writing in the second or third century) wrote that Pan collected the reeds:

> as though they had been the maiden's limbs and put them together as though to form a single body: and then, holding the pieces in his hands, kissed them, as though they had been her wounds. As he put his lips to them he groaned from love, and breathed down, upon the reeds while he kissed them; and his breath, pouring down through the holes in them, gave musical notes, and the pan-pipes found its voice.
>
> (1917/1969, pp. 405–407 [VIII. 6, 7–12])

His breath and her reed body together transformed – metamorphosed into music. She lost her autonomy, his love was unrequited, yet something new came to life out of the losses: beautiful music. Syrinx, as an archetypal image of innocence lost through panic, is transformed into a soulful melody of love.

In one version Syrinx does not remain stuck. She evolves to an even freer state than she was as a naiad of the river Ladon. In Nonnos, a Greek epic poet of the fifth or sixth century, Syrinx lived on as one of the Bakhoi (1940/1062b), one of the nymphs in Dionysus' retinue. After the panic she devolved to a vegetative state, but in this telling, Syrinx regained her freedom of speech and movement and then gained sexual freedom as well. "Syrinx escaped from Pan's marriage and left him without a bride, and now she cries *euoi* to the newly-made marriage of Dionysos" (Nonnos, 1940/1962b, p. 27 [XVI. 330–334]). In the ancient Bacchic revels, *euoi* (pronounced you-oh-ee) is a cry of impassioned rapture (Morwood and Taylor, 2002, p. 144).

She did not remain buried in the earth nor did she return as a virginal nymph. She was transformed into a feminine being with the right to choose her partner. In the myth, emphasis is placed on her having a voice and sexual freedom (Nonnos, 1940/1962b). She was able to enjoy running in states of impassioned rapture rather than running in a state of panic. In the same story that told of how the unmitigated phallic power, represented by Pan, experienced a vulnerable state of sadness and discovered a way to sublimate the frustration and sadness through music, the life giving nymph Syrinx was able to evolve rather than remaining frozen in a vegetative plant state. When the cacophony of echoes and wails of the nymphs and the pent up aggressions of Pan were transformed, the result was music and rapture.

Modern commentaries

Pan was not alone as a victimizer of the nymphs. Apollo, Zeus, and Poseidon were gods with stories of chasing terrorized nymphs (de Vries, 1984). But of all the Greek gods, it is Pan who is singled out most in modern analyses of myth as a rapist and murderer (Borgeaud, 1979/1988; Hillman, 1988; Schwartz-Salant, 1991). In his analysis in *The Cults of Pan* (1979/1988), Philippe Borgeaud, a historian of religions and one of the foremost scholars on Pan, interpreted Pan's behavior as "hopeless desire, rage, [and] murder" (p. 79). Syrinx, Pitys, and Echo are sympathized with as victims (p. 79). James Hillman, in his valuable contribution *Pan and the Nightmare* (1988), also defined Pan's aggression toward the nymphs reductively. He called them "a horror because it is an archetypal *transgression*. . . . Rape puts the body's drive toward soul into a concrete metaphor" (1988, p. 43). Nathan Schwartz-Salant (1991), a Jungian analyst, also labeled Pan a murderer and rapist. Here are Schwartz-Salant's thoughts delivered at a conference for clinical psychologists given at the Jung Institute in Chicago:

> The Pan force is extremely dangerous to women. He's a killer of women, like Echo, Syrinx, he kills them. He is a force that unites badly. He does not lead to union well. He is always defeated in love. He never has good love relationships, at best he has decent relationships with a

> male shepherd. He has no decent love relationships with women. . . . A demonic force.
>
> (1991)

Though there is one vase painting of phallic Pan chasing a shepherd, there are no specific stories depicting a sexual interest in males on Pan's part (Dover, 1978, p. 93). I am at a loss as to where Schwartz-Salant learned Pan had a happy relationship with a shepherd. Classical scholar Kenneth James Dover's exhaustive study of Greek homosexuality, aimed to "describe those phenomena of homosexual behaviour and sentiment which are to be found in Greek art and literature between the eighth and second centuries B.C." (p. vii), has only one reference to Pan. He refers to a terracotta vase where "Pan, penis erect, runs full-tilt after a young herdsman" (p. 93). This vase is an Athenian red-figure crater from about 470 BCE by an unknown artist referred to as the "Pan Painter." As the sole example of Pan chasing a male and with no textual references upon which to rest the assumption that Pan was attracted to males as well as females (Dover, 1978), let alone that "at best he has decent relationships with a male shepherd" (Schwartz-Salant, 1991), a first glimmer dawns of modernity's tendency to judge behaviors as either good or bad and avoid the complexity the Greeks were able to savor.

Further, Pan is not "always defeated in love" (Schwartz-Salant, 1991) and was often described as being in happy relationships with various nymphs. Examples include the first century author of *The Golden Ass*, Apuleius's (c. 125–180), inclusion of Pan in his story of Psyche and Eros: "Pan the rustical god was sitting on the river-side, embracing and teaching the goddess Echo of the mountains to tune her songs and pipes" (1915/1958, p. 237 [V. 25–26]), the Greek poet Aristophanes' (c. 448–380 BCE) dedication of *Women at Tesmorphia* "to Pan and his dear Nymphs" (2000, p. 579 [978–981]), and in Moschus (fl. c. 150 BCE) a Greek bucolic poet of the school of Theocritus, "Pan loved his neighbor Echo" (Edmonds, Trans., 1912/1977, p. 459 [V, 1]). Echo and Pan had two daughters (Bell, 1991). One, Iynx, whose name means love charm, is the source from which the English word "jinx" is derived. She incurred the familiar wrath of Hera who transformed her into a wrynecked bird (p. 173). Their other daughter was Iambe, who used her bawdy nature to rejuvenate Demeter after Hades abducted her beloved daughter, Persephone (p. 173).

Another happy love affair of Pan's was with the Titan goddess of the moon, Selene. In the Homeric hymn to the "long-winged Moon . . . white-armed goddess, splendid Selene" (Athanassakis, 1976, pp. 68–69), she is praised for her great beauty that causes "the dim . . . to glitter" (p. 69). Pan fulfilled his desire for Selene by wrapping himself in the skin of a white ram and "twas with gift of such snowy wool, if we may trust the tale, that Pan, Arcadia's god, charmed and beguiled you, O Moon, calling you to the depths of the woods; nor did you scorn his call" (Virgil, 1916/1999, p. 205

[*Georgics III*, 391–393]). The horned god was not entirely luckless in love in his own time. He loved and fathered as copiously as did the other Greek gods.

The Greeks understood Pan's wildness as more complex, and, within the context of his role as Pan *Lyterius*, the loosener, allowed his places of worship to be places where transgressions took place. This did not defile his sacred sanctuaries. The evolution of a negative concretization of Pan began with the rise of Christianity (Halford, 1993, p. 58).

Jungian scholar Susan Rowland (2002) addressed the question of concretization and reductionism in her modern articulations of the archetypal.

> In the case of feminist theory, if we regard the archetype not as an image whose content is frozen . . . but as a tendency to form and re-form images in relation to certain kinds of repeated experience, then the concept could serve to clarify distinctively female concerns that have persisted throughout history.
>
> (pp. 13–14)

If the polytheistic gods of the Greeks are reduced to simple equations their value is manipulated into a concrete, stereotypical shorthand. The modern languaging, inaccuracies, and additions to the myths suggest possible projection of unworked shadow material, and that these misconceptions are not isolated points toward a larger issue.

In the myths, Pan's sexuality, as with others of the Greek gods, is compulsive and, as Jung wrote, "compulsion is the great mystery of life. It is the thwarting of our conscious will and of our reason by an inflammable element within us, appearing now as a consuming fire and now as life-giving warmth" (1963/1970, p. 128 [*CW* 14, para. 151]). Pan is here a representative of the consuming fire of sexual desire that human contact can inspire. On the other hand, the nymphs personify the life giving warmth of nurturers in their roles as helpers during births and healings (Larson, 2001). Even the bare bones of the myths of Pan and the nymphs play with the tension in humans between the wild fire of an all-consuming passion and the vulnerability of a life giving, altruistic warmth. Without the passion, the myths intimate, empathy freezes (the nymphs devolve) and without the altruistic, passions are not satisfying. The self-involved Pan begets a self-involved nymph pining away for freedom. When Pan's aggression gave way to sadness he created music and Syrinx was released. Pan has the "ambiguity of a being whose power oscillates unceasingly between fear and seduction, disorder and harmony" (Eliade, 1987, p. 160).

Pan's myths tell us about action and passivity. When rejected he pursues. Rather than fall into a depressed state he presses on, creating panic. He does not abandon, he overwhelms. He projected his unwanted desire onto the nymphs and goddesses he chased. Pan attempted to rape – *there is no story where he actually succeeds.* When viewed as transpersonal psychic energy rather than as physical attacks, Pan's desire can be understood as a trigger for trauma, an anxious need projected into others that does not murder, but violates and frightens the victim into a vegetative state. As in contemporary trauma theory (Kalsched, 1996), the nymph has a traumatic reaction, which results in her literally becoming stuck. If this was a story of a woman, the result would be defined in Jungian terms as having become caught in a complex following a traumatic event or events. Such a cut off can leave the victim without an internal sense of safety or one reduced to the agoraphobic safety found only in certain narrowly defined areas, such as Pitys's pine tree or one's bedroom.

Pan's compulsive rush into life compares to America's aggressive expansion, which began as soon as the first European settlers arrived and has often produced traumatic reactions in those it has overwhelmed, either economically or militarily (Watkins & Shulman, 2010). America is mirrored in Pan's bucolic land of Arcadia, an isolated and idealized territory (Virgil, 2011) where the safety of Pan's isolation also allowed him to freely attack and traumatize virginal nymphs (Nonnos, 1940/1962a). Pan's Arcadian wilderness parallels the mythic landscape of America's "purple mounted majesties/ Above the fruited plain/ America! America!" (Bates & Ward, 2014). The American themes of endless frontiers and heroic independence in a vast land, well protected by its natural isolation and self-sustaining terrain, are central characters in the legends and tales that shape the national character of the United States (Guthrie, 2011; Smith, S. F., 2011) and parallel the mythic landscape of Arcadia. C. P. Segal's (1969) description of Arcadia as a trap "which reveals the insecurity and danger surrounding the dwellers in such a world" (p. 18) could have been a description of the legends of the American Wild West. Pan *Agreus* ("of the hunt") was a major god (Eliade, 1987, p. 160) in a sensuous and peaceful world, until his presence announced instability and the threat of impending danger.

In ancient times, Pan was the god of nature and so a protector. He oversaw the wilderness and the hunting and herding boundary areas surrounding civilizations (Farnell, 1909/1971). Pan protected a vast area of natural resources, but he also exploited these when he chose (Bulfinch, 1855). Like Pan, the United States has been exploiting its natural resources as policied in the founding vision of Manifest Destiny (Rosen, D. A., 2007). The current state of depletion of this policy shows up in problems such as the 6000 to 7000 square miles of a dead zone (oxygen deprived) in the Mississippi River delta area of the Gulf of Mexico. This has been caused by the exploitative overuse of agribusiness fertilizers, which led to massive runoff into the Mississippi River, which has destroyed all living organisms and is responsible for untold numbers of fish kills in the Gulf (Bruckner, 2011).

In Jungian theory, once a trauma splits the unity of the psyche into a complexed state, repeated attempts to break out of the cycle tend to recapitulate the trauma and result in reinforced barriers to well-being (Kalsched, 1996). The shell of the complex thickens and the archaic core decompensates further as long as the archetypal forces are held below the surface, like a cork under water. The natural tendency of the ego is to try to kill off the unwanted, archetypal shadow, and at the very least project it out on to other people, rather than committing to the plodding therapeutic work "to transform the shell by examining it in relationship to the archetypal core" (Whitmont, 1991, p. 67). According to cultural complex theory, this holds true for cultures as well as for individuals.

The myths of Pan with the nymphs Syrinx, Pitys, and Echo are concerned with just such traumatic regressions. In these myths, Pan ceases to be the nymph's protector and leader and becomes a predator. Innocence finds itself isolated and trapped by the demands of an indifferent Pan and, like the undeveloped core of a complex, they are unable to grow because they are now stunted behind the protective walls of a defense the very trauma has erected. Pan and the nymphs, in ancient terms, personify the traumatic cost of modern hypermasculine aggression.

Athenian Pan: panic and the battlefield

> There's no piping for me at high noon. I go in too great dread of Pan for that.
>
> *Theocritus* Edmonds (Trans.), 1912/1977, p. 11 [I. 16–17]

Pan's countenance, with hairy flanks and fierce brow, was often described as fearsome by the ancients (Flaccus, 1931/1963). However, this countenance did not develop until after he was first honored in Athens in the fifth century BCE.

> We know, however, of no figurative representation of the god antedating the diffusion of his cult outside Arcadia, nor do we have any literary testimony, with the exception of some dedications that retain only the name of the god. Not until the beginning of the fifth century BCE, and after the introduction of his cult in Athens, does the image of Pan take shape.
>
> (Eliade, 1987, p. 160)

It was as if when Pan increased in popularity, he became more embodied. In his *Histories* (1921/1960), Herodotus described Pan as one of the youngest gods as well as one of the most ancient (p. 453 [II, 145]), with the head and legs of a goat (p. 333 [II: 46]). Subsequently the ancients named him as a deity of herds of sheep and cattle (Ovid, 1931/1959, pp. 77–70 [II. xv. 267–283]), rustic and horned (Apuleius, 1915/1958, p. 237 [V. 25–26]), and a singer and master of the flute (Nonnos, 1940/1962b, pp. 23–27 [XVI. 282–336]). But Pan was also characterized as wanton, faithless, and vexing (Longus, 1916/1955, p. 121 [II. 39]). Roman satirist Lucias Anneaus Cornutus characterized his body as different from all the other gods:

> The lower part of this god is hairy, and recalls a goat, to designate the roughness of the earth. The upper part, however, is like a man, for heaven holds sway over the entire world, because in heaven itself reason is in place.
>
> (as cited in Merivale, 1969, p. 10)

Pan's panic-inducing presence is the most prevalent theme in his myths (Bulfinch, 1855). For the Greeks, panic was a significant integrant in the natural landscape (Segal, C. P., 1969). "Where even the place of refuge and peace is invaded, there is no safety, no escape from arbitrary force. In such a world innocence is never preservable" (p. 8).

Another central theme in Pan's myths is his representation as the instinct for self-preservation: he was a god of fertility, a warrior, and a sexual predator, using confusion and surprise attacks to get what he wanted. Both his enemies and the nymphs typically reacted to his advances with panicky retreats (Borgeaud, 1979/1988). These two themes, panic and self-preservation, are connected.

Mythos of panic and protection

In times of unrest in ancient Greece Pan emerged as a protector, allying with gods and men against outside aggressors (Pausanias, 1935/1961; Herodotus, 1921/1960). To achieve victory in battles Pan often worked in tandem with the nymph Echo to create panic and confusion. Pan's signature motif was to use stealth and surprise to overwhelm enemies, which would cause them to panic. He was deeply feared (Hillman, 1988). His sudden, unexpected threats of violence induced his allies' enemies to flee in panic (Sophocles, 1994).

In the second century CE, Artemidorus of Ephesus (1975) wrote an *Oneirocritica* ("interpretation of dreams") illustrating Pan's associations with panic and anxiety. He stated Pan "signifies confusion and tumult. He also signifies that the things in which a person takes pride will not remain secure" (p. 118). The battle myths of Pan give examples of his presence creating the kind of confusion and insecurity that leads to terror in a variety of ways, including organized attacks and an awareness of the effectiveness of infecting a group with a mob mentality. Polyaenus (1994) (born c. 100 CE in Bithynia), a rhetorician and author of *Stratagems of War*, recounted the myth of Pan's chaotic use of echoes while a general in service to Dionysus in India:

> Dionysus' [lost text] was in a hollow valley, when the scouts reported that an enemy band of 10,000 was camped against them. Dionysus was afraid, but not Pan, who at night signaled Dionysus' army to give their loudest yell. They shouted, and the rocks resounded and the hollow made the noise seem to the enemy to be that of a much greater force. Struck by fear, they fled. To honor Pan's stratagem we call Echo "friend of Pan," and we name the groundless fears that strike armies at night "panic."
>
> (p. 17 [1.2])

His tactics, like modern day strategic bombings and terrorist attacks, avoided great loss of life for his allies. The American battle slogan of the 2002 Iraq War "Shock and Awe" (Richey & Feldmann, 2003) would have made an apt descriptor for Pan's fear-provoking strategies. Pan's use of panic in his battle myths metaphorically expressed the instinct in nature that senses that fear is a more powerful weapon than strength or numbers.

Lucian (1913/1961), an Assyrian-Roman writer and rhetorician, (120 CE–c. 180 CE) described Dionysus's army as arranged with Dionysus in the center, Silenus (a son of Pan) on the right wing, and Pan in command of the left flank (p. 53 [Dionysus. 4]). "Dionysus' general was Pan, who discovered formation, called it a phalanx and formed left and right wings. For this reason, you know, handicraft workers represent Pan as having horns" (Polyaenus, 1994, p. 17 [1.2]). Here Pan was credited with creating the principal protective battle formation of Hellenic Greece, so strong, it was able to repel cavalry charges (Connolly, P., 1981) and was adopted by the Roman Legions as a method to be able to fluidly move from defense to offense and back again on the battlefield. Pan's strategy to use echoes to create pandemonium in enemy armies and other ingenious scenarios attributed to him makes Pan the power behind the throne in a number of myths.

Roman poet Gaius Valerius Flaccus (1934/1963) (c. d. 90 CE), in his rewrite of the *Argonautica*, told how under the darkness of night Pan tricks the outward bound ships of the enemy, causing the ship's guard to fall asleep. He then shifts the wind so they returned home unawares. Pan leaps in at night when consciousness is at its weakest – panicking the soldiers in the uproar, his enemy turn their defenses against their own soldiers.

> The god Pan had driven the doubting city distraught . . . Pan lord of the woodlands and of war, whom from the daylight hours caverns shelter; about midnight in lonely places are seen that hairy flank and the soughing leafage on his fierce brow. Louder than all trumpets sounds his voice alone, and at that sound fall helm and sword, the charioteer from his

> rocking car and bolts from gates of walls by night; nor might the helm of Mars and the tresses of the Furies, nor the dismal Gorgon from on high spread such terror, nor with phantoms so dire sweep an army in headlong rout.
>
> (p. 131[III. 46–57])

Pan was fearsome to his enemies, but an eager and loyal ally to his friends.

Pan, half god/half beast, also used noise and trickery to aid Zeus and overcome the Typhoeus. His relationship with the dragons Python and her consort Typhoeus, or Typhon, was ambiguous. Typhoeus was like Pan, half like a human and half like a beast, shaped like a man down to the thighs, with vipers for legs. Pan protected against the Typhoeus but he was also linked to the Typhoeus and the Python through kinship lines and behaviors (Kerenyi, 1998) and some background helps to make the situation clearer.

Plutarch explained the genealogical link in the story in which Apollo established himself at the oracular site of Delphi, previously occupied by the dragon Python. Apollo was following the Python, after having mortally wounded it, and "he overtook him when he had just died from the effects of the wound and been buried by his son, whose name, as they say was Aix" (Plutarch, 1936/1972, p. 187 [IV. 293C]). *Aix*, or *Aigipan*, is Greek for goat and Pan is identified with Aix and also said to be the son of Aix (Hyginus, 2013, *Astronomica, Part 1.* [II.13]). Pan's relationship to the Typhoeus and the Python suggest a very ancient origin for Pan as he is then related to the battle forces allied with the Titans, the gods who preceded the Olympians. Pan, the Typhoeus, and the Python express aspects of the psyche that are dangerous, chaotic, and unpredictable.

In Zeus's successful battle for Mt Olympus, Pan did not aid the old gods, the Titans. Instead he assisted Hermes in aiding the new, young god, Zeus (Kerenyi, 1998). Pan, or Aegipan, helped Zeus win his victory over the monster by blowing a conch so loudly it confused and panicked the beast (1998). "The real participant in this was Aigipan; the god Pan, that is to say, in his quality of a goat (*aix*)" (1998, p. 28). Zeus, "since he was very fond of him, he placed in memory the form of a goat among the stars" (Hyginus, 2013, *Astronomica, Part 1.* [II.13]). Pan was present, then, and essential, in the formation of the Olympian period and is linked through his relationship to the dragon with the matriarchal period of pre-history.

Plutarch (1996/2003a) explicitly tied Pan to the panic that overcomes groups of people in his essay on "Isis and Osiris." In the story Osiris is tricked into getting into a coffin that is then thrown into the Nile. The first to learn of the deed were "the Pans and the Satyrs who lived in the region around Chemmis" (p. 37 [356, D]). When the Egyptians learned what had been done to their great leader they lost courage "and so, even to this day, the sudden confusion and consternation of a crowd is called panic" (p. 37 [356, D]). Chemmis, also known as Panopolis, was a city in Egypt with a temple to Pan, so it is not surprising to have him turn up in this Egyptian myth.

The roles of protector and persecutor are never entirely divorced. At the battle of Marathon Pan was a persecutor to the Persians, while for the Athenians he brought victory (Artemidorus, 1975). He is credited with coming to the aid of the Athenians in their famous battle against Xerxes in 490 BCE. The Persians launched a seaborne attack on the Athenians after sacking Eretria (in the Aegean Sea) and moved their fleet into the bay of Marathon, poised to strike the final blow. The Athenians' last hope lay in their treaty with the Spartans, both city-states had vowed to come to each other's aid against the Persians (these two enemies were willing to work together against their greater enemy). A runner, Phidippedes, was sent across the mainland and down the Peloponnesian peninsula to summon Sparta. The Spartans turned him down. They were in the midst of a festival and would not risk the ill will of the gods by not completing it first. When the Spartans finally arrived at Marathon they were amazed to see the Athenians had decisively driven off the Persians (Connolly, P., 1981).

Phidipiddes had been running for days to accomplish this and would have been exhausted, sleep and food deprived, and dehydrated. These conditions have been found to encourage an eruption of the numinosum into everyday life (Corbett, 2004).

Herodotus (1922/1971) is the oldest extant writer who recounted the part Pan was imagined to have played in the victory:

> The [Athenian] generals sent as a herald to Sparta Phidippides, an Athenian, and one, moreover, that was a runner of long distances and made that his calling. This man, as he said himself and told the Athenians, when he was in the Parthenian hills above Tegea, met with Pan; who, calling to Phidippides by name, bade him say to the Athenians, "Why is it that ye take no thought for me, that am your friend, and ere now have oft been serviceable to you, and will be so again?" This story the Athenians believed to be true, and when their state won to prosperity they founded a temple of Pan beneath the acropolis, and for that message sought the god's favor with yearly sacrifices and torch-races.
>
> (pp. 257–259 [VI. 105])

When the Athenians prevailed in battle, Phidipiddes was believed and Pan was catapulted onto the world stage (Herodotus, 1922/1971). The Cave of Pan on the north shore of the Bay of Marathon was dedicated to him after the battle, and in Athens a ritual "torch-race in honour of Pan may have been stimulated partly by the recollection of the famous race of Phidippides in the course of which he met Pan on the mountains" (Farnell, 1909/1971, p. 382).

Pausanias (c. 110 CE-180 CE), a Greek geographer and incomparable source for the ways ancient Greeks thought about their world (Jones,

1918/1954) identified Pan's role as an aggressive provocateur and an arouser of instinct (Pausanias, 1935/1961). Pausanias traveled through the city-states and wrote his *Description of Greece* during the second century while the Greek religions were still actively practiced. "Pausanias appears to have gathered most of his topographical knowledge from his own travels, but he doubtless used in places the works of his predecessors, while his historical information is fairly reliable, being generally derived from good sources" (1918/1954, p. xv).

Pausanias (1935/1961) reported a battle between the Greeks and the Gauls. During the night a panic fell on the Gauls:

> For causeless terrors are said to come from the god Pan. It was when evening was turning to night that the confusion fell on the army and at first only a few became mad, and these imagined that they heard the trampling of horses at a gallop, and the attack of advancing enemies; but after a little time the delusion spread to all. So rushing to arms they divided into two parties, killing and being killed, neither understanding their mother tongue nor recognizing one another's forms or the shape of their shields. Both parties alike under the present delusion thought that their opponents were Greek, men and armor, and that the language they spoke was Greek, so that a great mutual slaughter was wrought among the Gauls by the madness sent by the god.
>
> (p. 503 [VIII, xxiii, 6–9])

The mytheme of "causeless terrors" bringing panic and madness in the night to the enemies of Pan echoes the description of Panic Disorder in the *Diagnostic and Statistical Manual of Mental Disorders* (American Psychiatric Association (APA), 2013) the standard for diagnosing mental disorders in the United States. Though some of the categories in the *DSM-5* are controversial and it has not resolved problems of reliability in diagnosing (Spiegel, 2005, p. 63), its compounded lists of symptoms for psychological disorders are accepted as accurate within the American field of psychology (APA, 2013).

A panic attack is defined as an "abrupt surge of intense fear or discomfort" (APA, 2013, p. 214). Symptoms include a pounding heart, sweating, trembling, sensations of shortness of breath or choking, nausea, feelings of chest pain, dizziness, derealization (feelings of unreality) or depersonalization (being detached from oneself), and fears of "going crazy" or losing control (p. 214). The diagnosis of panic disorder is given when an unexpected state of panic occurs more than once. "Unexpected refers to a panic attack for which there is no obvious cue or trigger at the time of occurrence – that is, the attack appears to occur from out of the blue, such as when the individual is relaxing" (p. 209). These symptoms are apt descriptors for the reactions to Pan by the Gauls. They were confused, felt they were going mad, and suffered a temporary loss of control.

American Pan

Panic and anxiety problems are common in early twenty-first-century America (Anxiety Disorders Association of America, 2007). Some psychological disorders correspond directly with the *zeitgeist* of their times. Panic disorder and others in APA's anxiety disorders group, Post Traumatic Stress disorder, Generalized Anxiety disorder, Agoraphobia, Obsessive Compulsive Disorder, and Social Anxiety disorder, are rivaled only in commonality by Major Depressive disorder and Persistent Depressive disorder. According to the National Institute for Mental Health (NIMH), "Approximately 40 million American adults ages 18 and older, or about 18.1% of people in this age group in a given year, have an anxiety disorder" (NIMH, 2013, "Anxiety Disorders," para. 2). These numbers include only those people who went to a doctor for their symptoms and were diagnosed and so it is likely that more than one in five American adults suffer from anxiety disorders.

In Pan's earliest days as an archetypal god-image, roughly 2600 years ago (Germany, 2005), panic was cultured within the same conditions in the psyche as it is today. In Jungian terms, panic is an unconscious and compulsive reaction to life, which can be modified, even transformed if the repressed core of the complex is freed up and becomes a conscious part of the personality or culture. Pan was a leader and protector when he allied with others, creating a shell-like phalanx to provide safety for his friends. He was not only a god of panic, but he did use surprise and noise when the best way to protect his allies was to panic his enemies. Pan demonstrates creativity, bravery, strategic cunning, loyalty, and a trickster nature in these myths, while his countenance expresses the need to conjoin the disparate parts of the self.

The structuring of Pan's myths, which include a fear-based control over the natural world, panic arousing tendencies, and fight-flight-freeze responses mirror both an underlying inflated attitude and a fear-based apocalyptic vision in the US that has developed out of America's superpower status in the world (Lifton, 2003). The tactics such a vision legitimizes include scapegoating and manipulation of the mainstream public as well as brutality toward the perceived enemy. A compensatory naivety in the American public aided in the formation of this protective vision. The belief in the country as not just the richest and most powerful, but also politically and morally the best, the myth of "exceptionalism" as an US birthright, is seen here as foundational to this complex (Lewis, D., 2012). The formation of the belief of America as exceptional has been fundamental in forming its unique mythic sense of itself. As a faulty central ideal, it appears to be unconsciously compensating for the dominant culture's fear of inferiority.

Chapter 5

Rites of healing and scapegoating in antiquity

Metamorphoses

The Homeric hymn to Pan

The Homeric hymns, dating from the late sixth to mid-fifth centuries BCE (Germany, 2005), are among the oldest extant written record of the stories of the Greek gods (Cole, 2004). "The Homeric hymn to Pan" (Boer, 1970, pp. 64–68) begins with Pan's birth. At the first sight of her son his strange appearance and noisy behavior upset his mother so greatly that she panicked and fled:

> She produced for Hermes
> a dear son –
> fantastic to look at,
> with goat-feet,
> and two horns,
> very noisy
> but laughing
> sweetly
> Its mother
> jumped up and fled –
> instead of nursing it
> she abandoned the child –
> she was scared
> as she looked at
> its brutal face! (Boer, 1970, p. 67)

Pan was shunned from birth for being singular and peculiar. Differences in his countenance from that of ordinary human beings branded him as grotesque. The hymn itself addresses this by making a point about the difference between the gods' reactions and the human responses to Pan. His mother had a subjective, judgmental reaction while Pan's father, Hermes, was "overjoyed in his mind" (Boer, 1970, p. 67) and flew him up to Olympus to show him off.

> And all the immortal gods
> were delighted
> in their hearts
> and more than anyone else even
> Dionysus,
> Bacchos.
> And they decided to call him
> Pan
> because he had delighted the minds of
> all. (p. 68)

Pan panicked his mother but charmed the gods (Borgeaud, 1979/1988). He did not fit his mother's picture of what a god should look like or how a god should act. He represents how the new often presents itself in a form traditional thinking finds frightening or repulsive because it is a threat to the status quo. The son of Hermes "should" look, smell, and sound a certain way, just as many a daughter's high school boy friend should not have tattoos, long hair, or a beard. But the gods see him with different eyes, they see through to his essence and are charmed by him.

Whether women or nymphs, in the myths feminine figures continued to run from Pan. He expresses sadness and anger when rejected. He personifies an archetype of hypermasculine power on the one hand, and another of the loneliness and disconnection from nurturing. He is most often seen in the retinue of other masculine gods such as Zeus and Dionysus or alone hunting in the wilderness.

Hypermasculinity often leads to a propensity to be callous toward the needs of the disenfranchised, dependent on dangerous behaviors for stimulation, spending much time and resources to become dominant, and routinely emphasizing strength and physical prowess over intelligence or compassion. Hypermasculinity begets social norms that support warfare and ignore the rights of women to have control over their own bodies. It thrives in a power system in which men and masculine values control society (Klein, 2012). One way to think about culture politically, from antiquity through modernity, is that we live in a world of ongoing colliding, hypermasculine groups. For instance, one could say that once Russia subsided as a threat terrorism emerged from the vacuum because hypermasculinity seeks high levels of competition.

The Greek sophist Philostratus, b. c. 190 CE, handed down the story of the consequences for a hypermasculine Pan when he was unwilling to dance in harmony with the Naiads, (water nymphs) "who shake dew-drops from their hair" (1931/1960, p. 177) and the Anthousai, the flower nymphs who "have hair that resembles hyacinth flowers" (p. 177). He went "beyond bounds in his leaping" (p. 177) and they tried to teaching him a dance "of a more delightful character; when he, however, pays no heed to them but, his garment extended, tries to make love to them" (p. 177). The story goes that:

> Formerly he used to sleep relaxed, with peaceful nostril and soothing his angry spirit with slumber, but to-day he is very angry; for the Nymphs have fallen upon him, and already Pan's hands have been tied behind his back, and he fears for his legs since the Nymphs wish to seize them. Moreover, his beard, which he values most highly, has been shaven off with razors which have been roughly applied to it.
>
> (p. 180)

This story amplifies a number of important points concerning Pan. First of all, he did not occupy a lofty hierarchal position, but was accessible. Second, Pan's sexual impulses often depict him as having made himself foolish. Third, he was taken to task for not being able to stay within the limits of dancing. Dance is as an expression of non-verbal communication, usually between the sexes, and, so can be seen as a way to engage one's opposite without confrontation. Pan went beyond the limits prescribed and even ignored the nymphs' attempts to teach him. He could not help himself and overdid it. Finally, he was held accountable for his weaknesses. Although other gods, such as Zeus, have stories of obsessive pursuits of nymphs, it is Pan and his retinue of satyrs who are taken to task for their wanton ways. Dionysus, the god most clearly expressing the divine nature of unbound ecstasy, is never seen in full blown myopic pursuit of the other. It is Pan who is so often painted and sculpted in full chase, ithyphallic, and mindless of all save his prey. His sexuality is closely related to his role as Pan *Agreus* ("of the hunt").

Yet the nymphs as a group were able to ensnare him and subdued his overcharged nature when it veered out of control. The nymphs mediate Pan's lust. When he refuses to learn, he had his beard "the sign of full manhood" (de Vries, 1984, p. 39), which "he values most highly" (Philostratus, 1931/1960, p. 180) roughly shaved. The nymphs have a lesson for Pan. If he does not behave willingly, he will be shamed into it. So to understand Pan, it is crucial to see him in the context of the many nymphs who shared his realm.

Without this nymph-like response to Pan energy, there is a paucity of nurturance in a hypermasculine system, whether ancient or modern, with heroes who are numb to pain and transformed into one-sided fighting machines. Rather than looking at their own and the others (whoever is seen as the enemy) lack of nymph-like participation in their everyday lives, instead many people, without necessarily meaning to or realizing it, are becoming more and more hardened, hypermasculine, as they witness the media's relivings of weekly random shootings, bombings, and massacres and then go to the movies and watch TV shows about the same.

A hypermasculine inflation of the archetypal protector and provider has become more predominant since 9/11. Perhaps this signals the patriarchy needs greater defense, and so, hopefully, foreshadows an underlying weakness, and thus an unconscious need to defend itself more and more. Besides these parallels, since hypermasculinity implies, requires really, being cut off from the sensitivity of the feeling function, it promotes self-centered complexes and behaviors in individuals and cultural complexes in groups. Hypermasculinity connects through competition, and thus loneliness and inadequacy underlie it (Klein, 2012).

Even today, the Greek god Pan holds an archetypal image that reflects this aspect of the psyche. He is remembered for his insensitivity, violence, attempted rapes, and selfish, self-absorbed behaviors. These are all elements of the habitual nature of Pan as relayed to us through the myths and legends of the early Greeks and Romans (Borgeaud, 1979/1988).

Pan embodied more than these best-remembered qualities. A god, half divine and half animal (Farnell, 1909/1971), he suffered the whip on his back for the good of those for whom he cared (Theocritus, 1999), divined the future (Borgeaud, 1979/1988), was a loyal ally to his friends (1979/1988), was named *All* by Zeus (Athanassakis, 1976), and provided the cipher of being a god who was proclaimed to be dead and yet was immortal (Borgeaud, 1983). Pan delighted the Olympians with his laughter (Athanassakis, 1976), played the pipes for the nymphs' nightlong, labyrinthine dances (Philostratus, 1931/1960), and provided sustenance for his cults from the herds and his lonely hunts (Pausanias, 1935/1961). Pan was a leader and protector when he allied with others, creating a shell-like phalanx to provide safety for his friends. He was not only a god of panic, but he did use surprise and noise when the best way to protect his allies was to panic his enemies. Pan demonstrates creativity, bravery, strategic cunning, loyalty, and a trickster nature in these myths, while his countenance expresses the need to conjoin the disparate parts of the self. He was above all an ancient fertility god (Farnell, 1909/1971). The goat-god Pan tracked alone through the wilderness, hunting down quarry or compulsively chasing after sex, uncorking dread and panic in those he pursued, who either froze or fled away (Nonnos, 1940/1962c). A recurrent theme, linking danger and ecstasy with Pan, echoes through his chthonic attributes.

Pan was said to have caused *panolepsy*, a seizure that brought laughter and ecstatic rapture. The nymphs were also, and more commonly, associated with inducing altered states in humans. Both *panolepsy* and *nympholepsy* were believed to be a gift that inspires. But these healing trances were also thought to sometimes cause a person to be carried off by Pan or a nymph and were feared. Untimely deaths were even attributed to them (Borgeaud, 1979/1988). In other myths, Pan's desire exploded into chase and created panic in the nymphs and goddesses who despised the outcast Pan. But, ironically, in Pan's hunting ritual and myths comes a possible way out of the compulsive side of hypermasculinity.

Scapegoating

Ektithemi *and spinal dysraphism*

There is a possible medical basis for the physical description of Pan and his retinue of *panes*. They may actually have been surviving outcasts. *Ektithemi*, an ancient Greek custom meaning to expose or set out (Patterson, 1985), was practiced on newborns with birth defects. Plato described this custom in 360 BCE in a dialogue on the nature of knowledge, *Theatetus*, in which Socrates said of a newborn:

> now that he is born, we must run round the hearth with him, and see whether he is worth rearing, or is only a wind-egg and a sham. Is he to be reared in any case, and not exposed? Or will you bear to see him rejected, and not get into a passion if I take away your first-born?
>
> (2011)

In early Greece, if children were born with deformities they were left for dead in isolated places outside the cities (Sailer & Kolb, 1995); in other words, in Pan's territory. "An exposed infant is a victim at an early stage, chosen because of the signs of abnormality which augur badly for his future" (Girard, 1982/1989, p. 26). Since children have been discovered who lived through such an experience (probably by surviving with the aid of wild animals, such as goats) as recently as the Wild Boy of Aveyron, a 12-year-old found in the forests near Toulouse in 1798 (Cattell, 1933), it is plausible that a few children survived their "exposure" after having been born with the goat-like deformities that accompany certain types of genetic spinal cord defects.

Professors Gary P. Williams and Lewis Leavitt (2004) suggest just such a genetic reason could account for the physical abnormalities in men who resembled Pan, the *panes* as they were called (Harrison, 1991), and who had survived in the mountains. A "Pan tail is based on an ancient observation of an abnormality associated with diastematomyelia," (Williams & Leavitt, 2004, p. 519) also known as spinal dysraphism, and is the result of a severed spinal cord. In this rare condition, humans are born with what amounts to a tail. Suffering from this condition, a boy's:

> calves would have become progressively thinner and he would habitually have risen on his toes to walk. His feet would have become rigid, in a "high-heels" position. They would have lost not just the flexibility of normal human feet but the architecture and sensation of human feet as well, as trophic ulcerations wore away the toes on which he initially walked, and as thick layers of callus and scar tissue developed in their stead. His gait might have become more and more spastic.
>
> (pp. 520–521)

Priapism occurs with this disorder (Williams & Leavitt, 2004, p. 521) and reinforces a possible historical explanation since Pan is so firmly associated with both fertility and wantonness. Urinary incontinence is associated with spinal dysraphism as well, a condition which people tend to find repulsive. The irksome state would probably have led to the reticence attributed to Pan to enter towns or civilized areas and to drinking as much wine as possible as a way to numb the pain (p. 521). All Pan's physical attributes save the horns on his head fit a description of spinal dysraphism.

These deformities describe the *panes*, the many goat horned Pan-men who became fashionable as attendants to Kore in the fifth century BCE (Harrison, 1991, pp. 277–278). A historical explanation for the countenance of Pan and the *panes* also could explain why they were identified as fearsome beings that are both a cause of panic and to be revered. They were cast out and repulsive, as was Pan by his mother, but also unique in their survival, which probably was considered the work of the gods in the animated world of the ancient Greeks. Pan personifies a scapegoat as well as a divine figure.

Holder of the opposites

Pan demonstrated the characteristics of the scapegoated, where "the further one is from normal social status of whatever kind, the greater the risk of persecution. . . . The very word *abnormal* . . . is something of a taboo; it is both noble and cursed, *sacer* in all senses of the word" (Girard, 1982/1989, p. 18). Pan carries the weight of the scapegoat. He is both monster and god. Today, a scapegoat is understood to be the carrier of a group's projected weaknesses (Perera, 1986, p. 8), while in ancient Greece the scapegoat was also regarded as a *pharmakon* (p. 8). It was the poison, the scapegoat, and the remedy (Dioscorides, 1934/1959, Ars Industrialis, 2017, "pharmakon").

The Greek formula for a *pharmakos* was either the ugliest, stupidest, or most reviled member of a community or, conversely, the leader, a king, or a god (Vernant & Vidal-Nauet, 1972/1981). "The divine king, the purifier and saviour of his people becomes one with the defiled criminal who must be expelled like a *pharmakos* or scapegoat so that the town can regain its purity and be saved" (p. 97). Jungian analyst Sylvia Perera (1986) stated that the split off energies in the scapegoat complex are "aggressive, sexual and dependency needs that erupt impulsively and compulsively" (p. 23). These fit with Pan's mythic themes as a hyper-aggressive force in nature.

Pan can be understood as a projection of what Jungian analyst Edward Edinger referred to in his discussion of the Self.

> The living experience of the Self is an aberration, a joining of opposites that appalls the ego and exposes it to anguish, demoralization and violation of all "reasonable" considerations. And yet the same event viewed from above is a coronation, demonstrating once again the reciprocal and compensatory relation between the ego and the unconscious.
>
> (1987, p. 137)

Such an explanation begins to make clearer the stark contrast between the disparate reactions to Pan, and most especially to the difference in the way the gods received him.

Squilling: a healing ritual

In Arcadia, Pan was originally worshipped as a god of the hunt and a protector of the herds (Farnell, 1921). If there was a poor hunt, ritualized containment of his cult's fear of starvation, in a rite called "squilling," was enacted (Borgeaud, 1979/1988). Through squilling Pan was honored, as were all the Greek gods, by a rite of sacrifice. In squilling, the cult approached Pan with both fear and aggression. This served as a way to come up against their own fears and aggressions in a ritualized manner. Squilling's purpose was to restore the balance of order in the cult, specifically the focus was on restoring an abundant supply of game so the hunters would be able to provide sustenance and the group would survive (Borgeaud, 1979/1988). The ritual itself uniquely served as a container for healing the traumatic emotions associated with fears for survival. For the Greek cults, this rite, like all rites, were "the basic experience of the 'sacred'" (Burkert, 1972/1983, p. 3). Harrison (1991) explained the ancient Greeks believed in

> the ridding of what is hostile and enhancing what is favorable with rites . . . primitive man has before him, in order that he may live, the old dual task to get rid of evil, to secure good. Evil is to him of course mainly hunger and barrenness. Good is food and fertility.
>
> (p. 1)

Theocritus, a native of Syracuse, preserved local traditions in his writings and recorded the oldest known reference to squilling in the third century

BCE (Borgeaud, 1979/1988). In his *Idyll*, "Harvest Home," the narrator, Simichidas, referred to a ritual that followed poor hunts: "This do, sweet Pan, and never, when slices be too few/ May the leeks o' the lads of Arcady beat thee black and blue" (Edmonds trans., 1912/1977, p. 103 [VII, 106–109]). If the kill was small or, worse yet, the hunters returned empty handed, the young men of the village would ceremonially circle around a statue of Pan and use large bulbous onions attached to their stalks, "squills," to whip Pan around the shoulders and genital area (Edmonds, 1977; Farnell, 1921).

When considered out of context, whipping one's god into helping seems a crude and bizarre rite. However, it gave the young hunters an outlet for their fears and anxieties, reminded them of their society's understanding that sustenance and life itself are gifts of the gods, and aligned them as the sons of Pan who, like them, was a hunter and so must learn to be invulnerable to pain, hardship, and loneliness. "Wilhelm Mannhardt put forth the theory that the scapegoat is 'originally' the vegetation spirit, who must be whipped and chased, and even killed, in order to be invigorated, to be born afresh" (Burkert, 1979, p. 68). Whipping was understood to stimulate life-giving power when performed with fertilizing boughs, as are those of the squill (Farnell, 1921, p. 33). "The object of this discipline was not punishment and insult, but stimulative magic whereby the life-giving power of the deity might be restored" (Farnell, 1971, p. 433).

The squill was a well-known variety of onion in Greco-Roman times (Aristotle, 1984; Dioscorides, 1934/1959). "The philosopher Pythagoras wrote a whole book about them, including an account of their medicinal properties" (Pliny, 1950/1971, p. 483 [XXX. 94–95]). Nicander, a Greek poet and physician from the second century BCE, related that "the many-coated head of the Squill, . . . fearfully inflames the flesh" (1953, p. 111 [249–254]). The squill was pungent (Pliny, 1950/1971, p. 481 [XXX. 93]), nettle-like (Bremmer, 2000, p. 282), and considered "contemptible, inedible, even deadly" (Parker, 1983, p. 231). Among its many ancient uses it was "a Catplasme for such as are bitten of vipers" (Dioscorides, 1934/1959, p. 213 [202]), a cure for softening the belly, moving urine, for coughs, asthma, warts, and much more. It was considered to be a purifier, able to ward off evil spirits, promote growth, and thought of as an all-purpose healing herb (1950/1971). The squill was long lived (Theophrastus, 1926/1977, p. 129 [VII. xiii. 4]). It was referred to as a *pharmakon* (Dioscorides, 1934/1959).

Pan's shoulders and genitals were the targeted body parts, suggesting the ritual is concerned with awakening strength and stimulating fertility. The endurance and physical strength of young men of the cult was well suited to hunting as long they were able to master the emotions puberty sets on fire. So for them to be the ritual performers may have had to do with an initiation into conscious awareness and containment of the more irrational sides of masculinity that are represented by Pan, a theme that will be explored in relationship to hypermasculinity in present day America.

Perhaps Pan's followers believed the irritant would be arousing by making Pan itchy and restless. There is considerable evidence that Pan was easily irritated in myth (Philostratus, 1931/1960, p. 167 [II, 11]; Edmonds, 1912/1977, p. 11 [I, 16–20]; Ovid, 1989, pp. 232–323). If he is to be aroused out of an implicit apathy (he was known to sleep until noon) by the whipping, then in this rite, the poison in Pan's hypermasculine aggressiveness and self-absorption is sacrificed as a remedy to restore order for the cult. In other words, the psychological let down of the poor hunt was transformed when the cult's aggression was safely contained.

Pan and the nymphs

Nymphs are very ancient and were much loved in the cults. Hesiod (2002) said they were here before Aphrodite or even the Titans. Pan and the nymphs are often found together in the sanctuary of a cave. Caves dedicated to Pan were widespread and many have been excavated revealing reliefs and dedications. There are far too many to specify each of them here. Two that reflect on the enduring archetypal nature of Pan are the Cave of Pan, the Nymphs, and Apollo (the Vari cave on Mt Hymettus) and The Cave of Pan on Mt Parnes. The Vari cave was found containing remains from worshippers including nearly 1000 fifth- and sixth-century CE Roman lamps and late imperial coins from the periods of Constantine to Arcadius. These indicate the reuse of the cave after it had been abandoned by the cult in the second century BCE. The Cave of Pan on Mt Parnes (both are in Attica), held coins from these two distant and distinct periods as well. Susan Alcock (1994) wrote this indicates the cult was revived after discontinuation during the initial rise of Christianity in that area. The caves provided a natural form of protection that Pan's followers would have resorted to in order to avoid detection and would have served the cult followers desire to be in places surrounded by images of Pan and the nymphs.

Alone the nymphs were Pan's prey, but when they banded together, as the Naiads and the Anthousai did to shave off his beard, they could mitigate his aggressions and soothe his hypermasculine spirit. When the nymphs united they were not in danger. This is reflected in the rites that took place in his many caves throughout the Mediterranean basin.

The circle dance

One rite enacts Pan dancing in harmony with the nymphs. A recent find of a tableau of terra-cotta figurines from the mid-fifth century BCE at the Corycian cave above Delphi depicts a wheel with spokes: Pan stands at the center about to play the syrinx while nymphs encircle him at equal points on the wheel – all are poised, ready to begin the dance (Pasquier, 1977). In this earliest known image of Pan and the nymphs, the nymphs surround him and yet they are also out of his reach, safely distanced by the wheel that unites them. Rather than the brutal predation for which Pan is remembered, a symmetrical harmony was achieved when the archetype of hypermasculinity and the causer of panic was kept in balance and contained by the soothing presence of the nymphs. The result is music and dance. This tableau depicts an ancient rite that was not isolated, but rather was performed in many caves in the region.

The earlier metamorphoses of the nymphs were devolutions – instinctive responses of panicked flight or freezing that resulted in a vegetative state such as a laurel bush or a pine tree – while the circle dance is an evolution from aggressive fights for personal fulfillments of desires by Pan and panicked reactions by the feminine figures, to a boundaried and centered, joyful exchange between the one and the many. The nymphs are not controlling Pan or influencing him by being warlike. The configuration suggests a relationship between nurturer and predator that involves being close but out of reach – contained and mutually receptive – approaching the opposite without anger but rather with joy and playfulness. In the circle dance the nymphs embody safety not only in numbers, but in an entirely radical approach. Not only non-violent but also non-rejecting, they dance with the would-be rapist. This has something to do with embodying the feeling function in an inclusive way, rather than anger or despair, a nurturing commitment to each other brings the hypermasculine into balance.

By beginning with the archetypal we can search for an approach grounded in wisdom that still holds up as true. It appears doubtful modernity can achieve containment of hypermasculine forces dominating politically on a global level, a reversal so desperately needed, by overcoming the hypermasculine using force or cunning or making a lot of noise with protests – this is playing its game. Rather the idea emerges of a dance or of a harmony, above all balance and safety are emphasized in the rite. Perhaps this points to a new paradigm, one that is darkly mirrored in the #MeToo movement beginning in 2017. If we look to the immense suffering in the world today and then back to the myths, this paradigm would have to do with creating safety by introducing the balance and harmony expressed in these circle dances to the modern world.

Pan's inherent healing forces

As an archetypal force, Pan carries the potential for wholeness as well as the pain that the splitting of wholeness causes. He is perceived as being a monstrous aberration, half animal and half divine, because of the ego's need to reject the loss felt when this split happens in a person or a culture. Humankind's relationship to its own chthonic nature is ambiguous and cryptic, and so it is often avoided. It is too dangerous even if also exciting; the desire to kill off the chthonic is personified in ritual. "Originally the scapegoat was a human or animal victim chosen for sacrifice to the underworld god to propitiate that god's anger and to heal the community" (Perera, 1986, p. 8). But in squilling, the chthonic god himself is sacrificed. Parallels can be drawn with the atonements made by Jesus for his people (Boardman, 1997). "Pilate took Jesus and scourged him" (John 19:1 Bible, King James Version), which led to his crucifixion. He cried out in anguish, "but I am a worm, and no man; scorned by men, and despised by the people. All who see me mock at me" (Psalms 22: 6–7). Pan and Jesus were offered as a sacrifice, scapegoats, in atonement for the lack of success of their followers. Pan is one of many god-images who sacrifice for the good of the whole. "The enigma of the *primitive* sacred [is] the beneficial return from the harmful omnipotence attributed to the scapegoat" (Girard, 1982/1989, p. 43). Pan *Skoleitas*, the winding or crooked, was also Pan *Lyterius*, the releaser or redeemer (Roscher, 1892/1988).

Squilling, as a community-based use of sacred space in which to contain fear, aggression, anger, and panic, offers a template for an alternative and less-hostile method to contain group anxieties. There is a tendency for a group to overwhelm individuality when threatened with traumatic circumstances. Rather than forming a protective cultural complex around anxieties and aggressively defending a weakened sense of self against an outer enemy, a transformation through sacrifice of aggression and self-interest is the solution indicated by this ritual.

The circle dance takes this theme another step. Now the *pharmakon* is centered and shifts from being poisonous and scapegoated to healer. The nymphs do not judge Pan – they dance with him, they do not need revenge, instead they see the best in Pan and because they all see it, the strength of their vision helps him become it.

American nymphs

Implicit in an inalienable right to freedom, so fundamental to the United States, is the possibility of an active and conscious struggle to become a more aware community. This positive social impetus is still alive in the polity of the US. It is visible in ethical movements such as the waning of resistance toward gay marriage and the momentum toward greater ecologic sustainability. When enough awareness creates critical mass it can tilt public opinion in a certain direction and then public opinion is an inexorable force, nearly impossible to stop.

It is too easy to dismiss America as inflated and greedy or boorish. The situation is much more complicated. The best and the worst in Pan meet in the United States. The best of Pan, a protector and provider god, and the worst of Pan, a self-absorbed brute, are reflected in America's story. When the most brilliant strands of the dominant American culture are separated out from those of the West in general, one can see more of the Greek god

Pan in the US. The wild west, the frontiers of space, innovative utilizations of natural resources, and freedom for individuals crown American contributions. Pan's dominion over the natural world and his life as a separate and independent god, his freedom from the restraints of civilization and, above all, the sense of space that separates him from others in his own territory, parallels some aspects of the *zeitgeist* of the dominant culture in the US. But perhaps the day is not far off when the culture awakens to the notion that the archetypal field the ancients called the nymphs, the many, the beautiful, the nurturers, will rise up together and join hands, offering up a new way to mitigate the complexed attitude in its aging, hyper distress.

Chapter 6

American history reconsidered using cultural complex theory

The most prominent motifs in Pan's myths include fear-based control over the natural world, panic-arousing tendencies, and fight-flight-freeze responses. These themes are the scaffolding of an American cultural complex, one that has had serious effects on American society and thus, the world. This complex, as Jung said of all complexes, is a splintered off part of the psyche, has an inner coherence or wholeness, holds some amount of autonomy over the ego-complex, acts as a disruption putting a person under stress and so is accompanied by strong feelings, and is not necessarily negative, but rather is an expression of a characteristic state of the psyche (1948/1960 [*CW* 8]). An underlying inflation and a hypermasculine attitude in the leadership in the US has caused splintering within the country and between the US and many other countries. A compensatory naivety in the American public has aided in the formation of a protective vision that has its own inner coherence. Research indicates the psychological state of the country is more pathological now than before the turn of the millennium indicating high levels of societal stress. One example of how American reactions to threats to its security are actually overreactions is the story (discussed in detail in chapter eight) of how in 2002 the US government believed it had the right to defy the UN's leadership and attack Iraq (World Press Review, 2012). Examples of the rising level of anger in the country are myriad, but one is the angry backlash toward the Democratic Party's commitment to diversity and globalism in voters who elected Donald Trump as a populist and isolationist president. These conditions are hallmarks of Jung's original idea of a complex.

I am suggesting that an anxiety-based cultural complex formed in the colonial period of US history and has been triggered by recent events. The belief in the country as exceptional was birthed out of the Puritan ethos, raised on the dogma of Manifest Destiny, and triggered out of latency by events in modernity. It is now in a highly reactive state and would appear to be unconsciously compensating for fears of inferiority. When shadow material locked in a cultural complex is exposed and threatened, as with the attacks on 9/11, it may erupt, revolutionize, instigate regression, or promote compassionate dialogues, but it can always be understood as a compensatory move by the unconscious to restore wholeness (Jung, 1946/1978 [*CW* 10]). The restoration of wholeness, seeing the whole truth rather than a partial truth, naturally revitalizes rejected parts of the psyche (Jung, 1948/1960 [*CW* 8]). This is, in part, why archetypal theory is highly valued today.

Exceptionalism

The origin of a complex is traumatic and so was the birth of the nation. The Puritans were escaping from a hostile living environment in Europe and faced severe hardships establishing a community, yet for them the discovery of the New World provided the Puritans with what they perceived as a *tabula rasa* on which to practice the new social order they believed their God desired. They saw this as an opportunity to create an outer life that matched their deepest inner values: a way of life that would reconcile cultural tensions between spirituality and free enterprise. "The changing of the course of trade, and the supplying of the world with its treasures from America is a type and forerunner of what is approaching in spiritual things, when the world shall be supplied with spiritual treasures from America" (Jonathan Edwards, as cited in Bercovitch, 1975, p. 156). The Puritan notion of their exceptionalism was birthed out of the idea that by adhering to their strict religious beliefs and contributing to the wealth of their community through free enterprise they would remain a chosen people.

At the core of a Puritan complex are the traumas begun by severe restrictions on practices of religion in seventeenth century English law. John Winthrop, governor of the Massachusetts Bay Company, led the first wave of Puritan immigrants, the Pilgrims, in making risky Atlantic crossings to begin a new life free from persecution. On the eve of their landing in 1630, he exhorted them to "be as a city upon a hill. The eyes of all people are upon us" (as cited in Greenberg, 2012, p. 43).

The Massachusetts Bay colony began as a theocracy. The Puritans conceived of their new home as a "fulfillment of scripture prophecy" (Bercovitch, 1975, p. 137) and "the American self as the embodiment of a prophetic universal design" (p. 136). Other colonists, such as those in New Amsterdam, viewed their new home as a mercantile adventure in cooperation with their Old World home, while southern colonial writers in Maryland and Virginia colored the New World more as a Romantic utopia: "the territories already under cultivation spread before the 'ravished' planter like so many 'Beauties of naked Nature'" (Louis B. Wright, as cited in Bercovitch, 1975, p. 137).

Puritans brought on, even encouraged the disdain and persecution they suffered for their beliefs; shunning their neighbors led to their rejection. For these sects, to be hated by "reprobates" was a sign that they were of the elect. The protective shell of the complex began to form even as the fledgling country met with early success. The archetypal core of the complex (the notion that the Puritans were the elect and closer to God) was protected by shunning, which, in reality, is a defense system. Like many people who are the target of projections and thus scapegoated, the Puritan's motivations contained a transparent revenge fantasy, the fantasy that all those they shunned were destined for everlasting hell. This increased the pressure to make virtue a non-negotiable element of Puritan life. Winthrop warned if the new Americans did not live up to strictly held Puritanical virtues, "wee shall shame the faces of many of God's worthy servants, and cause theire prayers to be turned into curses upon us till wee be consumed out of the good land whither wee are goeing" (Winthrop, as cited in Greenberg, 2012, p. 44). They *had* to see themselves as destined for greatness, and relied upon high standards and stoicism in the pursuit of this goal. In psychological thinking, the one-sidedness of their lives and perspectives created a split. Greatness was non-negotiable and so relatedness, compassion, and mercy for others were split off into the unconscious to aid in the protection of this notion of Puritan greatness.

For the Puritans themselves, the experiment in theocracy failed and Puritanism as an organized religion faded away in the mid-1700s. Modern America could take a lesson in what *not* to do from the way the Puritans brought about their own demise through harsh and oppressive tactics. Their chosen ideology compelled them to respond in an uncompromising way when challenged by reformers, such as Roger Williams, who was banished when he called for a "wall of separation" between church and state. He was forced to lead his followers to what is now the state of Rhode Island (at that time a wilderness mainly inhabited by Indians). Besides banishment the Puritans used torture, imprisonment, and the Salem Witch Trials to enforce their standards for a pure life. The community eventually rejected the uncharitable severity of the psychology of Puritan life, though many of the Puritan's political reforms, such as a system of justice based on a jury of peers, held strong, the church itself dwindled in numbers and hence in political influence after the death of its last charismatic leader, Cotton Mather in 1723.

Puritan beliefs still unconsciously influence modern American beliefs, not only in superficial ways such as a clichéd understanding of American prudery, but also in the idea that wealth is the greatest sign of success, that one is expected to work tirelessly, and that control of sexuality is more important for a culture than restrictions on violence. The central core of an American anxiety complex, that America has an exceptional destiny, did not die with the decline of Puritanism; instead it continued to find new justifications for its existence.

French historian Alexis de Tocqueville (1840) originally conceived of the label of American exceptionalism for this attitude: "The position of the Americans is quite exceptional, and it may be believed that no other democratic people will ever be placed in a similar one" (pp. 36–37). This standard is based on the notion that America is fundamentally different from other nations because it was formed out of a revolution without an antecedent basis in feudalism. De Tocqueville based this premise on his experience of Americans as a society believing in "liberty, equality, constitutionalism . . . and a special destiny to lead the world toward liberty and democracy" (Wood, 2011, pp. 2–3).

Though no longer named as "God's will," implicit in US president's foreign policies is the notion that America has the right to impose its values on others. Abraham Lincoln (1862) said saving the Union was "the last best hope of earth" (para. 4). At the close of World War I Woodrow Wilson (1917) addressed the US Congress and redefined his policy of interventionism because "the world must be made safe for democracy" (para. 7).

The doctrine of exceptionalism still guides American political policy. The administration of President George W. Bush invoked exceptionalism without naming it as such. For example, Bush implied American spiritual superiority while describing why the US is not an empire, saying "We may be the only great power in history that had the chance [to be an empire], and refused – preferring greatness to power and justice to glory" (1999, para. 64). Bush sought to legitimize the political ideology, known as the Bush Doctrine, that the US has a duty to keep the world free for democracy.

> The Bush administration defends its pursuit of this unlikely goal by means of internationally illegal, unilateralist, and preemptive attacks on other countries, accompanied by arbitrary imprisonments and the practice of torture, and by making the claim that the United States possesses an exceptional status among nations that confers upon it special international responsibilities, and exceptional privileges in meeting those responsibilities.
>
> (Pfaff, 2007)

But Bush is not alone. For example, in 2013, President Obama (New York Times, 2013, para. 3) relied on exceptionalism as his rationale for bombing Syria. "But when, with modest effort and risk, we can stop children from being gassed to death . . . I believe we should act. That's what makes America different. That's what makes us exceptional" (para. 35).

President Donald Trump, whether consciously or not, reconnected to the Puritan roots of exceptionalism by tying economic wealth to how great the country is in his inaugural speech. "We do not seek to impose our way of life on anyone, but rather to let it shine as an example," he declared, "We will shine for everyone to follow" (Trump, 2017). These quotes demonstrate the ongoing usage of exceptionalism and its link to the early Puritan vision of America as a theocracy where political decisions are based on a religious belief with the mission to dictate how all should live. These beliefs are problematic because they create a system that encourages American citizens as well as other cultures to see the US as exceptional and because they consistently avoid allowing the disenfranchised their own voice.

Manifest Destiny

In the colonial era, the Puritan's belief in their superiority morphed into the geopolitical policies of colonization by the government. These were guided by the notion of a "Manifest Destiny." The same pattern underlies this belief since at the core is the same assumption of superiority. The belief in such a god given-destiny gave the colonists and pioneers confidence and inspired qualities still admired: fortitude and ingenuity among them. But, psychologically, Manifest Destiny is a one-sided, self-centered way of thinking.

The strategy of Manifest Destiny, which justifies taking land away from those already inhabiting it, was in place long before the *Democratic Review* named it a Manifest Destiny. Though this is certainly not an exclusively American principle, Manifest Destiny proposed that divine sanction made an *obligation* to expand US territory across the North American continent, including Canada, Mexico, and the Caribbean. This principle made a virtue of the appropriation of resources, while the disregard for the freedom and rights of others was blamed, as shall be discussed, on the scapegoated victims. This, it will be demonstrated, is an example of a hypermasculine attitude of ignoring the rights of others.

Manifest Destiny facilitated the growth of the US over the course of its first century. The colonies of the eastern seaboard achieved rapid economic success, catalyzing the growth of a continental US in only 74 years from the establishment of the nation in 1776 to California advancing to statehood in 1850. In 1823, the Monroe Doctrine made law of the strategy later named Manifest Destiny, stating the US had revised its foreign policy regarding European nations and that interference through further colonization of North and South America would be met with American resistance (Monroe Doctrine, 1823, para. 1–3).

One of the outstanding land transactions of the period was the Louisiana Purchase, orchestrated by Thomas Jefferson in 1803. In his second Inaugural Address of 1805, Thomas Jefferson (1805), though not a member of a Puritan congregation (he called himself an unorthodox Christian), embraced a Puritan ethos when he dismissed the sovereign rights of the First Nations:

> The aboriginal inhabitants of these countries I have regarded with the commiseration their history inspires. Endowed with the faculties and rights of men, breathing an ardent love of liberty and independence . . . they have been . . . reduced to limits too narrow for the hunter's state, humanity enjoins us to teach them agriculture and domestic arts.
>
> (para. 8)

This was Jefferson's strategy to appease Americans fearful of the effects the Louisiana Purchase would have on Indian hostilities. It made a virtue of the aggressive politics of moving native peoples off their homelands, which never faltered until the Indians were limited to "reservations" and their children sent to Indian schools where their customs and language were forbidden (Hoefel, 1999). Jefferson believed resettlement and reeducation of the native peoples was sufficient rationale for the dislocation that American expansionist policies demanded.

The making and breaking of treaties between the many nations of Native Americans and the French, English, and early American governments is a well-known story. One early example will suffice. In 1793, after a long and indelicate negotiation over the lands of the Ohio River Valley, a united confederation of sixteen tribes met in council and wrote to the US commissioners:

> BROTHERS: We know that these settlers [colonists who were encroaching on their land] are poor, or they would never have ventured to live in a country which has been in continual trouble ever since they crossed the Ohio. Divide, therefore, this large sum of money, which you have offered to us, among these people: give each, also, a proportion of what you say you would give to us, annually, over and above this very large sum of money: and, we are persuaded, they would most readily accept it, in lieu of the lands you have sold them.
>
> (as cited in Greenberg, 2012, p. 51)

There is really no longer any debate over these treaties. At first, many Native American peoples attempted to help the foreign arrivals. For instance, in 1607, Chief Wahusonacock of the Powhatan Confederacy who helped found Jamestown, the first permanent English settlement, asked Captain John Smith, "Why will you take by force what you may have quietly by love? Why will you destroy us who supply you with food?" (as cited in McLuhan, 1972, p. 66). Then they tried to resist the flood that followed. The Shawnee chief Tecumseh argued, "The way, and the only way, to check and stop this evil, is for all the Redmen to unite in claiming a common and equal right in the land, as was at first and should be yet; for it never was divided, but belongs to all for use of each" (as cited in McLuhan, 1972, p. 85). Eventually, in increasing numbers, they fought back, even though they recognized it was hopeless. "My heart is a stone: heavy with sadness for my people; cold with the knowledge that no treaty will keep the whites out of our lands; hard with the determination to resist as long as I live and breathe" (Tecumseh, as cited in McLuhan, 1972, p. 116).

Not all the European born settlers were at odds with the many indigenous peoples they found already inhabiting their new homeland; reports of white settlers who came to the Americas and had warm relations with their new Indian neighbors abound (Hill, 1993; Meyer, 2005). Colonial Americans were often Europeans who immigrated because of religious persecution and advocated for tolerance for all peoples. Interracial marriage was not uncommon on the frontier. Some tribes were primarily agrarian, such as the Choctaw of Mississippi River Valley, and remained on good terms with the white settlers/neighbors. Even some nomadic hunting tribes did not clash with the newcomers. For instance the Cheyenne and Arapaho remained neutral until 1856, when hostilities broke out between a band of Northern Cheyenne and the troops at Fort Laramie (Hoig, 1982, p. 5).

In 1849 John Sutter discovered gold in California. Over the next four years, this led to a massive migration by immigrant settlers across the North American continent; over 350,000 settlers followed the Oregon Trail and the Santa Fe Trail across what is now the western US (Meyer, 2005). This migration effectively began the Indian Wars (2005). Demonizing messages aimed at Native Americans rapidly caught hold following the Civil War as new waves of immigrants headed toward the "Promised Land" out west. Applying an aggressive use of the notion of a ManifestDdestiny, a scorched earth policy, to destroy the Indian nations who stood in the way of the expansion was eventually approved and legalized by the authoritative organs of the United States (Meyer, 2005).

These wars spanned 40 years, began before the Mexican American War, and outlasted the Civil War (Hill, 1993). The tension between the races reached a fever pitch as the last free lands of the Native Americans began to be wrestled away from them. The wars were waged in what was then the Indian Territory, the Great Plains of the United States (Meyer, 2005). This vast area had become a co-mingled home to three earlier migrations of Native Americans that were also caused by the incoming tides of immigrants. For 100 years Native American peoples had been driven off their traditional lands and into the Indian Territory in the center of the country – the area now called the heartland. From the southwest the Pueblo Indians and the Apaches were pushed into the Great Plains following the arrival of the early Spanish invaders. In the Santa Fe region in 1680 the Pueblo Indians successfully revolted against their Spanish overlords and drove them out for a time. The Spaniards left behind their cattle and Iberian mustangs. Some of the horses escaped and formed wild Mustang herds, another significant symbol in the American mythic ideals of freedom and courage. The diaspora of southwestern Indians when the Spaniards returned followed the horses onto the Great Plains (Meyer, 2005).

Along with the Pueblo Indians of the Southwest, Eastern woodland tribes were forced west across the Mississippi River, especially after the loss of the French and Indian War in 1763. At the same time, tribes such as the Crow and Kiowa, were pressed eastward from the Pacific Northwest and regions of Montana and Wyoming, as miners and cattle ranchers expanded their investments in those regions (Meyer, 2005). These nations transformed themselves into the nomadic horse cultures of the Great Plains.

The woodland tribes quickly adapted to life on the plains and became adept at horsemanship. The other nations followed their lead. By the early 1800's seven Indian Horse Warrior nations had battled each other and created peace treaties for territories on the Great Plains. These were the Sioux, Cheyenne, Apache, Cree, Kiowa, Comanche, and Arapahoe. The Native Americans of the Plains formed seven distinct nations with separate languages, within these nations or tribes were many separate clans or bands, for example within the Chiracahua Apache nation there was the Bedonkohe band and the Chokonen band. Bands did not always get along, and many treaties were formed and broken (Meyer, 2005).

However, there were customs and a code of honor considered sacred by all Native Americans (Meyer, 2005). One aspect of the code of the horse warrior societies was to fight for honor and prestige, stealing horses and counting *coup* on a living enemy. It was considered a greater honor to touch an enemy and get away unhurt (a coup) than to kill an enemy (Goodwin, 1998). The bravery to withstand torture or any other distress was the most highly regarded trait of a warrior (1998). Raiding parties, also called war parties, would form sneak attacks and steal horses and goods as well as torture, kill, or kidnap their white or Indian enemies (Meyer, 2005). As the great Shawnee Chief Tecumseh put it, the "white intruders become more greedy, exacting, oppressive, and overbearing . . . are we not stripped day by day of the little that remains of our ancient liberty?" (as cited in McLuhan, 1972, p. 69). Finally, the tribes united on the Great Plains and made their stand against the settlers. The Native American strategy of surprise attacks on settler's homes panicked the colonists.

> For the whites one disturbing facet of the Indian Wars was the individual tactic of random raiding and killing. Rather than attacking the whites who had actually injured them they took out their anger by raiding any available homesteads, wagon trains, or military patrols. Innocent settlers and travelers were terrified by the threat of their families being tortured or mutilated.
>
> (Meyer, 2005)

This form of warfare was considered part of the warrior's code of honor (2005). Their fierce attacks on frontiers people, cavalry forts, and the rivers of wagon trains engendered fear in many and led to the wars that brought their downfall (2005).

Projection of savagery onto Native Americans

The white settler's projection of aggression and savagery onto the Indians is entirely misleading, not because the Indians did not torture their victims, but because the colonial Americans did as well. There are numerous accounts of brutality by the cavalry and vigilante groups (Goodwin, 1998;

Meyer, 2005). For instance, in 1862 Geronimo's mentor, the Chiracahua chief Mangas Colorados, was killed by the 7th US cavalry while inside their fort. He was decapitated, his head boiled, and then sent back east for display (Geronimo, 1996).

The following are eye-witness reports of the 1864 Sand Creek Massacre of a village of Arapaho and Kiowas. Robert Bent, US Cavalry guide said, "When we came in sight of the camp I saw the American flag waving and heard Black Kettle tell the Indians to stand around it. . . . I saw a white flag raised. These flags were in so conspicuous a position that they must have been seen" (as cited in Hoig, 1982, p. 192). In another example of hypermasculinity, the desire to fight overcame the rule of law and the soldiers attacked without mercy.

> I saw the bodies of those lying there cut all to pieces, worse mutilated than any I ever saw before; the women cut all to pieces . . . with knives; scalped; their brains knocked out; children two or three months old; all ages lying there, from sucking infants up to warriors. . . . By whom were they mutilated? By the United States troops.
>
> (John S. Smith, Congressional Testimony of Mr John S. Smith, 1865, as cited in Scott, R., Editor, 2004, p. 192)

> Fingers and ears were cut off the bodies for the jewelry they carried. The body of White Antelope, lying solitarily in the creek bed, was a prime target. Besides scalping him the soldiers cut off his nose, ears, and testicles – the last for a tobacco pouch.
>
> (Hoig, 1982, p. 153, footnote 9)

Samuel G. Colley, Indian agent reported: "None denied that they were butchered in a brutal manner and scalped and mutilated as bad as an Indian ever did to a white man. That is admitted by the parties who did it" (as cited in Hoig, 1982, pp. 177–178).

The Indian Wars were won after the US Cavalry adopted Kit Carson's strategy to destroy the villages, killing the women and children. Carson also promoted the destruction of their food sources, which led to the infamous slaughter of the huge herds of North American buffalo (Meyer, 2005). This strategy undermined the success of the Native American war parties. The last great battle was at Wounded Knee in 1890 (2005). After the Indian wars ended, all Indian children were taken from their families on the reservations, put in segregated schools, and punished if they spoke their native tongue or practiced their familial religions (Hoefel, 1999).

Geronimo

The Chiracahua Apache Chief and shaman, Geronimo, exemplified a sacred code of honor in his fierce battles with the US. Geronimo had visions from an early age and was first a shaman for his tribe, only becoming a warrior after his family was killed (Goodwin, 1998). In 1851, 400 Mexican soldiers attacked his village killing his mother, wife, and daughter (1998). In his autobiography he stated that for a year "I did not pray. . . . I had no purpose left" (Geronimo, 1996, p. 77). Geronimo wrote that his power would come to him and show him what to do in his visions. This is what led him to fight for his homelands, which, during his lifetime, were first occupied by Mexico and then annexed to the US (1996).

Geronimo said he "talked to the air, the giver of life" and saw that "everything is invested with life" (Goodwin, 1998). Geronimo believed "the sun, the darkness, the wind are all listening to what we have to say" (as cited in Goodwin, 1998). To say that a person has "strong medicine" means that he or she can hear and understand what the spirits of the Earth are saying to him or her (Geronimo, 1996). In Geronimo's worldview, healing and fertility were understood to be directly related to an animated natural world. There was no separation between the natural world, the world of humans, and the gods. The gods walked right into the world people inhabited, whether they could see or comprehend them or not. Of course, these ideas were heretical to the early Christian settlers (Geronimo, 1996). The missionary's efforts were a source of consternation for the Native Americans. Sa-a-go-ye-wat-ha, or Red Jacket, a Seneca chief asked:

> You say that you are sent to instruct us how to worship the Great Spirit agreeable to his mind; and if we do not take hold of the religion which you white people teach, we shall be unhappy hereafter. You say you are right, and we are lost. How do we know this to be true? We understand that your religion is written in a book. If it was intended for us as well as you, why has not the Great Spirit given to us – and not only to us, to our forefathers – the knowledge of that book, with the means of understanding it rightly?
>
> (as cited in McLuhan, 1972, p. 61)

The Christian ideas left no opening for the traditions that had contained the Native American people for countless generations. Geronimo's Chiracahua Apache people thought he had "special access to the power in the land" and that he had "the power of coyote running around, pretty soon over here, over there, can outfox anybody. Soldiers would ride right by him" (Yuzos as cited in Goodwin, 1998). His legendary bravery came from his faith in the powers of nature. He felt certain he had the right to hold onto the lands where Apaches had lived since their ancestors, the Asian Athabascans, migrated across the Bering Strait into the area. Though dating is unclear as to when that happened, it was certainly sometime before 1541 when the early Spanish explorer Coronado reported encountering the Apache (Riley, 1995, p. 190).

Geronimo is still a legendary figure (Goodwin, 1998; Hill, 1993). Melferd Yuzos, a Chiracahua Apache living in New Mexico, said he had

> risked everything for his home and way of life. Most of his power isn't handed down to no one because it is said that most of his power is dangerous and he didn't want no one to have it and so he just took most of his power with him.
>
> (as cited in Goodwin, 1998)

Power and spiritual strength are considered to be inseparable in the Apache culture (Geronimo, 1996).

Through newspapers coverage, Geronimo's defiance of the US Calvary and government policies was closely followed nationwide. Fear of Indians and especially Geronimo sold papers. When Geronimo and 400 followers jumped the San Carlos Reservation in 1886 (he surrendered, went onto reservations, and then left many times), the Arizona paper, the *Daily Tombstone* in an extra edition reported:

> It is stated, this morning that Arizona is in a state of terror, that murderous Apaches are cavorting over the territory, killing, burning, and destroying wherever they go. These hopeless and indiscriminating savages don't have a way of life except to kill others.
>
> (Daily Tombstone Extra cit. 1886, as cited in Goodwin, 1998)

For years "hysteria aided by lurid and exaggerated newspaper accounts swept the southwest and the entire country" (Meyer, 2005). The Senate directed the War Department (the US Cabinet department responsible for the US Army from 1789–1947) to send 5000 troops into Mexico to capture the wily Geronimo (Goodwin, 1998). They never did, though they spent three years trying (Geronimo, 1996). When Geronimo surrendered for the final time, he was persuaded to accept the terms of surrender offered to him by Lt Charles Gatewood for the sake of his exhausted band. At that point it had dwindled to only 39 men, women, and children (Geronimo, 1996).

The capture of Geronimo marked the closing of the western frontier. But Geronimo lives on as a symbol of how fierce bravery and cunning can panic an enemy (Hill, 1993). Even on Geronimo's deathbed when his nephew, Daklugie, asked if he had any regrets, he said, "I should never have surrendered. I should have fought until I was the last man alive" (Leach and Levy, 2014, p. 226).

After his final surrender in 1886 the band was shipped off by train (Goodwin, 1998). A lynch mob mentality swept across the country; the crowds that gathered trackside as the train rolled across the Arizona territory calling for Geronimo's blood. The Army decided not to have him tried in Civil

Court in San Antonio, Texas for fear he would by lynched and instead took him to St Augustine, Florida. There he became a prisoner of war, which he remained until his death from pneumonia in 1909.

Seven years later, Geronimo's band of Bedonkohe Chiracahua were finally allowed to join the other Apache in the Indian territory (now Oklahoma). On this train trip rather than lynch mobs, cheering crowds gathered along the tracks, begging for autographs and pictures at the whistle stops. His reputation reversed from "indiscriminating savage" to hero in seven years. Though still a prisoner of war, he made many appearances, even riding in Teddy Roosevelt's inaugural parade.

Americans feared Geronimo when he was a force they felt unable to control and could not understand, one who might cause sudden and terrifying harm. He was depicted as the aggressor, the Other, the Pan of his day. Overreactions to Geronimo are visible in how greatly he was feared and then, once he was corralled, in how greatly he was, and is, revered. "The hero is always the embodiment of man's highest and most powerful aspiration. . . . In the American hero-fantasy the Indian's character plays as a leading role" (Jung, 1931/1978a, pp. 47–48, [*CW* 10, para. 100]). Geronimo came to be thought of as an exceptional man: courageous, defiant, independent, unpredictable, and filled with wild abandon. Americans resonated strongly with these qualities, wanted to be like him or at least be thought of as being like him. Once subdued his resistance, so feared, rapidly became an iconic symbol of the fierce strength of the US military. The American foundational myth of a free and courageous people, a "land of the free and home of the brave" mirrors Geronimo's life story.

Even once Geronimo was revered by the American public, he was misunderstood and seen through a distorted mirror of projection. Geronimo was also a shaman and a healer, and must have enjoyed marriage since he married at least six times. The more relational sides of his personality are mostly forgotten. They do not fit the mold of the hypermasculine American hero but he is one personification of the defenses of the Pan complex. The symbolic meaning of Geronimo for Americans inspired the cries of the WWII parachutists yelling "Geronimo!" as they leapt into the uncertainty of the black skies over Europe. It was also the code name for Osama bin Laden in the 2011 Navy Seals surprise attack on his compound in Pakistan. In the sort of stumbling about and miscues that signal an active complex, the Navy Seals who found and killed Osama bin Laden, gave him the code name Geronimo, much to the chagrin of Native peoples (Memmott, 2011). The distortions of the viewpoint within the complex first over-exaggerated a savagery in his defense of his people, then, in a degraded form of the First Nations tradition of counting coup, having contact with a fenced in Geronimo became an American pastime. False representations of the man and misuse of his life story are examples of the selective thinking in the complex.

American Pan

An interlinking and long-lived system of nations, both agrarian and hunting societies, were ignored by the immigrants who survived severe hardships in order to be freed from want, to find religious freedom, and to avoid persecution. They all but destroyed the pre-existing culture. The nature of an unconscious complex set the stage for the scapegoat to become a persecutor. The colonists had suffered under persecutory laws and from famine in Europe and then came to the New World and persecuted and starved Native Americans. The colonists wanted a place to raise a family and used brutality to achieve this, while faulting those who already inhabited the land for savagery. Rather than blame the participants and take sides, it is time to see the systemic nature of a complex at work. This cyclic, negative pattern can be expected to continue until the wounded core beliefs evolve from the undeveloped state that they have been limited to by the complexes defense system.

Dismissing these stories as past mistakes allows the projecting to continue. Viewing Native Americans as inferior and stupid has continued, as example consider the films and TV westerns so popular in the early twentieth century. In the box office hit and cult classic directed by John Ford, *Stagecoach* (Wanger, 1939), Native Americans are characterized as being like children, in *The Old Overland Trail* (White, 1953) as a race the world would be better off without, and in *The Great Sioux Uprising* (Goldstein & Cohen, 1953) as evil. Rapists and murderers are also epithets used in these scapegoating stories of the role Native Americans played during the "taming" of the Wild West. Such blatant racism is no longer politically correct, but ignoring the civil rights of Native Americans in political standoffs such as the 2017 battle to stop the Dakota Access Pipeline at Standing Rock reservation in South Dakota continues. The negative projections and microaggressions have not stopped and the complex is central to this problem.

Though the Eurocentric culture of the settlers of the United States is hardly the only example of one culture's destruction of indigenous people, it can serve as a tool to study the psychological ramifications of the cultural shadow in a dominant culture. The colonists and pioneers stood up to the threat to land ownership by wearing the mask of a god-given Manifest Destiny based on their righteous exceptionalism. In the end, it was actually the sheer numbers that won out.

In a complex the faulty beliefs in the protected core, in this case American superiority, are shut off from growth by the defense system. New perspectives are unwelcome. The beliefs and accompanying emotional aspects of a person or a culture are protected within the core and remain naive and unchanged. As Jung found, they also represent an archetypal truth, personified in a symbolic way. This describes the current state of American politics. The complexities of modernity cry out for adjustments to create ways of life with tolerance and spaciousness for all peoples.

The traumatic exodus from Europe by the colonists was birthed in the rejection of religious views but led to the same sort of rejection by the colonists. To my mind, this is a significant addition by cultural complex theory to historical understandings. In psychological thinking, an unconscious cultural complex settled into the pioneering *zeitgeist* of the European colonists, which they projected onto Native Americans, among other disenfranchised groups. This underlying notion that Americans have the right to be free even when it impinges on others reflects the theme in the myths of Pan that might makes right and that he has the right to do what suits him when he is in his realm (Nonnos, 1962a, pp. 477–479 [Book I. xiv, 67–95]; Propertius, 1912, p. 49 [I. XVIII, 20]). This reflects the worst in Pan's mythic motifs.

In Pan's myths from both his Arcadian and Athenian period he is a protector and a persecutor. At times he protects the nymphs at others he persecutes them, he protects the Athenians and persecutes the Gauls. His own self-interest and the interest of his allies are what matters and since personal gain trumps compassionate consideration in this world view, Pan never offers a diplomatic alternative and simply takes what he wants.

The isolationist Monroe Doctrine reflects Pan's isolation in Arcadia and the Christian-based doctrine of Manifest Destiny established justification to destroy the First Nations as did the advent of Christianity for the Greek cults. Psychologically, isolation allows a complex to grow since solitary ruminating about perceived hurts feeds the wound and easily leads to the desire to take revenge. Passions can feel unmanageable and even become addictive, like the desire to wiggle a loose tooth, complexes are like caves in the mind, places where hidden thoughts spring up. Lurking fears seem more real when no one challenges them.

Paradoxically, isolation can also lead to creativity, such as with Pan's invention of the syrinx and American ingenuity on the prairie. When the negative emotions met in isolation are faced and contained they can lead to fertile, innovative ideas. Again here is Pan, with his attribute of fertility, reflected in the belief of America as a place of new possibilities and points of view that bubbled up into consciousness out of the necessity to create new solutions when suffering in states of isolation. A crucial key to the ongoing development of exceptionalism as a driving force in American history was not only the military successes to protect the citizenry but also the economic success of the country, in the eighteenth, nineteenth, and early twentieth century, fueled by its vast resources and the cultural belief in innovative ingenuity. The aggressive drive in all sentient beings concerns procreation and protection of those creations as the pull toward life (Jung, 1963/1970, pp. 457 *ff* [*CW* 14, para. 654 *ff*]). Pan was responsible for the herds and the hunt and so the sustainability of his cult was dependent upon his ability to find new fertile valleys where game and grazing was plentiful and to be inventive with what he had. From Ben Franklin's spectacles to Henry David Thoreau's better pencil to John Moses Browning's semi-automatic rifle, American confidence also led to continual successes, large and small.

Wealth rapidly accrued from the combination of available resources and a climate of pioneering and risk taking, and this then brought further migrations of hopeful future millionaires.

But the protective shell of the complex gradually became *overly* protective of the core belief that the US is better, or the best, a vulnerable belief to have because it is impossible to sustain over time. Like much unconscious material, once it becomes conscious it sounds obvious. But when it is a cutoff, emotionally laden complex, in this case one that encases a culture, it is not obvious, it is masked by the very qualities that make the culture feel unique. The courage of those Europeans families to climb into tiny ships and sail west is impressive. Those men and women and others like them come to America to start fresh and feel, whether rightly or wrongly, the hope of a better future. But when this drive ignores the rights of others it lacks empathy, reflection, and caution. As Jung put it when describing a person caught in a complex, "The only appropriate term would be the judicial concept of diminished responsibility" (1948/1960, p. 96 [*CW* 8 para. 200]).

There are a number of similarities between Pan and the Native Americans. They used similar strategies in battle, developed a similar relationship to the divine in nature, and were projected upon as demonic. They were feared for their use of strategic and explosive sneak attacks to defend themselves and to gain status (Meyer, 2005), as did Pan. Pan used surprise, sudden attacks, and panicked his enemies on the battlefield. Native Americans worshipped nature and Pan was a nature god. Pan's cult and the Indian nations were hunters, healers, diviners, and both groups lived in an animated, polytheistic world (Borgeaud, 1979/1988; Meyer, 2005; Goodwin, 1998). Native Americans lived in close harmony with nature by listening and communicating with the natural world around them. They only took what they needed and did not endanger the natural world's ecological balance for their own purposes. As a pastoral god of nature and fertility, Pan naturally lived in harmony with his landscape and took from it what he needed. In his introduction in the Homeric hymns he is described as the one:

> who's got
> all the snow crests
> and mountain ridges
> and all the rocky roads
> . . . and often
> he runs across
> a great white mountain range
> and often
> he comes down
> the side of mountains
> killing animals.
> He has a very sharp eye. (Boer, 1970, pp. 64–65)

Also like Pan, Geronimo's mystic power as a shaman is largely forgotten (Goodwin, 1998; Geronimo, 1996). Pan communicated with his cult by divination, as did Geronimo with his gods. Pan's use of divination, rarely mentioned in the literature, figured largely in the legend of the death of Pan (Plutarch, 1936/2003b, p. 403 [419D]). Pan was said to have taught Apollo divination and in many sites sacred to Pan, such as Lykosoura in Arcadia and the Corycian caves near Delphi, artifacts related to prophecy have been found (Borgeaud, 1979/1988, pp. 108–109).

Pan, "the one who loves noise" (Boer, 1970, p. 64), asks to be heard in many ways. These included using cacophony in battle, in divination with voices (in some cases), in music with his pipes, and in many circumstances with echoes. Native Americans used music and dance to unite themselves in harmony with the land and the Great Spirit (as some nations referred to the invisible forces that surround us) (McLuhan, 1972). Pan is remembered in the earliest writings for his joy and celebration in the simple pleasures of music and dance. In the poet Pindar's (b. 518 BCE) words, "O Pan, ruler of Arkadia/ and guardian of the holy shrines,/ companion of the Great Mother,/ the holy Graces' delightful/ darling" (1997a, p. 333 [fr. 95.1]) and "I wish to pray to the Mother, to whom, along with Pan, the maidens often sing before my door at night" (1997b, p. 253 [Pythian 3.78–80]). Pan's joy was expressed in his music and dance. War cries and elaborate divination ceremonies are also well known Native American expressions. Pan's courage and strategic intelligence were respected, and he was sought after as an ally in various myths.

Also, he appeared, as did the Native Americans, to be rough, rustic, and savage to those who opposed him. Like Geronimo, Pan's very presence caused panic. In both views, there is no concept of a separation between the world of nature, the world of humans, and that of the gods. Pan's power, as Geronimo's, came directly from his instinctive and natural urges to protect and care for himself and for his cult, which led him to easily outwit his enemies.

Further, the hatred and scapegoating of Native Americans is reminiscent of current attitudes expressed by psychologists James Hillman (1988) and Nathan Schwartz-Salant (1991), and classicist Phillipe Borgeaud (1979/1988), singling out Pan as both a rapist and murderer as well as early Christian beliefs in Pan as the devil. Finally, Pan was said to have died but has continued to surface in movements such as the Romantic period in the nineteenth century (Merivale, 1969) and in modern dramas such as Guillermo del Toro's *Pan's Labyrinth* (2006a), while Geronimo lost his power and his way of life but has lived on as a symbol of fierce courage.

The complex is triggered

The United States experienced a long period of fertility and prosperity for its people. This era either has come to an end or else is going through a remarkable period of reinventing itself. Presently, the need to adjust to changing circumstances in the globalization of the planet are in direct conflict with a sizeable portion of the American electorate's denial that that this era could be ending, as it did once for the British Empire, and before that for the Roman Empire, and so on back through history. Indeed, an ending is actually an inevitable outcome for any one country to be the most powerful nation in the world. No one stays the champ forever.

In the summer of 1969, the moon landing riveted the world's attention, once again, on America's seemingly endless ability to achieve astounding success. The moon landing may turn out to be the pinnacle of America's rise. The Space Race with Russia was considered "won" when Neil Armstrong and Buzz Aldrin got to the moon first. Perhaps since it was no longer a contest, funding for the Apollo program and space exploration dried up four years later. Ironically, four weeks after the landing, the gathering of 400,000 at the Woodstock Music Festival also became an iconic event; widely acknowledged as the nexus of the counter culture. These two, nearly simultaneous events, both encouraged the continuation of the enduring sense of the multifaceted, multidirectional American spirit as innovative, even revolutionary, and still at the center of the world stage.

The success of America had been a rising force that, though it had its ups and downs, had a steep, upward trajectory until the mid-twentieth century. Following America's decisive entries into both World Wars, the reluctance America showed to enter both wars was forgotten when the resources and "Yankee" confidence it brought to its allies enabled crushing defeats of the enemy. As Churchill famously quipped, "You can always count on Americans to do the right thing – after they've tried everything else" (US National Churchill Museum, 2017). Though isolated and yet with superior might, they managed to save the free world. The post-war era brought even greater prosperity and glory to the US as the Marshall Plan helped Europe off her knees and American technology rapidly developed products and American social psychologists collaborated with corporations to devise advertising that made those products coveted the world over. It seemed it would never end. America prospered and the GNP rose in a bubble of its own making.

Only the Russians and the threat of nuclear destruction worried some, but most Americans were content to focus on establishing a stable life for their families and paid little attention to the buildup of arms, the rapid changing of governments in Southeast Asia, or even the Space Race until the night in 1957 when Sputnik flew over the country. Even then, it seemed inevitable the US would overtake the Russians. And so the events the turbulent late sixties, antiwar protests and loss of the Vietnam war, and the civil rights movement were absorbed into the mainstream like bumps in the road while riding in a tail finned fifties Cadillac.

But then the world turned. Since the early 70s, the US has found itself floundering in one moral dilemma after another. So many issues surfaced at once as Watergate, the oil embargo, paralyzing inflation and interest rates, Iran Contra, the Watts riots, insensitive dismantling of the system of state mental institutions, and greater degrees of violence all began to combine to unsettle the complacency of the American people. Activism by Russell Means and the American Indian Movement brought world attention to Indian rights through the occupations of Alcatraz Island in 1969 and Wounded Knee in 1973. Women's rights, AIDS, gay rights, black power, random shootings, terrorism, global warming, housing bubbles, oil hungry empire building, and the election of President Trump have left America's invincibility suddenly exposed, vulnerable, and looking fairly absurd.

One photograph taken during the Apollo 8 moon landing was of the Earth from outer space. This wondrous first look at the Earth rising above the moonscape, opened up a new perspective for the people of the Earth. Technology married to innovative spirit gave us a new way to see our home – as a whole. One could say the *telos* ("aim") of the space race became entwined with the *temenos* ("sacred space") of the Woodstock Nation in that first dawning of the notion of the whole Earth as our true homeland. This image energized a new unifying principle, begun by American enterprise, but now grown into a global one. By the following April in 1970, the first Earth Day brought 20 million Americans to the streets to bring awareness to the need to care for the environment. By 2015 over a billion people participated in Earth Day in over 190 countries. The moon landing seeded an emerging awareness of how exceptional the Earth is and so, rather than how exceptional America is, a new ideal has begun to root.

Now why would this be? Why would America be able to get it right in the end for over 200 years but now lose its way? America has begun to sound tiresomely narcissistic, insisting too loudly on its greatness and its need to be center stage, it feels dangerous, blundering around in the Mideast and Asia, upsetting delicately balanced tensions by using its abundant might to attempt to stomp out threats, and it begins to seem less relevant to peaceful progress since it cannot contain the anger of its disenfranchised nor the greed of its corporate bellies and seems to daily grow more anxious and focused on protection. It is like a 250-year-old California Live Oak in a severe drought. Still tall and full of life, but surrounded by fields of dead chaparral and rocks, all the same dull brown; still strong, but vulnerable.

Woodstock's counter culture watched the dominant culture's gradual usurpation of its radically transformative libido and ideals, so eloquently captured in the final episode of the wildly popular TV series *Mad Men* as Don Draper, having fallen to his nadir, lands at an Esalen-like center in Big Sur. Then, based on an actual Coke ad that was conceived of in 1971, with "American gumption," revitalizes his career by turning the give-peace-a-chance message into a slogan for Coke. In the few generations between Woodstock and *Mad Men* the basis for success shifted from innovations to cynical self-reflection. Capitalizing on past successes, like gladiators reliving Roman conquests in the Coliseum, has risen to the fore.

The defensive structure and underbelly of the hypermasculine complex has remained blind to its effects on other's alternate approaches to community, governance, and spirituality. Rather they are viewed as undesirable because they are different. This xenophobia becomes a justification for forcing those others, today as with the Native Americans in the nineteenth century, to conform, leave, or be destroyed. The complex becomes manifest, and is an American destiny, because today this level of force is being met with greater and greater resistance. President Trump's "Make America Great Again" slogan suffers from the same myopic vision. Whether it is instigated by altruistic concern or by American economic interests protecting their global investments abroad, US militant defense of global democracy is a modern application of Manifest Destiny.

At the core of the complex the fear of not being good enough and thus shunned is defended against by projecting those feelings onto the other, whether that is the Native Americans or Hillary Clinton or the mayor of San Juan, Puerto Rico. The hidden insecurity that Americans are not actually particularly exceptional triggers anxiety over defense and security. The insecurities remain hidden and impel grasping at even greater achievements to avoid detection from within the complex. Others, outside of America, see it much more easily.

America can still drink up the bitter dregs of the outmoded concepts of exceptionalism and Manifest Destiny. This means, essentially, accepting a place as one among equals in the global body politic. If the culture stubbornly continues to tell itself it is the greatest one on Earth, America's over identification with a hypermasculine, inflated belief in its own greatness (a negative side of an archetype if ever there was one), then it is likely it will continue to trigger a complex. Jung (1931/1978a) felt the following statement was so significant he italicized it in full: "*I would like to suggest that every psychic reaction which is out of proportion to its precipitating cause should be investigated as to whether it may be conditioned at the same time by an archetype*" (p. 32 [CW 10, para. 57]).

Currently, the nation, regardless of political party affiliations, is caught in a hypermasculine struggle to protect itself from further shock by building stronger militaristic defenses. On the one hand it struggles to comprehend why others see it as an aggressive bully rather than a benevolent leader, while, rather ironically, on the other hand it has built the greatest weapons stockpile in the world (Sipri, 2014). The US continues to peer into a distorted mirror of its own making and tells itself not only that it is great and with President Trump that it will be great again, but that it is better than others with statements by its leaders such as, "America has a continued extraordinary role in leading the world towards peace and prosperity" (Obama, 2009 April, para. 50) and Bush's statements following the 9/11 attacks, "We will not be secure as a nation until all of these threats are defeated. Across the world, and across the years, we will fight these evil ones, and we will win" (Bumiller, 2001, para. 2). Complexes thrive in an atmosphere where unquestioned beliefs interpret all evidence as proof of their validity.

America

In the United States today, a less than hopeful mood hovers inaudibly and invisibly in the air and can be observed in contemporary America's intense collective emotional reactions to threats to its security. The turn of the millennium in the US was bookended by the school shootings at Columbine High in 1999 and the bombings of the Pentagon and the World Trade Center in 2001. The Y2K scare scarred the moment of the actual turn with intense media coverage transmitting numerous possible disasters (Quigley, 2005). The media cautioned that banks could close down, and that air traffic, emergency systems, and food supplies might be interrupted. The *Wall Street Journal* alone covered the upcoming event 262 times (pp. 262–263). Meanwhile, aiming to ease bond traders fears, the "Federal Reserve Bank of New York auctioned Y2K options to primary dealers" (Sundaresan & Wang, 2008, p. 1022). The contrast to the turn of the nineteenth century when "a millennial hope was in the air, yoked to the expectation of massive technological, political, and social change" (Aronson, 1999) contextualizes this new chapter in American history. In the United States, instead of millennial hope, the event was tinged with millennial anxiety and fear (Mueller, 2005, 2006; Richey & Feldman, 2003; Furedi, 2007).

An insecure fixation on being the strongest and richest country in the world is causing anxiety and friction within the country and between the US and other nations (Lifton, 2003). These beliefs are being challenged by recent upheavals in the world today (Stein, 2004) and are understood here to have triggered a latent cultural complex. This complex is best tracked by observing reactions in the political powers that be, the media, and public opinions and behaviors of Americans following events that were unexpected and shocking, Pan-like sudden outbursts of hypermasculine power. The Columbine massacre of 1999, the terrorist attack on 9/11, and the ongoing apathy toward an epidemic of rape in the military are prototypes of this pattern in hopes of charting a course toward greater wholeness and a more compassionate attitude toward sharing the resources of this planet.

The belief in itself as exceptional was a catalyst for America's rapid rise as a nation, but the complexities of the modern age have overwhelmed the naïve and one-sided nature of these concepts and it is now consequential for the welfare of the global community that they be understood as central to a cultural complex. Today, it appears America is unable to consciously consider its changing role from the One, the most powerful and greatest, to a place as one-of-many-countries. It is time to explore what is holding back new, transformative ideas along these lines.

Chapter 7

Random shootings

American reactions to the massacre at Columbine

Introduction

On April 20, 1999, Eric Harris and Dylan Klebold entered their school, Columbine High in Jefferson County, Colorado, and shot to death 12 students and one teacher, while injuring 24 other students. Nothing quite like this had happened before. Moments like Columbine, as the massacre has come to be called, can be turning points for cultures, with the responses to a disaster sometimes more significant than the disaster itself. While there could have been a period of sober national reflection on how the community had failed these boys, instead a media-led charge interpreted the two as monstrous prodigy who, with their families, were solely to blame for the loss of 13 innocent lives. Reactions in the community served to amplify the notion that the shootings were personal vendettas carried out on innocent members of the community. Minor changes in Colorado gun control laws and defensive measures such as lock down drills and tighter security in public schools were the sole solutions eventually reached due to the politically charged climate surrounding guns in the country.

But, it will be shown, much was missed in the rush to fix blame, determine motive, and eulogize those who performed heroically during the rampage. A reactive rather than a reflective climate followed the massacre. Why did the United States get caught in fear-based reactivity? Protecting the identity of the country superseded the need to understand the individuals, in this case the disenfranchised teenagers. Condemning Klebold and Harris as an anomaly made them the scapegoats for an unconscious feeling in the country that it is not standing on the moral high ground it has always wanted to believe it occupies. This is a theme that runs through modernity's plague of random shootings and random terrorist actions.

What the senseless killings really were was a way to get attention from an indifferent society. The police recognized the revenge motive did not fit the facts within days. Dylan Klebold and Eric Harris actually wanted to blow up the entire school, but the bombs in the cafeteria did not explode. They wanted to kill as many people as they could and their motivation was to create so much notoriety that their story would reach others who would copy them and begin a revolution (Harris and Klebold, 1999). What brought them to such a state of mind?

These two boys were regularly bullied, scapegoated, and met with apathy at their high school. They internalized these attitudes and the bullied became the bullies. They developed a hypermasculine attitude while simultaneously fearing their lives would never become better. This attitude is reflected in their individualistic, militarist, and rapacious behaviors (Larkin, 2007). These behaviors sadly mirror the worst in Pan, whose myths, in part, are based on the motifs of rejection, bullying, soldiering, and rape fantasies (Borgeaud, 1979/1988). The Greek god Pan aptly personifies the unconscious tension of a cultural complex that was triggered and played out through the lives of these two boys.

A complex is invisible to individuals while they are caught in it (Jung, 1948/1960 [*CW* 8]). They see the problem as coming at them from the outside rather than caused by internal blockages (Jung, 1910/1989a). The anxiety this instills naturally leads to attempts to split from and defend oneself against outside "evil" forces, such as Eric Harris and Dylan Klebold. Hence the common response to destructive forces is to destroy them, in other words to use violence and aggression against violence and aggression. In complex theory, the goal is to transform the destructive elements in a complex by examining the defensive shell and its relationship to the traumatized and regressed authentic nature that shelters in the core. This will transform the core of the complex itself into a "constructive and helpful impulse" as the trauma is gradually resolved (Whitmont, 1991, p. 67). Transformation rather than extermination of destructive elements is tantamount to psychological health.

> We have to realize, quite dispassionately, that whatever we fight about in the outside world is also a battle in our inner selves. In the end we have to admit that mankind is not just an accumulation of individuals utterly different from one another, but possesses such a high degree of psychological collectivity that in comparison the individual appears merely as a slight variant. How shall we judge this matter fairly if we cannot admit that it is also our own problem? Anyone who can admit this will first seek the solution in himself. This, in fact, is the way all the great solutions begin.
>
> (Jung, 1910/1989a, p. 393 [*CW* 18, para. 927])

Are American efforts to contain the problem of eruptions of violence missing the taproot of aggression while debating whether to weed the offshoots of gun control and rights to privacy? In the mid-1930s Jung observed "a sort of collective psychosis taking hold in Germany, a society-wide state of psychic possession. . . . Under these conditions the psyche is ripe for releasing behavior that is primitive, irrationally driven, and highly charged with affect and emotion" (Stein, 1995, p. 12). "Primitive, irrationally driven, and highly charged" are apt adjectives for school shootings of innocents by their classmates, as well as for the intense reactions by the community. The reactions resulted in little action and remained fixated on blame. Why were the boys so frustrated and why did nothing really change?

Eric Harris (1981–1999)

Born April 9, 1981, Eric was an only child. His father was in the military when he was a young boy so they moved every few years. He reported painful memories of the moves causing the loss of his childhood friends for whom he cared deeply. Eric excelled at schoolwork and loved sports, but was small in stature and not chosen for teams. He was unpopular with girls. These failures compelled him to journal about his low self-esteem. His high school diaries show a boy who had mastered deceiving adults and was brimming with intense hatred aimed at whomever he perceived as having slighted him (Harris, 1998–1999). He had a preoccupation with weapons and indulged in violent, sexual fantasies. Eric talked about how people made fun of his face, his shirts, and his hair when he was growing up (Kass, 2009, p. 135). He was particularly sensitive about the teasing he got for having a slightly concaved chest. In Eric's journal he ranted about those he hated and his own exceptional abilities (Harris, 1998–1999). His pent up aggression and pain prompted him to fantasize over and over again about how his classmates would feel when he got back at them (1998–1999).

Eric was seeing a therapist and taking an anti-depressant (Adams & Russakoff, 1999, para. 7). He had been in trouble with the law and was eventually arrested and put on probation (Cullen, 2009). Eric had no plan for his life following high school. His failings resemble those of many disenfranchised youth – it is the intensity of his feelings that are greater than most. That intensity led him to plot, practice, and initiate a surprise attack. His parents reported to the police that they had no idea that he was building an arsenal in their basement, snuck out many nights running "missions" to test his bombs, or that he published a Nazi-oriented blog (Cullen, 2009; Kass, 2009).

Eric has a striking resemblance to the aspects of Pan that represent the rejected, foolish parts of ourselves. Like Pan, Eric's life was filled with awkward attempts to be noticed that ended up causing more embarrassment instead of satisfaction. The theme of hubris and foolishness, youthful folly, is ripened in Pan in a story where Midas retreats to the country to become a follower of Pan after he shuns the riches brought on by his "golden touch." One night Pan had the nerve to challenge Apollo to a contest to determine which was the better musician. "Pan croons songs at soft nymphs/ plays light tunes on wax reed flute:/ dares rate Apollo's music after his,/ provoking a contest (mismatched). . . . Pan blasts wild reeds: barbaric music/ delighting Midas" (Ovid, 1989, pp. 232–233). Apollo is quickly declared the winner, while Midas is jeered at and taunted by the other gatherers for remaining loyal to Pan. To complete his humiliation, Apollo causes Midas's ears to "increase in length, grow hairy, within and without, and moveable on their roots; in short, to be on the perfect pattern of those of an ass" (Bulfinch, 1855, p. 71). The theme of being a rejected dolt is peppered throughout the myths of Pan and the stories of Eric's short life.

But Eric's inner life is also reminiscent of Pan's auto-arousal when observing a nymph alone in the woods. When corralled within an individual's imagination, eroticism can wander into uninhibited fantasies without causing any harm to others. Usually people feel shame or embarrassment about harboring blatantly selfish fantasies where the objectified "other" becomes a victim. But Eric shows no such feelings in his journals where he writes about his desires to rape and abuse women.

The most self-evident link to Pan is the connection to war and battles and thus to the planned, military-like massacre. Also like Pan, the two lived on the edge of their society at Columbine High and sheltered in a basement away from the light, just as Pan lived at the edges of the civilized world, in dark caves on mountain peaks, and in huts in hidden, shady glens, a solitary and, oftentimes, melancholy god.

Dylan Klebold (1981–1999)

Dylan Klebold grew up in a suburb in the foothills of the Rockies. He was so shy the girl he was secretly in love with never even knew about his feelings (Klebold, D., 1997–1999) until after he died (Larkin, 2007). He was an awkward-looking kid, tall with big feet. In his journals he expressed constant pain, embarrassment, humiliation, and many gradations of sadness over and over again – so he was certainly sensitive. He blamed himself for all his failings (1997–1999). Dylan's self-hatred was a form of whipping, his inability to speak up for himself and his pain speaks volumes about the abyss he lived in, unable to articulate a cry for help. He does not appear to have reached out to anyone about all this.

Eric and Dylan left behind several home videos that are known as The Basement Tapes (Harris and Klebold, 1999). In The Basement Tapes, the school videos, and violent papers Dylan wrote for class assignments, it becomes clear that imagining violence was one of his only pleasures. He had classic signs of depression (feeling helpless, hopeless, and suicidal) but he kept them inside. In his journals Dylan repeatedly expressed his self-hatred and the pain he felt over his lack of friends (Klebold, D., 1997–1999). While Eric's diary (1998–1999) is filled with hypermasculine misogyny and fear of loss expressed with such hatred that, in comparison, Dylan's drunken and sometimes romantic ramblings (though interspersed with fantasies of cruelty) evoke sympathy.

As a teenager Dylan, alone, regularly drank vodka in his room at night (Klebold, D., 1997–1999). He hacked into the school computer system and stole the student body's locker combinations to be able to get back at kids (Kass, 2009). He and Eric went out on "missions" in the early hours of the morning to test pipe bombs and vandalize his neighborhood, was arrested for breaking into a truck and stealing electronic equipment, and attempted to blow up his school (Klebold, D., 1997–1999).

Years after the shooting, Susan Klebold, Dylan's mother, wrote an article for *Oprah* magazine because she needed to express her painful reactions to her son's crimes (Klebold, S. 2009). The article focused on her feelings and her defense of herself based on points with which others had attacked her. In the article she failed to address how Dylan evolved from the healthy elementary school kid she raised into a repressed, inarticulate teenager, what responsibility she had for what Dylan did, or to ask the community for forgiveness. Her purpose appeared to be the desire to clear her name, rather than writing out of care for Dylan even so many years later. Like Dylan, Pan represents the archetype of a melancholy figure, rejected by his mother, suffering from unrequited love, and ritually whipped when he failed his cult.

Evidence of bullying at Columbine

There is considerable evidence bullying was a problem at Columbine High before the massacre (Cullen, 2009, p. 158; Klein, 2012; Larkin, 2007; Kass, 2009). Eric and Dylan were bullied, probably on a daily basis.

Examples of Eric's and Dylan's ordeal, as reported by Columbine students, include:

> In January 1998, Harris and Klebold were surrounded by a large group of football players and squirted with ketchup packets from the cafeteria. RH [star wrestler at Columbine] suggested that because Harris and Klebold were always together they were a homosexual couple. "That happened while teachers watched. They couldn't fight back. They wore the ketchup all day and went home covered with it."
>
> (A. Prendergast as cited in Larkin, 2007, p. 87)

"They got their share [of being picked on], just like everybody else of that unpopular crowd, but again, they knew their place" (as cited in Larkin, 2007, p. 79 [May 1, 2003]). Another student told of a time, "a bunch of football players drove by, yelled something and threw a glass bottle that shattered near Dylan's feet. I was pissed, but Eric and Dylan didn't even flinch" (p. 15). Eric and Dylan "were publicly taunted with epithets questioning their masculinity; they were called 'pussies,' 'queers,' and 'fags'" (p. 171). A classmate witnessed, "Once they got a cup of fecal matter thrown at them" (Vanderau, 2013).

Dylan was publicly booed when called up on stage at school. He was being recognized as the recent state champion at the national forensic debate qualifications (Klein, 2012, p. 32). A female student described them as "marked for abuse" (Larkin, 2007, p. 15) and said that it was better not to talk to them or else the "jocks" would punish you. When she was a freshman she talked to Dylan and a jock:

> slammed her against the locker and called her a "fag lover." None of the students came to help her – and when asked later why she didn't report the incident to the administration, she replied, "it wouldn't do any good because they wouldn't do anything about it."
>
> (p. 15)

The bullies would, like Pan, suddenly and aggressively overpower their victims. Stories of this sort of extreme bullying at Columbine High (which only made the news after the massacre) include *The Washington Post* writers Lorraine Adams and Dale Russakoffs' (June 12, 1999) investigation.

> Columbine High School is a culture where initiation rituals meant upper-class wrestlers twisted the nipples of freshman wrestlers until they turned purple and tennis players sent hard volleys to younger teammates' backsides. . . . The homecoming king was a football player on probation for burglary.
>
> (para. 1)

The themes of hopelessness, panic, and hypermasculinity are reflected in these stories.

The existence of a rigid hierarchal social order in the school appears to have been common knowledge amongst the students. In an interview, a Columbine student told a reporter all the kids were saying the same thing, "*They got the wrong people. Everyone said that – cheerleaders, ballplayers, wrestlers, they all said the same thing*" (as cited in Larkin, 2007, p. 82 [May 13, 2003]). The shooting victims were kids who were well-liked, kind, happy children, and not the bullies that the students assumed Eric and Dylan were retaliating against because of the way they had been treated (pp. 82–83).

Principal DeAngelis stated that bullying was rare at Columbine (Larkin, 2007, p. 93), but apparently the administration turned a blind eye to the bullying in the halls and the cafeteria. Students routinely reported dramatically higher incidences of school violence and drug abuse than the administrators

(p. 93). By refusing to see what students reported as daily occurrences, the administration created a situation where the jocks could humiliate and harass Eric and Dylan with virtual impunity (p. 81).

Hometown pride in championship sports teams allowed a system to ignore harassment, effectively handing the team players power over the rest of the student body (Kurtis, 2008). Like America's goal to be the greatest country in the world, many local schools invest in athletics as a way to achieve stardom. The star athletes "ruled" the halls because they could. Before the shooting the school condoned bullying by ignoring it, which is substantiated in many student reports of instances where teachers stood by and watched; " 'Boys will be boys,' they'd say, and laugh" (an anonymous student as cited in Larkin, 2007, p. 89). This is the sort of atmosphere that made it feel safe enough for a football player to tell a reporter, "Columbine is a good clean place, except for those rejects" (Klein, 2012, p. 15).

As one time friend of the boys, Brooks Brown, put it, "Eric and Dylan are the ones responsible for creating this tragedy . . . However, Columbine is responsible for creating Eric and Dylan" (Larkin, 2007, p. 107). The humiliation the two suffered was instrumental in formation of a social status group of two with an ideology that affirmed racism, their own exceptionalism, and the right to enjoy acts of violence without consequences.

Marginalized masculinity

Marginalized masculinity appears to be a factor in the outbreak of school and other random shootings in the US (Newman & Fox, 2009). Eric and Dylan were two young white men who did not benefit from white privilege. White privilege, loosely defined as social advantages based on race, benefits whites disproportionally by allowing access to power, choices, and opportunities (Vang, 2010). Eric and Dylan felt their opportunities to date and to be rewarded for their intelligence and creativity were dwindling (Harris, 1998–1999; Klebold, D., 1997–1999). As high school progressed they saw others reaping rewards based on their physical prowess and good looks while they were snubbed, bullied, and in Eric's case unable to lose his virginity (1998–1999; 1997–1999). Dylan ridiculed the world as zombies (Klebold, D., 1997–1999) while Eric wrote lists of targets to bully and concocted gruesome rape fantasies (Harris, 1998–1999). Together they made up vigilante stories they videoed for homework projects that glorified killing and sadistic torture (Harris & Klebold, D., 2013). Eric wrote a paper for school researching gun control laws as a way to learn how to most easily obtain an arsenal (Cullen, 2009, p. 99). These reflect their search for a creative outlet for their intelligence and romantic feelings, which had turned destructive.

In a well-planned retaliation, they concocted a narrative they believed would seed fear into everyday activities of the survivors, by murdering them in the quotidian halls of their high school (Harris and Klebold, 1999). They randomly killed and maimed, even filling bullets with nails. In this way they forced the world to notice their rage, low social status, and grievances. In the end, Dylan and Eric took the same unchecked hypermasculine values of the school bullies to the next level and made themselves fearsome and subsequently are the ones who became infamous for it, while the others got away with it.

What the other students failed to realize is that Eric and Dylan knew they would get the attention they desired if they slaughtered innocent people and they did this on purpose. Eric's journals are often written with the expectation that he will have an audience. "All right you pathetic fools listen up" (Harris, 1998–1999, p. 26 [para. 009]).

If they had planned a precision attack on the jocks they could have aimed to blow up the gym during a game, or if they had been after the social elites they could have bombed the senior prom the Saturday before the shootings. Instead they chose the library and the cafeteria at lunchtime when the most students were targets and when the fear factor would be at its highest (Cullen, 2009).

Columbine was a political act. The boys did not target the hostile jocks that they felt deserved their retributive justice; they targeted the entire social structure of their high school. Apparently, they saw no other way out. In The Basement Tapes (Harris and Klebold, D., 1999), made shortly before the attack, Eric and Dylan sum up their motives. They wanted the chaos they felt internally to explode into the world around them, to start a chain reaction and inspire other kids to use their methods to destroy anyone who had hurt them (Harris & Klebold, D., 1999). They seduced others to hero-worship. This is openly evidenced on numerous Internet websites (for a list see Vaughan, 2001). Eric and Dylan dreamt their act of terror would "kick start" a revolution (Harris & Klebold, D., 1999). Eric left intact his journals, notes and plans for the attack, videos, and a blog site. He knew they would be found and wanted the attention notoriety would bring (Harris & Klebold, D., 1999). These would appear to be the dreams of terrorists.

This act of domestic terrorism led to an increase in rampage shootings on and off campuses in North America, Europe, Australia, and Argentina with perpetrators having referred directly to Columbine as their inspiration (Larkin, 2007). Random shooters are not letting themselves be forgotten because they keep replicating. The boys who attempt the school shootings have some traits in common; their social needs are not met, they are secretive, they are isolated, alienated young men with an intense desire to inflict pain, usually upon the entire culture, and so indiscriminately fire their rage at innocent targets (Siegel, 2012, p. A16).

This is a high price to pay for a cultural complex. But murdering and rape are key epithets that run through this exploration and here the two boys identified with them. By 2009 in school shootings worldwide, 500 students, parents, or faculty were dead or wounded overall (Klein, 2012, p. 2). The same ideology that justified the reactions to 9/11 on a global scale, that the US has the right to retaliate by "shocking and aweing" others into submission, is displayed here. The boys believed the school deserved to suffer because they had suffered. This level of morality is the modern equivalent of a "divine right" to a Manifest Destiny for the early European settlers, who took the lands and resources they coveted, and demonized those who were in their way.

An underlying cultural complex

Singer (2004) theorized that a cultural complex creates a type of group false self, a daemon, who protects the wounded inner core. In this sense, Eric and Dylan's repressed sensitivity was protected by a hypermasculine defense. Eric and Dylan's story reflects themes from myths of both Pan and the nymphs. At times, Pan ceased to be the nymph's protector and became their predator. Innocence found itself isolated and trapped and becomes traumatized, regressing and hiding in a vegetative state. Echo and Pitys were never able to spring the trap and again be free in the bucolic woods of Arcadia.

But labeling Eric and Dylan as Pan-like or nymph-like concretizes the complex. When caught in a complex one moment one is over reactive and defensive, the next one has retreated and obsesses over the cruelty of others (Kalsched, 1996). Both reactions are a part of an unconscious identification with a splintered off complexed part of the psyche. Eric and Dylan's aggression and selfish behavior acted as the protective daemon for the complex while the split between their inner and outer lives demonstrates the split nature of one.

Pan expressed an isolated, lonely, self-absorbed, and aggressive archetype, with no qualms about using violence to dominate others (Borgeaud, 1979/1988). Pan's myths articulate a code of aggressive hypermasculinity. He lived a solitary life where the value of women was often disregarded; he was a soldier/general, and a hunter. Like Dylan and Eric, Pan fared better in isolation then in the civilized world where he was ridiculed for his looks, his music, and his rustic nature (Ovid, 1989; Bulfinch, 1855). Pan's locations reflect a recurring theme of dwelling in isolation. "Although shrines were sometimes built to him [Pan] in cities, his sanctuaries were more often to be found in wild and isolated places, on mountainsides, in grottos and in caves" (Schofield, 2005, pp. 9–10). Dylan and Eric lived their secret lives in the dark, sneaking out at night on "missions" and vandalizing their neighborhoods. They could see no way out of the lonely darkness they inhabited. "Suicide gives me hope, that i'll be in my place wherever I go after this life. that ill finally not be at war w. myself, the world, the universe – my mind, body, everywhere" (Klebold, D., 1997–1999, p. 3 [para 2]).

Pan *Agreus* (of the hunt) was the god of a sensuous, peaceful world, until his presence announced instability and the threat of eminent danger (Eliade,

1987, p. 160). His wilderness also parallels the mythic landscape of the Columbine area; pastoral, sparsely populated mountainsides with great expanses for roaming undetected, but still home to black bears, mountain lions, and gray wolves. Even the name "Columbine" signifies the beauty and resilience of the Rocky Mountains. The columbine is a delicate but hardy wildflower with a "fairylike woodland quality" (Clark, 1981, p. 184). The community presents itself as serenely bucolic on the surface as well, but the savage aggression of a frontier bully culture waits in ambush and expresses danger and an omnipresent insecurity that has become a part of modern America life (Lifton, 2003).

Caught in the hubris of the Pan archetype Eric, Dylan, *and* the school bullies, needed to believe they were a type of hypermasculine, godlike men. Eric wrote, "I feel like God and I wish I was, having everyone being OFFICIALLY lower than me. I already know that I am higher than most anyone in the fucking *welt* in terms of universal Intelligence" (Harris, 1998–1999, p. 26 [005]). An incomplete picture of Eric and Dylan's buried sensitivity is found in their journals. The vegetative state of the nymphs following Pan's aggressions expressed the same numbed sensitivity as the boy's internal state – Eric's "I wish I was a fucking sociopath so I didn't have any remorse, but I do" (Harris and Klebold, D., 1999), and Dylan's "me is a god, a god of sadness/ exiled to this eternal hell" (Klebold, D., 1997–1999, p. 9 [paras. 3–4]). They are examples of a hidden, traumatized state of paralyzed innocence at the core of the complex. This would suggest that in order for systemic change to begin the country will need to examine paralyzed beliefs about itself that are keeping it trapped in an archaic state of deluded and unconscious innocence.

Following the repetitive nature of a cultural complex (Singer & Kimbles, 2004), research has found that not only did hypermasculine boys gain status through bullying aggression before the shootings at Columbine, after the shootings this code reestablished itself (Meadows, 2003, p. 57; Larkin, 2007, p. 33). By 2003, the hierarchal social system at Columbine had reverted to bullying. This suggests the problem is systemic and that the solution of zero tolerance for a few isolated troublemakers is inadequate. The inadequacy of this solution may explain why school shootings are still on the rise in the US. It also suggests a need for approaches that consider this problem at a deeper level than merely determining blame and creating stronger physical defenses against "misfits." Bullying is a direct result of the competition inherent in the naïve principle of exceptionalism.

The archetypal core

The unconscious and repetitive nature of a complex can become more visible when seen through the structure of myth. Patterns bridging the painful details of reality then come into focus. By using myth to interpret current events the hope is that the repetitive nature, selective memory, and knee-jerk reactions stimulated while in a cultural complex will be tempered as awareness of the pattern within the culture grows (Kimbles, 2003). At the core of a cultural complex is an unconscious archetypal identity (Singer & Kimbles, 2004, p. 6). Disowned aspects of this identity are cast off onto out-groups or onto rejected members of the group itself (Kimbles, 2003). In this case, the primary affect was fear and disbelief, and the shooters and teenagers "like them" were scapegoated in order to reassure the community. When seen through comparison to the archetypal qualities attributed to Pan, it becomes clearer why intolerable anxieties caused by the Columbine shootings required a scapegoat to relieve the country's anxiety.

Pan's mother found him monstrous (Boer, 1970, pp. 64–68) even though he signified "all" to Zeus and the Pantheon. He panicked humans and so quite naturally they shunned him (1970). From his beginning in the Homeric hymns, Pan is directly related to the nymphs with whom he danced and cavorted. But he also terrorized them. Sudden surges of desire would compel him to chase after them with the intention to rape (1970; Borgeaud, 1979/1988). The nymphs escaped through transformation into a clump of reeds or a tree or an echo, but always to a state with less self-determination (Borgeaud, 1979/1988). These couplings suggest a pattern of conjoined innocence, panic, and hopelessness. Those who run from terror in panic survive, but the price for panic, according to the myths, is devolution, or in modern terms a traumatized state of mind. The pattern of ignoring the needs of the disenfranchised and then panicking when those needs erupt, the myths suggest, leads to losses of personal freedom and autonomy.

Pan is an archetypal representation of the human capacity for egocentric selfishness that lived deep in the wilderness, or as an archetype of human nature, deep in the unconscious layers of the psyche. Like the school shooters, when Pan's needs were shunned, fear and panic ensued. The panic that was birthed in the boys' hearts by the bullying they endured at school, devolved into stagnation about their futures and then a dramatic death wish in them both. These feelings eventually burst forth and caused the massacre. After the dust has settled on these types of shootings, the real work begins for the survivors who have witnessed events that they then relive in flashbacks and nightmares. Otherwise, the chances increase that the survivors become caught in the same kind of moralistic rejection of others who are different that generates the power in the cultural complex.

At times in myth Pan was a bully, at others he was a scapegoat. When Pan was a scapegoat he contained the cult's anxiety and survival needs through ritual. The purpose of Pan's rite of squilling in his cult was to restore the balance of order when the hunt went badly by allowing the frustrated hunters to release their aggression and fear of failure. This helped to contain the aggression, panic, and hopelessness engendered by fear of starvation (Borgeaud, 1979/1988). But in the American school system the children who are scapegoated and bullied often bully others in hopes of finding entrance into an in-group (Klein, 2012). Uncontained anxiety and fears are cruelly projected onto those perceived as weak. School rallies to end bullying or teacher and administrative interventions into specific situations often make things worse for the more fragile teenagers (2012).

Perhaps the violence will not stop until the social structure itself has been identified as a key element in the bullying cycle. The difficult and painful work of containment of projections might then begin, even as aggression and fear were contained in the rite of squilling in the cults of Pan.

The role of social influences in constellating a cultural complex

In 1999, there were three story lines about Columbine that dominated the media and consequently affected social discourse. They all reinforced anxiety and confusion in the American public. These discourses supported and strengthened the complex by blocking more nuanced ideas or viewpoints. This, I am suggesting, led to stagnation in the culture.

The three story lines are that Eric and Dylan were part of an underground group set on getting revenge at the jocks for the bullying that had plagued them for years, the parents were to blame for their neglectful disregard of their sons activities, and the evangelical right aggressively adapted the meaning of the event to be about their own perceived persecution. Researchers found the media formulated these narratives by hyper-focusing *en masse* on sensationalist issues that activated fear in their audience and avoided more complex issues, such as how to address the cultural norms complicit in the event (Ogle, Eckman, and Leslie, 2003). The shell of a complex creates blocks in the energetic field: pathways that do not lead to connections or learning but instead to repetitious thoughts and compulsive behaviors (Kalsched, 1996, p. 91). Thus, the avoidance of the more difficult issues, it is argued here, led to apathy in the American public. In order to understand the reactions Americans had, and did not have, to the Columbine massacre, it is essential to consider the role of the media.

The media's role in American reactions to Columbine

During unexpected moments of great turmoil, such as natural or man-made disasters, in effect, the media become the eyes and ears of a culture. People are "glued" to the coverage during crises. Traditionally, news sources were expected to remain unbiased and simply report the facts, but they are now openly biased (Nyhan, 2012; Knickerbocker, 2012). For example, in an interview at The World Economic Forum in Davos, Switzerland on January 27, 2007 Rupert Murdoch of *News Corp/Fox News* was asked if there were agendas he wanted to shape and he answered, "Well, we've basically supported the Bush policy" (The World Economic Forum Davos, Switzerland 2007).

Even though crises transform the TV or computer news feeds into the center of many family homes, a recent Gallup poll (Morales, 2012) found most Americans have little or no trust in the media. Confidence in the media has been steadily falling since the Watergate era (Holtzman, Schott, Jones, Balota, & Yarkoni, 2011). In a Gallup poll only 8% answered they have a great deal of confidence in mass media (Morales, 2012).

The opinions of the news outlets produce bias by over or under reporting of stories as well as through "commentaries." The media not only reports news but also inevitably shapes the story through choices in coverage and oversimplifications due to space or time limit considerations. The media may buckle under to profit-driven motives and pressures to produce immediate conclusions or solutions to a problem (Ogle et al., 2003). One of the consequences of bias is that sources go beyond reporting, implying judgments through tone of voice or descriptive phrasing and by giving commentary. This influences the public about what choices to make. By suggesting what should be done they are not only following a story, the media leads toward particular outcomes. Media bias regarding causes and needed change during a crisis is significant if it influences public opinion because public opinion drives political change.

Since the media has chosen to create fan bases by skewing the news toward one or another political agenda, it is blocking movement toward change by obfuscating issues in ways that lead people to polarize and adopt oversimplified opinions. The polarization has led to political stagnation in Washington, DC. Voters "believe" one side or another as factual. Media bias has thus contributed to the protective shell of a cultural complex by being the mouthpiece for a psychic shield, insulating its readers or listeners from any responsibility for the problems in the culture, regardless of whether they are biased toward conservative or progressive values. This direction continues to gain traction as one side will currently claim the other is reporting "fake news."

Each random shooting brings a public outcry, but nothing seems to change. Evidence of a deep-seated problem can be seen in the alarming rate of people killed by guns in the US (Richardson & Hemenway, 2003, para. 1). There are 19.5 times more killings in the US than in similar high-income countries in the world (2003, para. 1). On an average seven children a day die from gunshot wounds (Brody, 2013, p. D7). After Columbine, the 2007 Virginia Tech massacre had an even higher number of students killed (Barak, 2005) and in 2012, at the Newtown, Connecticut massacre, the 20 children killed were all only six or seven years old (Siegal, 2012). Over time, the massacres must be ever greater in numbers or grotesqueness in order to command the attention of the general public. If attention is what the shooters are seeking (even if only in part), then it is reasonable to expect that the magnitude of the events will continue to increase. This disturbing aspect fits the facts as witnessed in the random shootings in Las Vegas in October, 2017 when 58 were killed at a concert and the 17 lost in Parkland, FL in 2018. As the incidents worsen, both fear for one's loved ones and apathy toward more bad news increases in the general public. The defensive shell of the complex thickens and the paralysis of the sensitive core of the complex deepens.

Immediately following such shootings, the television media coverage breaks off its usual programming and reports the real time action of the event. The nation huddles around television sets and computer screens absorbing the trauma. In this vulnerable state the media's handling of the coverage influences the country. On the day of the Columbine shootings, people reported feeling as if they were witnessing the shootings in real time (Cullen, 2009). Within hours the reportage froze the two shooters into "monsters" (Cullen, 2009). Reporters focused on "this spooky Trench Coat Mafia [TCM]. It grew more bizarre by the minute. In the first two hours, witnesses on CNN described the TCM as Goths, gays, outcast, and a street gang" (p. 72). Diane Sawyer on the ABC show *20/20* reported, "the boys may have been part of a dark, underground national phenomenon known as the Gothic movement and that some of these Goths may have killed before" (p. 156). But they were not Goths nor were they members of a Trench Coat Mafia, rumors that were never dispelled (2009). Eric and Dylan just liked to wear long coats and wore them that day to hide their shotguns.

In an example of bias, possibly due to the strength of the LBGT culture's voice, though there were two rumors that immediately formed following the shootings, that Dylan and Eric were gay and that they were Goths, the media avoided the early rumor that the two boys were gay and concentrated on the Goth rumor as a way to characterize their deviance (Cullen, 2009, p. 72). The jump to labeling them as some sort of anomaly, or monstrous "bad seeds" created a feeling of distance and safety since "they" are not like "us" (Zimbardo, 2007, p. 6). Jungian analyst Robert Johnson cautioned, "The tendency to see one's shadow 'out there' in one's neighbor or in another race or culture is the most dangerous aspect of the modern psyche" (1991, p. 27).

Media sources repeatedly warned that if this could happen in white middle class Jefferson County, Colorado it could happen anywhere. The media concentrated on minor details such as the appearance and dress of the two shooters. They described these as markers of troubled children and spun fear inducing and "personalizing" themes warning parents to watch for signs that might suggest violent tendencies (such as black clothes!) (Ogle et al., p. 15). The conclusion, stated as "fact," that unless parents and the education system properly police children more violence will result, created unresolvable anxiety and left the country looking for quick answers (Ogle et al., 2003). The obvious, easy target was the revenge motive for the two boys.

The media misreported the purpose that Eric Harris and Dylan Klebold had for committing the crime and reinforced a story line that Eric and Dylan's motive was to revenge themselves by targeting the jocks. Those errant myths prevail. The intense, affect-laden reactions of viewers and readers were shaped by the repetitious images of the massacre and the opinions of the media (Cullen, 2009; Larkin, 2007). Their actual plan had been to blow up the school; killing as many random people as possible. The boys were failed bombers (the ignition fuses on their two 20-pound propane bombs were faulty) aiming at the student body, rather than revenge shooters (Kurtis, 2008; Tonso, 2009; Larkin, 2007).

For investigators, the two large bombs found in the cafeteria made it clear that the boys' target were not specific enemies. The sheriff's department and the FBI realized the attack was indiscriminate, and so, much more disturbing in terms of motive (Cullen, 2009, p. 124). Never the less, the media-led public consensus that they had targeted victims prevailed as the motive in the public imagination (p. 151). The discourse also projected a simulacrum onto the perpetrators focusing primarily on whether they were actually evil, Satanic, or only mentally ill. The reportage was compelling to a horrified and fascinated public, encouraging the profit-driven news industry to exploit the victims and create instant heroes out of some of the murdered children (Moore, 2002).

Substantiating the popular expression "if it bleeds it leads" (Glassner, 1999, pp. 21–55) Columbine received unprecedented news coverage in the week following the event. Fifty-three separate stories aired on ABC, CBS, and NBC (Maguire, Weatherby, & Mathers, 2002). With this much coverage, the details of the event were repeated countless times and CNN and Fox News charted the highest ratings in their history (2002). A week afterward, *USA Today* was still running ten separate Columbine stories in a single edition and it was nearly two weeks before the *New York Times* printed an issue without Columbine on page one (Cullen, 2009, p. 178). The volume of coverage lends itself to compulsive watching with cliffhangers before commercial breaks on TV and promises for "new" news soon. A "herd mentality" created a stampede of sensational and disturbing stories with coverage allocation and content amongst the network channels closely resembling each other (Maguire et al., 2002).

The media's bias toward pigeonholing Eric, Dylan, and their parents directed viewers toward inflamed reactive affect and, since the boys were dead, led to the families becoming the chosen scapegoats. By casting out a scapegoat, the school, the community, and the country could see themselves as blameless. "The goat shall bear all their iniquities upon him to a solitary land" (Lev. 16: 22). Perhaps this helps to explain the baffling reluctance following the massacre to change policies or laws, save for small safety measures (Newman & Fox, 2009).

The notion of a cultural complex helps to make intelligible why a specific group of people will tend to identify as a whole in a crisis (Kimbles, 2000). Consensus that the cause was a few neglected, "evil" boys helped the country feel protected from the threat of further mayhem. By shaping public opinion with biased reporting about the boys and their families, the media unknowingly reinforced the shell of the complex and, in a sense, herded the public to a central position that failed to ask whether the community had a responsibility for shaping a culture in which children can become so alienated.

Columbine coverage ended abruptly. A string of deadly tornadoes hit Oklahoma, and the national press corps left town in a single afternoon (Cullen, 2009, p. 213). The school would return periodically to national headlines over the years, while the investigation slowly plodded along, replete with lawsuits and best sellers. But the narrative of what had happened was set by the media in the weeks after the shootings and never really changed.

Reactions in the Columbine community and the country

Within weeks the reactions in the community and the country coalesced around three conclusions: that the two boys were on a mission of revenge for having been bullied and rejected (as previously outlined), that the parents had failed in their job as parents, and that the evangelical right was targeted. The rapid formation of these opinions indicates the reactive atmosphere that followed the shootings. Then, after the initial panic, the country returned to an apathetic attitude toward the problems of gun control and the lack of low cost mental health services.

The ban on purchasing semi-automatic weapons was allowed to lapse *after* Columbine (Fuchs, 2012, para. 2). Such world-weary listlessness evokes poet Robert Frost's "Pan with Us," "Play? Play? – What should he play?" (1933, p. 36). America's old "can do" attitude, was not seen in the post-Columbine US relationship to guns. Restrictions could not be agreed upon and stagnation followed apathy. "He tossed his pipes, too hard to teach/ A new-world song, far out of reach" (Frost, 1933).

Not only after Columbine but after each incident of school rampages, outrage and calls for greater gun control have led to frustration when the new proposals bog down in political stagnation. This lack of enthusiasm has stymied reform and handed control over to lobby groups such as the National Rifle Association (Siegal, 2012). Kalsched (1996) suggested that the shell of a complex is a self-defense system that interprets impulses to change as threats. Gun ownership is perceived as a right in the US and perhaps this is why gun control has been unobtainable. The proliferation of small arms in America is one aspect of the widespread anxiety. Disinterest in public forums on the development of social skills that are inclusive rather than based on hierarchal tiers of social groupings in school age children in America has prevailed.

Over reactions and vicious public arguments followed Jefferson County's initial flush of self-disclosure to the media, they focused on blame rather than change (Cullen, 2009). A number of law suits against the parents, the school, and the Jefferson County Sheriff's department were begun. Then, a wall of silence followed. The community went into a defensive state that was symbolically enacted when the school reopened. The parents formed an actual wall out of themselves that shielded their children from the media as the students filed into school in an attempt to protect their children from further questioning (pp. 270–271).

Jung theorized that once a complex is activated it becomes predictable in the overreactions it motivates (1948/1960, p. 94 [*CW 8*, para. 198]). He also wrote that the reasoning in the split off complex has an inner coherence within itself and holds some autonomy over a person who is caught in it (1948/1960 [*CW* 8]). With help from the media's influence, an unconscious ethos guiding the solutions to violence in the US reflects these sorts of overreactions. Like a gunfight in the old west, if the "bad" guys are dead, the community is felt to be safe again.

The Klebolds and the Harrises

The second story line in Columbine was that the parents were to blame. They were the obvious target since the boys were gone. The Klebolds called their lawyer within hours of the event. "'Dylan isn't here anymore for people to hate,' he said. 'So people are going to hate you'" (Cullen, 2009, p. 91). He was right. One year later a Pew Research Center poll found they were considered the primary source of blame by 85%of the US population (Nagy & Danitz, 2000, para. 2). Two days after the attack, then Florida Governor Jeb Bush "challenged parents to spend more time with their children as a bulwark against future Columbines" (para. 4). By the end of the week, a Gallup poll found 25%of Americans believed the families should face criminal prosecution (Gillespie, 1999, para. 1).

Hostility and attacks against both families closely followed Eric and Dylan's massacre and suicides (Cullen, 2009). Hate mail and hate phone calls plagued them. The community sued both sets of parents and won large settlements. The suit against the shooter's parents by many of the families of the children killed (some of the parents sued separately) led to a compromise to depose Eric and Dylan's parents as long as what they said would be kept private. Others then sued to hear what they had said, arguing that this might prevent further tragedies and a judge finally, years later, decided the information could be released in 20 years, or in 2027 (2009).

Essentially, Eric Harris and Dylan Klebold's parents defense was to freeze. They never made any statements taking responsibility for their sons' behavior nor regretting any of their own actions. They never made any public statements at all, after an initial apology for what their boys had done.

Tom and Sue Klebold and Wayne and Kathy Harris denied any knowledge of their sons' plans, recent activities, or weapons stash (Cullen, 2009). Their sons had been arrested together for breaking and entering and had been suspended from school multiple times. Dylan was known to have a severe temper and a problem with alcohol but none of their parents suspected they might be up to something (2009). They never noticed the guns, bombs, and ammunition in abundance in their drawers and closets, nor the blatant clues left out in plain sight (Kass, 2009).

> Dylan and Eric brag about hiding their tools of death – and about the close calls along the way. Eric shows the camera a black tackle box with his bomb-making equipment stowed inside. They boast about concocting their plan under the noses of unsuspecting parents and friends.
>
> Dylan recalls a time when his parents walked into his bedroom while he was trying on his trench coat to see if it would hide his sawed-off shotgun. "They didn't even know it was there."
>
> (Harris and Klebold, D., 1999)

The night before the shooting the gun shop called Eric's house to say his ammunition order had arrived. Wayne Harris answered the phone and told the man he had not ordered the bullets but never questioned his son (Kass, 2009). Eric bragged about carrying his gym bag, the "terrorist bag," into the house with a gun butt sticking out. His mom assumed it was his BB gun (p. 136).

When Dylan's parents were called in to school by a teacher concerned about a gory story he had turned in, the teacher reports Tom and Sue Klebold were not worried about it (Kass, 2009, p. 154). Tom Klebold could not remember the last time he had been in his son's room.

In a film the two boys shot for a school project, Eric's mother sits at her kitchen table as they walk by in trench coats, wielding guns, smoking, and swearing (REB-VoDKA, n. d.). However, questionable issues are always easy to judge in hindsight and the Harrises and Klebolds are not alone in trusting their teenage children despite red flags. Both families appeared to have allowed their boys a degree of independence often afforded to American children.

When the sheriff's department came over, search warrant in hand, at 1:15 on April 20th, Wayne and Kathy Harris asked for immunity before they would talk to them (Kass, 2009, p. 224). At first they tried to refuse entrance. "The cops found them uncooperative" (Cullen, 2009, p. 68). In the basement and in Eric's room evidence was everywhere; a sawed off shotgun barrel, a page from *The Anarchist Cookbook*, journals, memos, and videos (2009).

Both sets of parents may have unconsciously taught their sons to blame others rather than themselves by example. Both pairs of parents blamed others as bad influences when their boys had misbehaved before the shootings (Kass, 2009). Eric's parents blamed Brooks Brown and his parents for Eric's behavior and felt they were persecuting him (2009). When Eric was suspended for hacking into the school computer and getting locker combinations his father blamed the computer teacher, Mr Long, telling him, "you trusted my son too much" (p. 84). Dylan's parents blamed Eric and downplayed Dylan's motives (p. 95). "A year after the shooting the Klebolds told Marxhausen [their pastor] that Dylan was infused with idealism and righteousness that led him to rebel against the injustices and imperfections of the world such as the social tiers he experienced at school. . . . They put the onus on Eric [for the massacre]" (pp. 211–212).

The slowly produced evidence from the investigation by the Jefferson County Sheriff's department described how trusting, perhaps even naïve, they were about their boys' private lives. Perhaps the lack of critical judgment on the part of the parents helped constellate callousness and a predatory nature in their sons, but this argument alone would suggest that any parents who fail to check their children's closets, drawers, and journals are negligent. Where to draw the line on privacy and freedom for children, especially once children have rebelled and behaved in ways that are dangerous for themselves or others, is a debate that might have followed these events, but did not.

The lack of a narrative for the Harrises and the Klebolds creates another failure. Their silence gives no way to understand and hence to connect with them. It might have been a different story if eventually they had shared with the traumatized country their own trauma, pain, and confusion. They froze in a state of unresponsiveness, caught in a grief, one would imagine, without end. Like the nymphs, the parents disappeared into the landscape by avoiding contact with the survivors, their families, and the general public.

The defensive shell of a complex serves to protect the authentic self, or core, during a traumatic event, but later the defensive wall can become a self-destructive retardant for a person or culture (Singer, 2004). The defensive shell the families retreated into protected them from the outside world. But as a construct in a complex, not speaking up about the secrets and the pain hardened the walls and reduced the chance that more penetrating insights might evolve. In this sense, the Harrises and the Klebolds also helped to strengthen the complex and so unwittingly increased the chances the repetitious and explosive nature of the complex would erupt again.

The evangelical right

The third story line concerning Columbine was that religious persecution was the basis for the attack. A cultural complex is likely to constellate when conflicts arise in groups based on religious differences (Kimbles, 2000, p. 155), as was the case between liberal Protestants and evangelicals in the area (Larkin, 2007, p. 14). The evangelical right led the way in specifically identifying Eric and Dylan as "evil." But they were not alone. They were portrayed in the media as " 'evil' perpetrators of a 'massacre' of innocents' " (Spencer & Muschert, 2009, p. 1381) and were named as evil by even the principal of their high school, Frank DeAngelis (Larkin, 2007, p. 53).

This was in contrast to the public image of the victims. The "martyrdom" of Cassie Bernall is useful as a case in point.

> Images of the students emphasized their ages and, often, their religious faith – both of which appeared to serve as proxies for their innocence. Cassie Bernall served as an iconic figure in this regard: She was young, she was female, and she was a "strong Christian" – all of which provided for claims to her "martyrdom."
>
> (Spencer & Muschert, 2009, p. 1381)

As such, the polarizing "evil" of Eric and Dylan and "innocence" of their victims reflexively reinforced each other and created an oversimplified, black and white narrative that bound the culture to an in-group/out-group dynamic and reinforced dogmatic beliefs in the evangelical community.

A defense of Christian evangelical religious beliefs was aggressively and opportunistically inserted into the national discussion of Columbine (Larkin, 2007; Cullen, 2009; Kass, 2009). Beginning with the orations at the memorial services, evangelicals defined the Columbine shootings in religious terms. The clergy used the event as a tool for recruitment. At Cassie Bernall's funeral, her pastor "saw the opportunity in the tragedy to unabashedly save more souls. 'Pack that ark with as many people as possible,' " he told his congregation (Kirsten as cited in Cullen, 2009, p. 178).

The evangelical ministries held that due to their beliefs they were Eric and Dylan's target, even though only three of the twelve children killed were born-again (Cullen, 2009; Larkin, 2007). They believed their innocent children were persecuted because of their faith, just as early Christians in Rome had been (Cullen, 2009). The evangelical ministries in the US are a fundamentalist culture, in which Satan is an actual living monster in the shadows, impatient to kidnap innocent souls (Cullen, 2009, p. 30). The repression of the god of nature and the adaptation of his countenance into Satan's are a compelling plumb line linking the archetypal energetics of Pan with a cultural complex in the Columbine shootings.

Dylan shot Cassie Bernall in the head while she hid in the library. Sixteen-year-old Craig Scott was hiding nearby with two others who were shot to death. Craig thought he heard Dylan ask her if she believed in God, and that she had said yes right before he shot her (Crowder, 1999, paras. 1–5). The story spread rapidly through the churches and the media. As interviewing went on in the first days and weeks, the story was repeated and writers assumed kids were informing the media. But it was the other way around (Cullen, 2009, p. 151). The media was telling the students the story and then they were repeating it to each other.

The story became a psychological touchstone in the midst of the horror. It took on such a life of its own that the media ignored the truth when it came out shortly thereafter. It turned out that Craig Scott was mistaken. Val Schnurr had been rushed to the hospital and was not interviewed in the days following the tragedy. Dylan shot her and she sustained injuries to the chest, arms, and abdomen after being riddled with shotgun pellets (Cullen, 2009).

Val dropped to her knees, then her hands. Blood was streaming from thirty-four separate wounds. "Oh my God, oh my God, don't let me die," she prayed.

> Dylan turned around. This was too rich. "God? Do you believe in God?"
>
> She wavered. Maybe she should keep her mouth shut. No. She would rather say it. "Yes. I believe in God."
>
> (Cullen, 2009, pp. 224–225)

Dylan reloaded but was distracted and she managed to crawl to safety.

Craig had innocently confused Val with Cassie (Cullen, 2009). The media ignored her and that the story was an erroneous one reported by a traumatized child. This suggests an unconscious need for a hero, another archetype that surfaces in every one of these modern day massacres. The facts here were simply not as important as the mythic. Criminologists Victor E. Kappeler and Gary W. Potter (2005) theorized that what makes a crime narrative mythic is the identification of innocent and often-helpless victims, the appearance of brave and virtuous heroes, a threat to legitimate and established norms, and the identification of a deviant population responsible for the crime (2005, pp. 22–26). The need to make meaning out of Columbine by finding some hope, some heroic moments, led to the fixation on the story of 17-year-old Cassie Bernall by the evangelical ministries and the media.

Cassie's martyrdom was a positive story that people could hold on to amid the negativity of the shootings. The strength attributed to her, believing that if she died she was going to her maker to be born again, offered psychological relief. Jung theorized that an archetype, in this case of a redeeming hero, is a structure within the collective unconscious that surfaces as a symbol when it is needed for the cohesion of a people or a person (Samuels et al., 2005). He concluded that there is an aspect within the unconscious that makes meaning of life, which is projected onto natural phenomena, in this case, onto Cassie Bernall.

Eric Harris and Dylan Klebold were split off from the community and banished as anomalies of evil. They were viewed by evangelicals not as symbolic of evil, but as evil incarnate, in a modern passion play in which the slain students were assigned the role of martyred heroes and the boys became the henchmen of Satan (Spencer & Muschert, 2009). For the evangelicals Cassie, Eric, and Dylan's story fit an archetypal role that is actually similar to Eric and Dylan's worldview. The difference is who is black and who is white in these opposing viewpoints. The moral elitism of the evangelical right mirrors the moral elitism of Eric and Dylan, whose journals show their belief in their own superiority over, as Dylan called the world, "the zombies" (Klebold, 1997–1999). The intolerance that Eric and Dylan showed everyone is a mirror image of the intolerance of evangelicals toward everyone who hold other spiritual beliefs (Larkin, 2007, p. 14, pp. 60–61). They became the projected shadow of evil for each other.

As D. H. Lawrence wrote in "Pan in America," Pan's interpretation as the Christian devil was "a most strange ending for a god with such a name. Pan! All!" (1936, p. 23). A belief that some humans are irredeemable, in other words, evil, underlies the branding of Eric and Dylan. This position contradicts the basic Jungian tenet that out of redemption of the shadow comes the possibility for growth. The understandable instinct to hate and try to kill off the shadow in oneself, or in a cultural complex, members of the society, actually does the opposite and empowers them. The way out of this impasse, using complex theory, is to continue the work begun here and drain the complex of energy by analyzing the symbolic meaning of the culture's history and its relationship to both the archaic core insecurities and the daemonic protection that have congealed around the complex (Whitmont, 1991). When a deeper meaning is found, the complex, like a hurricane once it hits land begins to weaken and become a reservoir filling rainfall, here the truth that we all have the potential to be heroes or monsters, would lessen the need to blame.

The community

Compassion for the seemingly monstrous perpetrators of the massacre was met with rage (Spencer & Muschert, 2009). For example, when a carpenter from Illinois, Greg Zanis, felt compelled to build 15 crosses to commemorate those who had died at Columbine, he included two for Eric and Dylan. He drove to Colorado and erected them on Rebel Hill, at the back of the Columbine campus. "News media immediately singled out these two crosses, framing the issue as a controversy" (p. 1374). The crosses had black plastic bags put over them and were continually graffitied until they were ripped down three days later (2009). 15 crosses imply the pain of the community was caused by misunderstood kids; the removal of their two seems to imply the boys were considered coldblooded murderers and deserved to be vilified, or better yet, forgotten (2009).

The arguments that a social hierarchy was not a problem for the students at Columbine High, that Eric and Dylan's parents were too neglectful or too liberal, that they did not deserve a cross, and that Eric and Dylan were focused on killing the jocks and the evangelical Christians can be more clearly understood when viewed as a cultural complex. The strong feelings that were expressed in the media, at the funerals, at the site of the crosses, and in the student interviews indicate the extreme levels of stress the community was under. Each argument has an inner coherence and consistency, but ignores aspects of reality, has an intensely affective component, lacks compassion, and uses projection. These characteristics obfuscate clarity.

In the US, the southern and western states are particularly prone to settling arguments with guns. The zeitgeist of the Wild West, and the Rockies in particular, formed early in the history of the US. It still reveres a collective set of characteristics indicative of fierce individualists (Kass, 2009). In the early years of colonization, the Rockies were a haven for violent advocates of individualism who expected no help from others and understood that everyone must take care of themselves and their families. Those who chose to settle matters with a gun not only survived, but were glorified. They have become symbols of what it means to be an American (p. 23). Annie Oakley, Wyatt Earp, Buffalo Bill are iconic figures who were legendary for their skilled marksmanship and live on as symbols of fearlessness and of life as adventures. For example, Buffalo Bill Cody, who got his nickname after killing 4,280 buffalo in 17 months (Cody, 2011, p. 97), is buried on Lookout Mountain in Jefferson County, 20 miles from Columbine High.

Today at Columbine, the student population is mostly college-bound, middle class, white Americans (Klein, 2012). The spirit of the Wild West is preserved in the high school's emphasis on winning and physical prowess, which is principally promoted through sports (Larkin, 2007). "The culture of hypermasculinity reigned supreme: the administration was dominated by coaches" (p. 209). For example, the Rebels, the Columbine football team, won their state championship in 2000, 2001, and 2003 (2007). Larkin found fierce support for the school and for the community as a whole. The prevalent attitude in Jefferson County is that it sees itself as deserving a "squeaky-clean" reputation (2007).

Karen L. Tonso, an ethnologist, observed the shocked, and defensive tones of the parents of the Columbine students. They believed their school was safe and that their children were at the very best place they could be (2009, p. 1275). "Ultimately, in rejecting the complicity of the school, its staff, and administration, the Columbine community was left with little else but to leap to the conclusion that the shooters must be insane, individuals incapable of rational thought" (p. 1275).

Jessica Klein concluded that the murders are a direct outcome of oppressive social hierarchies (2012). She stated there are "inextricable connections between school shooting outbursts, the 'everyday' violence of bullying, and the destructive gender pressures and social demands created by the larger culture" (p. 3). She and Larkin attribute this to the peer group structure, which was quite typical at Columbine with jocks and cheerleaders at the top of the hierarchy and ethnic minorities, nerds, loners, punks, Goths, basically any kids who are different, at the bottom (Klein, 2012, p. 3; Larkin, 2007, p. 63).

Students at Columbine were easily able to identify themselves within this structure suggesting it is readily visible (Larkin, 2007, p. 63). The dominant jocks, perched at the top of the pyramid, were three boys known to the administration, faculty, and students (p. 68). The gender politics of the popular crowd was sexist (p. 74). There was a great deal of amorphous movement between the popular crowd and the majority of students, save with the outcasts with whom no one would associate (p. 74).

Like Pan, their peers shunned Eric and Dylan and the other outcasts at Columbine High for being different. The community looked the other way. They felt alternatively bullied or invisible – and consistently rejected by girls (Harris, 1998–1999; Klebold, 1997–1999). "Eric Harris and Dylan Klebold and their bullies were in fact living in a typical American high school culture where, in a microcosm of an authoritarian state, kids were made to conform to constrained parameters of acceptable behaviors that were often vicious and hostile" (Klein, 2012, p. 13).

Jefferson County is not an isolated incident of hypermasculinity causing suffering in the US school system (Blumen, 2010). A study of 432 gifted children found that 67% reported being bullied by the time they reached the eighth grade and that many had specifically been teased about their school performances (Broodman, 2006, para. 1). A study published by the American Medical Association found that "the prevalence of bullying among US youth is substantial" and that "youth who are bullied generally show higher levels of insecurity, anxiety, depression, loneliness, unhappiness, physical and mental symptoms, and low self-esteem" (Nansel, Overpeck, Pilla, Ruan, Simons-Morton, & Sheidt, 2001, paras. 5, 10). How many children quietly choose to "dumb down" and cease to try to excel so that they will have a happier social life?

Some of the children who have perpetrated school shootings found that excelling at academics, which should have been a source of respect, became a social problem instead (Klein, 2012, p. 31). Eric was said to be one of the smartest students in his class at Columbine, both intelligent and articulate, and Dylan was also considered very smart, though an under achiever (Cullen, 2009). Eric was even recognized by major video-game manufacturers for the computer programs he wrote for the on-line games Doom and Quake (Klein, 2012, p. 32). Yet Eric saw no future for himself and did not even apply to college (Cullen, 2009).

During an interview with Michael Moore, singer Marilyn Manson was asked, " 'If you were to talk directly to the kids at Columbine and the people in the community, what would you say to them if they were here right now?' to which he replied, 'I wouldn't say a single word to them – I would listen to what they have to say, and that's what no one did' " (2002).

Unresolved problems

Eric and Dylan's attitudes are reminiscent of themes in Pan's myths with the nymphs. Eric, like Pan, rushed into love and frightened off the object of his desire. The girls Eric desired rejected him (Harris 1998–1999). He aggressively pursued them, but his unrelenting advances frightened them off. He wrote in his journals about his sadistic fantasies in which he, essentially, annihilated women through sex. On the other hand, Dylan was incapable of expressing his feelings directly to the girl he repeatedly declared his love for in his journal (Klebold, 1997–1999). Dylan, like Echo, was unable to speak up for himself. He was unable to act on his deepest feelings. For both, the feelings overwhelmed them and they turned to violence as an expression of their darkest feelings. For both, their journals indicate their feelings built up inside them and became intolerable (Harris, 1998–1999; Klebold, 1997–1999). These unrequited feelings led to despair and anger, which erupted in the school massacre. Relationships with women were stunted in them both and they turned to violent, militant revenge fantasies to ease their internal states. Rejection by women appears to be a factor in the psychological make-up of unmitigated hypermasculinity and the relationship between shooters and their family of origin is an area of research worth pursuit. In this case hypermasculinity served to protect and freeze the sensitivity at the core of a complex in the boys. The cultural complex in America reinforces unresolved opinions about women in the culture.

Psychological research is needed to help stem the bullying and homicidal violence in America. The United States has the highest number of murders of any industrialized nation (Moore, 2002). In 2010, 12,996 deaths due to gun violence were recorded in the US (Nationmaster, 2018). Certainly there are other countries, such as Germany and Great Britain, with long histories of bloodshed. Yet only 722 people were murdered in the United Kingdom in 2009 (Nationmaster, 2018) and 690 in Germany in 2010 (Nationmaster, 2018). These are far below the numbers in the United States, even when adjusted to take into account the percentage of the population.

One could postulate that the difficulty in procuring firearms in these countries explains the huge gap. In 2013, the estimated number of guns in civilian hands in the US was about 310,000,000 (Gunpolicy.org, 2013). If guns make a place more safe, the United States should be the safest country in the world. But the facts bear out that it is not. Why?

Perhaps the numbers of firearms are making people more afraid instead of feeling safer; persecuted rather than protected. Evidence of fear mongering by the media, private enterprise, and politicians suggests that it is fear that results in Americans at home and globally choosing to take up arms as a means to an end (Moore, 2002). To quote a gun owner interviewed shortly after 9/11 in *Bowling for Columbine* (2002); it is an "American responsibility to be armed . . . [and] a dereliction of duty if you don't."

School shootings leave a reverberating question mark behind. Why do they do it? A rush to find answers after Columbine overwhelmed careful, nuanced responses (Frymer, 2009). Many faulty conclusions were formed that have hardened into beliefs and an opportunity for national growth was missed. Nations *can* come to terms with their faulty notions, such as a god-given right to enslave others. When the dominant culture in America takes more responsibility for the anxiety and rage that triggers these outbreaks, like an end to slavery, this too can change. "Whatever we fight about in the outside world is also a battle in our inner selves" (Jung, 1910/1989a, p. 393 [*CW* 18, para. 927]).

In a cultural complex, people become rigidly polarized into an in-group and out groups; stereotypical thinking and mutual negative projections are promoted by the structuring. Kimbles predicted a complex is activated by "the projection onto some group of reviled 'others' of disowned aspects of the groups identity" (2003, p. 219). The projections strengthen the unity of the in-group. "In order for consciousness to perform its function of moral discrimination adaptively and accurately, it must increase awareness of personal and collective shadow motivations" (Stein, 1995, p. 10).

This was not the case following Columbine. "In its more abstract senses, *Columbine* has become a keyword for a complex set of emotions surrounding youth, risk, fear, and delinquency in early 21st Century United States" (Muschert, 2007, p. 365). The situation actually rapidly grew darker as only two years later the shadow of 9/11 fell across the nation, changing things irrevocably. The longer the complex remains unconscious it has a degree of control over those who believe in the repetitive ideas that fuel it, but once awareness begins to grow the story can be changed.

Chapter 8

American reactions to 9/11

Panic and naiveté

Columbine was barely in the rear view mirror before the millennial Y2K scare stirred up anxiety. 9/11 followed a year later, causing shock and panic that triggered even greater anxiety in the country. The traumatic reactions to 9/11 that followed altered both laws and attitudes in the US and put the country on an emotional high alert for years. A fear-based apocalyptic vision began to dominant the culture as perceptions of America's safety and stability came into doubt. Laws were swiftly passed curtailing freedoms. A frightened and docile public accepted the rapid changes, as the majority of Americans chose to allow the "experts" to decide what was best, which included waging simultaneous wars in the oil rich Middle East.

Pan's mythic motifs mirror both an underlying inflated attitude and a fear-based apocalyptic vision in the US, a vision that developed out of America's superpower status in the world (Lifton, 2003). The tactics such a vision legitimizes include brutal treatment of the perceived enemy, scapegoating, manipulation of the mainstream public through the use of euphemisms, and the co-opting of nationally-based sentiments. A compensatory naivety in the American public aided in the formation of this protective vision. The belief in the country as not just the richest and most powerful, but also politically and morally the best, the myth of "exceptionalism" as an US birthright, has been foundational in the formation of these attitudes.

Complexes tend to constellate other people's complexes. In cultures they can create a stagnating polarization of tensions. The collective anxiety complex in the US appears to be unconsciously colluding with complexed aspects of the movement referred to here as radical Jihadism. Identifying radical Jihadists, the American people, or any other group, as the "Pan element," or thinking in terms of labeling one group as being Pan-like and another as nymph-like, oversimplifies the archetypal and moves toward the stereotypical. Rather than invent yet another set of labels, the objective here is to learn what underlies the increase of anxiety and violence in the US and why this shadow material is affecting other groups.

Jung posited that suffering is required to heal a psychological split caused by rejection of the exposed truth of an event. This suffering helps revitalize rejected parts of the psyche (Jung, 1948/1960 [*CW* 8]). When shadow material locked in a cultural complex is threatened, as it was in the US with the attacks on 9/11, it may erupt, revolutionize, instigate regression, or promote compassionate dialogues, but can be understood as a compensatory move by the unconscious to restore wholeness (Jung, 1946/1978b [*CW* 10]).

September 11, 2001

> When we got to about 50 feet from the South Tower, we heard the most eerie sound that you would ever hear. A high-pitched sound and a popping noise made everyone stop. We all looked up. At th[at] point, it all let go. The way I see it, it had to be the rivets. The building let go. There was an explosion and the whole top leaned toward us and started coming down.
>
> I stood there for a second in total awe, and then said, "What the f – -?" I honestly thought it was Hollywood [Jeff Birnbaum recounts his experience].
>
> (Lucy, 2003, para. 11–12)

> You have two 110 story office buildings. You don't find a desk. You don't find a chair. You don't find a telephone, a computer. The biggest piece of a telephone I found was half of a keypad, and it was about this big: (makes a shape with his hand about 4 inches in diameter). The building collapsed to dust [Description of what New York Fire Fighter Joe Casaliggi found in the rubble at the WTC].
>
> (Cassaliggi, 2013)

Anxiety

On September 11, 2001, a multipronged, suicidal terrorist attack using airplanes filled with ordinary passengers felled the Twin Towers of the World Trade Center in New York City and crippled the Pentagon in Washington, DC, killing nearly 3,000 people. It would be difficult to find a person alive today who does not know this. Americans woke that autumn day in the general state of complacency to which they had become accustomed (Colvin, 2001; Irish, 2002), but once the disbelief wore off, that complacency rapidly morphed into fear. That fear has driven the country to adopt ever greater protective measures, such as the US Patriot Act or building a wall on the Mexican border, acts which have changed the American landscape.

There is ample evidence for a rise in anxiety disorders following 9/11. Two months later Post Traumatic Stress Disorder (PTSD) was diagnosed in 20%of New Yorkers living near the WTC (Galea, Ahern, Resnick, Kilpatrick, Bucuvalas, Gold, et al., 2002). This is considerably higher than the 3.6 percent of New Yorkers suffering from symptoms of PTSD the year before the attack (Cohen, Kasen, Chen, Gordon, Berenson, Brook, &

White, 2006). Following the attacks PTSD symptoms were diagnosed in one in ten of New York City residents (Marshall & Galea, 2004; Osborn, Johnson, & Fisher, 2006).

In general, PTSD and panic-based reactions are unfortunate byproducts of war. However the US was not at war, making the attacks psychologically as well as literally emerge, like a panic attack, "out of the blue" (APA, 2013, p. 209). The magnitude of the fall of two 110-story buildings one after the other, the surreal sight of airplanes filled with passengers used as weapons, the horror of the hundreds of falling bodies, and the reality that nothing like this had ever happened before created an extraordinary level of dread and disbelief. The strike, sudden, unexpected, and overwhelming codes the event, archetypally, in Pan's territory.

One of Pan's epithets is Pan *Phorbas*, the terrifying one. Pan was greatly feared by his enemies because of his use of surprise and confusion as fundamentals of war. C. P. Segal (1969) portrays figures like Pan in the wilderness of Arcadia as like a trap "suddenly and unexpectedly sprung" (18). The shock of such a sudden and cataclysmic explosion is reminiscent of the surprise attacks of Pan, who used noise and confusion to create disarray in his enemies. Just as the sound of the rivets at the WTC disoriented the firefighter, the sound of an approaching noisy, monstrous Pan created "madness" and led his Gallic enemies to kill their brothers on the battlefield before running in panicky disarray (Pausanias, 1935/1961, p. 503). Pan forcefully dominated his landscape and is an archetypal representation of the impulse to impose oneself upon others with his, as Farnell (1909/1971) describes them, "rustic and uncouth" (p. 431) powers. Like the US, he is a rescuer if you are his ally. If you are not, his methods of imposing his will are oppressive.

The US has historically been in control in war due to its massive power base, most famously turning the tide in World War I and II, but on 9/11 the roles were reversed. Terrorists succeeded, using Pan's method, surprise and confusion, to fell American military and economic power bases. They dramatically imposed their presence on the American psyche. Pan's battle strategy, to use cunning with force to incite "shock and awe," has historically been one of America's strengths, but not this time.

The response to the attacks was immediate and dramatic. On September 11th[h] President George W. Bush's first directive to his chiefs of staff was that "Everything is available for the pursuit of this war" (Clarke, 2004, p. 24). On the evening of September 11th Bush addressed the nation: "America was targeted for attack because we're the brightest beacon for freedom and opportunity in the world. And no one will keep that light from shining. . . . We will make no distinction between the terrorists who committed these acts and those who harbor them" (2001, paras. 4, 9). A line was clearly drawn, but against an enemy who added new dimensions to war because it has no borders, no nation, and no adherence to any known "rules of engagement." Bush was trying to define the perimeters of the enemy. He had the unfortunate task of trying to corral quicksilver; as al-Qaeda, the suspect at that point, was well adapted to splitting apart and re-forming seemingly invisibly.

These elements find an echo in the myths of Pan. Polyaenus (1994) credited Pan with introducing psychology into warfare. Pan taught the Greeks to manipulate the enemy's emotions and was "the first to put fear into the enemy by means of cunning and art" (p. 17 [1.2]). Not even "the dismal Gorgon from on high spread such terror, nor with phantoms so dire sweep an army in headlong rout" (Flaccus, 1934/1963, p. 131 [III. 57]). He is regarded as being the inventor of new tactics in warfare. New tactics, such as using airplanes as weapons, are bound to create a lasting and fearful impression. In the second century, Macedonian Polyaenus wrote his *Stratagems of War* (1994), which he dedicated to the emperors Marcus Aurelius and Verus to aid them in their own warfare. He attributed Pan with the invention of the phalanx, a formation that allows an army to more easily shift from offense to defense, and undoubtedly also first caused dread in those who faced it.

Pan was a fearless strategist and employed the unexpected in many wars (Pausanias, 1959). He made victory without the aid of his hunter's keen eyed marksmanship (Germany, 2005) or by deploying massive levels of force, but rather by undermining expectations and horrifying his opponents. In Jungian thinking, these tactics, to achieve a vision of safety for a person or a culture through the annihilation of the threat, is a psychic red flag. It alerts one to the presence of shadow and the ego's obsessive urge to get rid of it. Clearly success is desired once one is attacked. But a more permanent success and long-lived state of peace for a country are not going to be achieved using Pan's strategies. Like the Native Americans counting coup, these types of hit and run or rather bomb and run tactics encourage perpetual battle and feed hypermasculine propensities.

September 12, 2001

Apocalyptic visions

The day after the attack Bush and Secretary of Defense Donald Rumsfeld asked for an investigation into Iraq's complicity with al-Qaeda (Clarke, 2004, 30; Lifton, 2003, p. 9). All hesitations, and there were many even within the White House and Pentagon, were swept aside (Clarke, 2004; Woodward, 2004). A plan, based on fighting wars in "multiple, simultaneous major theaters" (David & Grondin, 2006, p. 39), was immediately implemented. This plan had been drawn up in 2000, *before* the attacks.

It was titled "Rebuilding America's Defenses: Strategies, Forces, and Resources for a New Century" (David & Grondin, 2006) and called for military forces to:

> defend the American homeland; fight and decisively win multiple, simultaneous major theater wars; perform the "constabulary" duties associated with shaping the security environment in critical regions; transform U.S. forces to exploit the "revolution in military affairs."
> (p. 393)

Following the attacks, martial justice was encouraged in Bush's speeches, "We have seen their kind before" (2001c) the terrorists are "barbaric . . . a new kind of evil. . . . This crusade, this war on terrorism" (2001b). It was a verbal prologue to a long, protracted war, that at this writing still continues 17 years later.

The controlled anger of the government voices encouraged war as the patriotic and righteous answer. American psychiatrist Robert Jay Lifton (2003) interpreted this plan to make the world "safe for democracy" as a messianic message and sees modernity as caught in a "worldwide epidemic of violence aimed at massive destruction in the service of various visions of purification and renewal" (p. 1). He understands an apocalyptic vision as an impulse to destroy the world as it is, with the idealistic belief that by doing so the world will be purified (pp. 4–5).

An apocalyptic vision of destruction and renewal includes the ideal of a golden era, like the bucolic Arcadia of the poets (Ovid, 1955/1986; Theocritus, 1999) or President Trumps's notion to "Make America Great Again," how things were back in the good old days, whenever that was, which is now to be restored by the believers through purification (Lifton, 2003, p. 78). It is a "response to one's enemy's pursuit of absolute purification, [and so] one seeks to purify absolutely in turn; in the name of destroying evil, each side seeks to destroy not only the other but enough of the world to achieve mystical rebirth" (p. 39). These sorts of idealistic yet selfish schemas are apparent in the beliefs Hitler sold to the German people, radical Jihadists desire to take over the Earth, President Trump's deportation of immigrants, and genocides in many regions. More noble pursuits languish when resources and energy are focused on hypermasculine goals of being the best, the strongest, or the purest people.

Aggression

Pan was brutal. In the third century BCE the poet Theocritus explained "he's one o' the tetchy sort; his nostril's ever sour wrath's abiding-place" (Edmonds, trans., 1912/1977, p. 11 [I, 16–20]). Roman poet Valerius Flaccus wrote "Sport it is to the god [Pan] when he ravishes the trembling flock from their pens, and the steers trample the thickets in their flight" (1934/1963, p. 131 [III, 46–57]). He raged against Echo and "in a desperate fury, like so many dogs and wolves, tore her all to pieces and flung about them all over the earth her yet singing limbs" (Longus, 1916/1978, p. 163 [III. 23]).

Pan's aggressiveness mirrors the pursuit of an apocalyptic vision regardless of its effect on the innocent. He was solitary and chthonic. He lived outside the civilized world in a wilderness that afforded him great expanses in which to pursue his desires unchecked. At times he focused his aggression on the nymphs. The pattern in the myths follows this recurring storyline: Pan chases a nymph, out of fear she asks for help, and is metamorphosed. She is still alive but in a different form, transformed by the interaction. In her new form she has less power of volition. She devolves. Over and over in the Pan/nymph myths, the torpor and despair of the nymphs follows explosions of Pan power.

This schema parallels American reactions to 9/11. The citizens of the US, shocked and in fear that another strike was imminent, froze and passively allowed the government to rapidly move forward with preplanned preventative aggression, regardless of the loss of freedoms for the public (Clarke, 2004). After the explosive attacks the need to feel safe overwhelmed the public. This enabled "unquestioning willingness to accept whatever the leadership said was necessary to fight terrorism" (2004, p. 1). Safety, it can be argued, replaced freedom as a pillar of American decision-making.

The American leadership set the stage to harness a Pan-like brutality, arrogant and self-serving, out of the prevailing sense of outrage in the US. The government then exploited the public's fears to achieve its own goals. Attacking Iraq was an opening for the planned overthrow of its government, with Iran and North Korea next on the list (Clarke, 2004). Bush identified these nations as the "axis of evil" (as cited in Clarke, 2004). As long as they could be defined as "the terrorists who committed these acts and those who harbor them" they were fair game in a preventative, global war to protect democracy (Bush, 2001a). Bush relied on the doctrine of American exceptionalism to justify a vision of a globalization of democracy.

Exceptionalism and inflation

Jungian analyst Murray Stein (1995) stated Jung "felt deeply that fanatical ideologies of any sort were demonic because they depended for their existence upon identification with archetypal images and upon grandiose inflations, which crippled individual accountability and destroyed moral consciousness" (p. 20). He went on to suggest that ideologies with these qualities need to be deconstructed using psychological interpretations to better understand those immersed in such systems, since this could help restore consciousness to "proper dimensions" (p. 20)

The underlying conceit that America has a divine right to do as it sees fit regardless of others is reflective of Pan's tendency to use his gifts to control others. Pan was the principal god of Arcadia (Borgeaud, 1979/1988). Like America, Arcadia is naturally isolated by its physical location. The terrain of Pan's isolated wilderness parallels the mythic landscape of America as a land of endless frontiers. The idea of a spacious land, well protected by its natural isolation and gifted with self-sustaining resources, is a central character in legends and tales that shape the national character of the United States (Guthrie, 2011; Smith, S. F., 2011). But, according to complex theory, the one sided complex that justifies constant expansion and seeing the world as endless wild frontiers will inevitably constellate a split out of which will emerge a compensatory force (Jung, 1948/1960 [*CW* 8]) – whether through the actions of other peoples or through natural forces. It would appear that time has come. The pursuit of a one-sided vision of some past/future golden age is an attempt to avoid the split. It is a flight from the realities of modernity.

Manifest Destiny and exceptionalism also parallel the inflated radical Jihadist's belief that they are destined to "seek the destruction of Western democracy and the conversion of the world to their concept of Islam" (Aaron, 2008, p. 1). Radical Jihadists vow to lead the world out of the impurities of secularism and into a new world birthed out of a revolution (as was the US) (2008). This justifies destroying the "corrupt" world through acts of terror (2008). In this, America and radical Jihadists resemble and mirror each other. Understanding this dynamic as a collision of unconscious complexes is the first step toward developing greater tolerance and then working toward better communication between the sides.

Safety

The vast expanses of America and Arcadia created a safe boundary for both for a long time. This spaciousness has become a psychological truth as well as a geographical one. In Greek myth, the contrast between a bucolic landscape and its unseen dangers served "to intensify the sense of the victim's helplessness. Where even the place of refuge and peace is invaded, there is no safety, no escape from arbitrary force. In such a world innocence is never preservable" (Segal, C. P., 1969, p. 8). When the airplanes smashed the Twin Towers the illusion of safety, already endangered by Timothy McVeigh's assault on the Oklahoma City Federal Building in 1995, the Y2K scare, and the Columbine massacre in 1999, could no longer be preserved. Bush told the country, "The world has changed because we are no longer safe" (2001c).

The search to restore the lost sense of security aided the creation of US government policies such as the US Patriot Act of 2001 (FinCEN, 2012), HIPAA standards for privacy (Health Information Privacy, 2012), and zero tolerance standards at public schools (Zero tolerance, 2012). The safety that was once a given became something hoped to be restored through policy-making.

The splits caused by a complex, Jung found, create their own reality: the behaviors have an inner coherence or wholeness to them, hold some amount of autonomy over conscious choices, and act as a disruption, creating continual fear and stress (Jung, 1948/1960 [CW 8]). The anxiety Americans felt, it will be shown, was exploited to drive policy. Fortunately, an activated complex has the potential to become conscious; in the case of a cultural complex, if it is to succeed, that process will happen in individuals one at a time (Kimbles, 2000).

September 21, 2001

Manipulation

In the reactions to 9/11, the federal government implemented a course of action to keep people focused on consuming as a way to relieve anxiety (Arndt, Solomon, Kasser, & Sheldon, 2004). Bush initiated this in an innocuous way in the first hours after the attack when he told his aides "I want the economy back, open for business right away" (Clarke, 2004, p. 24). But then, days after the attack Bush began to encourage the public to stay entertained by comments such as to "Get down to Disney World in Florida. Take your families and enjoy life the way we want it to be enjoyed" (Bush, 2001c).

The American public escaped into distraction enough to effect the statistical terrain. "Americans bought homes and cars in record quantities. They also snapped up appliances, furniture, and electronic gadgets. From October through December, consumption soared at a 6% annual rate" (Zuckerman, 2002). They worked hard at losing themselves. "People went to enormous lengths to distract themselves from the tragedy – by drinking, gambling, renting videos, watching television, and shopping" (Pyszczynski et al., 2003).

The urgings of the President and the obedient response of the American consumer seem absurd on the surface. A terrible event deserves the time to process the emotions stirred up by such an occurrence. But escape makes more sense when complex theory is applied. Pan, as the archetypal significator of such a complex, was known to denote "confusion and tumult. He also signifies that the things in which a person takes pride will not remain secure" (Artemidorus, 1975, p. 118). Perhaps, out of insecurity, Americans isolated and became benumbed through consuming. Opioid addiction, a long ignored problem, increased and continues to rise dramatically in the US, numbing users from suffering the many pains reality brings us all (National Institute on Drug Addiction, 2017). Rather than attending to the animosity and fear aimed at the US from outside its borders, segments of the American public chose to freeze into a state of indifference toward the innocent people of Iraq and Afghanistan. Others split into a Pan-like defense of the country, promoting the inflation of defenses to "shock and awe" the rest of the world.

Meanwhile, euphemisms began to spring up like weeds. While the re-languaging of the "war on terrorism" often began inside Washington's beltway, the euphemisms usually came into common usage when "embedded" in the mainstream media. The circumlocution obfuscated the brutal reality of distant battles for the American public. It reflected the "unconscious tendency to make the autonomy of the complex *unreal* by giving it a different name" (Jung, 1948/1960, p. 99 [*CW* 8, para. 206]). Being an aggressor became a "pre-emptive strike" and a "surgical strike" meant bombing city streets. Friendly fire and waterboarding speak for themselves. "Collateral damage" meant dead people. An estimated 500,000 Iraqi children's deaths were the collateral damage caused by Operation Desert Storm and the economic sanctions against Iraq (Perice, 2006, p. 121). In an interview in 1996, Leslie Stahl asked then Secretary of State Madeleine Albright:

> "We have heard that a half-million children have died. I mean, that's more children than died in Hiroshima. And you know, is the price worth it?"
>
> Secretary of State Albright: "I think it is a very hard choice, but the price – we think the price is worth it."
>
> (as cited in Perice, 2006, p. 121)

Ralph Slovenko, a psychiatrist, plays with the sanitization of initializing Weapons of Mass Destruction: "Euphemisms that mislead or deceive are known as doublespeak (or we might say, WMD – words of mass deception)" (2005, p. 533). The American public swallowed the experts' words and remained numb to the loss of innocent lives the war required. This shored up the defensive shell of the complex as it reformed out of the shattered psychic framework left behind after the fall of the Twin Towers. Americans were and are led by their leaders to consider American lives more valuable than those of other nationalities. The shell of the complex strengthens when a threat is considered imminent and the enemy is perceived to be outside of the complex.

During the days immediately following the attacks experts began to express beliefs essentially geared to keep the anxiety about personal safety alive. "Today's terrorist can strike at any place, at any time, and with virtually any weapon" (Office of Homeland Security, 2002, p. 1). This type of rhetoric filled the public imagination with fear and dread. For example, for a short period "unknown unknowns" were suddenly objects of concern (Furedi, 2007). An unknown unknown, an outcome that a planner could not conceive of while determining a course of action, became a news talk show item after Rumsfeld (2006) repeatedly made statements such as, "There are unknown unknowns – there are things we do not know we do not know" about the radical Jihadists. After the news of the attack broke on television and internet news sites, the message was established that the chance of another attack was possible; what was possible quickly became probable, and from there morphed into an inevitability (Furedi, 2007).

Once a trauma splits the unity of the psyche into a complexed state, a defense system will develop protective reactions (Kalsched, 1996). The anxiety, triggered by the iconic images of the two planes swallowed by the towers, was inflamed by the alarmist rhetoric. The mild and indirect rewording of the consequent bombing and killings blunted the gruesome reality of the distant wars. The anxious state of the country tended to recapitulate the trauma and resulted in reinforced barriers, while the euphemisms reinforced a regressive pull towards numbing distractions. The defensive shell thickened, and the core decompensated even further.

October 26, 2001

Scapegoating

On October 26, 2001, the US Congress voted to authorize the US Patriot Act, which was designed to make intelligence gathering within the US easier, create more control over international finances, and broaden the discretion of law enforcement and immigration officials to detain and deport suspected terrorists indefinitely (FinCEN, 2012). One consequence of the Patriot Act has been widespread abuse of suspected terrorists in the US.

> Jonathan Turley, a professor of national security and constitutional law at George Washington University . . . an expert in prison law, said . . . that the use of the dogs to frighten detainees in the New Jersey jail underscored "the trickle-down effect" of the disregard for immigrants' civil rights that top government officials showed after 9/11. "It trickled down through military intelligence, through low-level personnel and to sheriffs," he said. "Suddenly people who were predisposed to the use of such harsh measures thought they had license to use them, and 9/11 gave them a great appetite."
>
> (Bernstein, 2006, paras. 6–7)

The rhetoric engendered by the government and repeated in the media combined with the fearful state of many Americans and produced projections of evil onto Arab-Americans and Muslims. Like Pan's presence causing the "sudden confusion and consternation of a crowd" (Plutarch, 1936/2003a, p. 37 [356, D]), the country was infected by a mob mentality. In this state it is much easier to be led into believing things one would not otherwise accept as truc. Jung spoke about this in his writing on *participation mystique*:

> Practical experience shows us again and again that any prolonged preoccupation with an unknown object acts as an almost irresistible bait for the unconscious to project itself into the unknown nature of the object and to accept the resultant perception, and the interpretation deduced from it, as objective.
>
> (1948/1967b, p. 204 [*CW* 13, para. 252])

Recent studies of the brain have confirmed Jung's thinking. The mirror neuron system "is behind both *understanding* and *mimicking*. . . . While the understanding process usually involves the attenuation of original emotions, the mimicking process often leads to escalation and mob psychology" (Khalil, 2011, p. 86).

Such a psychology soon curdled into a climate of hate in the US. "Something about the current state of America has been causing far more disturbed people than before to act out their illness by threatening, or actually engaging in, political violence" (Krugman, 2011, p. A19). Arab-Americans were targeted as scapegoats. With no evidence of any connection to terrorism, hundreds of Muslim, Arab, and South Asian men were rounded up on the basis of racial and religious profiling and subjected to unlawful detention and abuse. Scapegoating resulted in "widespread labeling of opponents of the war, or even those insufficiently enthusiastic about it, as 'unpatriotic,' 'un-American,' 'traitors,' or if they were in foreign countries 'anti-American' and 'enemies of America' " (Lifton, 2003, p. xi). Scapegoating also led to the suspension of rights and torturing of imprisoned, suspected terrorists at, among others, Guantanamo Bay Naval Base and Abu Ghraib prison (Kugler & Cooper, 2010), and to racial profiling of Muslims (Shahshahani, 2011; Swiney, 2006).

> Among other documented abuses, many of the men had their faces smashed into a wall where guards had pinned a t-shirt with a picture of an American flag and the words, "These colors don't run." The men were pushed against the t-shirt upon their entrance to MDC and told "welcome to America." The t-shirt was smeared with blood, yet it stayed up on the wall at MDC for months.
>
> (ccrjustice.org 2009, paras. 1–4)

This occurred in the state of New York.

Kimbles stated that when fear becomes the primary affect that organizes a culture's reactions to an event, it can lead to scapegoating (2003, p. 227). A chilling reminder of how deep the resentment toward the Muslim community runs is reflected in the efforts in 2010 to stop a building committee in New York City from approving a Muslim community center, Park51, dubbed the Ground Zero Mosque by its opponents, because it is situated two blocks from the WTC. Leading up to the vote public exchanges reached a fever pitch when Mark Williams, a leader in the neoconservative Tea Party movement, declared, "The monument would consist of a Mosque for the worship of the terrorist's monkey-god." Williams, once a frequent guest on CNN, wrote this on his website (Hutchinson, 2010). "But Mr Williams was not the only critic. Many families of Sept. 11 victims fervently opposed the proposal, saying they were offended by the idea of building a prayer space so near the site" (Hernandez, 2010).

Beginning in 1980, the American-Arab Anti-Discrimination Committee (ADC) had organized to defend the rights of Arab peoples in the US. The ADC targeted the stereotypical portrayal of Arabs in film and on TV. "Hollywood has had a consistent record of Arab stereotyping and bashing. Some in the Arab-American community call this the three B syndrome: Arabs in TV and movies are portrayed as either bombers, belly dancers, or billionaires" (Qumsiyeh, 2013, para. 1). From *The Sheik* (Melford, 1921) to *Arabesque* (Donen & Holt, 1966) to *Rules of Engagement* (Rudin, Schmidt, Schroeder, Webb, & Zanuck, 2000) people of Arab descent have been consistently stereotyped in American made films.

Stereotyping is an oversimplified and formulaic opinion that is an accumulation of one's own unwanted attributes, which are then projected onto others (Colman, 1995). The stereotyping of people of Arab descent in the US began in tandem with the creation of the "Middle East" (a Eurocentric name) after World War I and the defeat of the Ottoman Empire. The region was partitioned in 1948 into British and French Mandates and the country of Israel was established. Some of the motivation was for the dominant western cultures to retain control of crude oil found in the region. Control of oil continues to dominate the politics of the region and the world today. The beginning of the downslide of American economic power, and economic power is to a great extent, true power, can be traced to the Oil Embargo of 1973 when the Arab nations at last wrested away from the colonial powers nearly complete economic control of the price of oil. Much resentment for the colonial behaviors of Great Britain, France, and the United States have built up and been voiced by both moderate and radical Arab groups. Decades of distrust and discrimination have, at least in part, led to terrorist activity by radical Jihadist groups. "Humiliation can in itself cause increased levels of commitment and recruitment to 'the cause' " (von Hippel, 2002).

Kimbles (2003) discussed dynamics that are represented when a culture is unconsciously influenced by a group complex. "The constellation of repressed aspects of group identity and the projection onto some group of reviled 'others' of disowned aspects of the groups identity. Both of these dynamics are operative whenever collective shadow processes shape cultural history" (p. 219).

Squilling

In ancient Greece scapegoat rituals were performed in times of great need, such as famine or drought, as well as during annual festivals (Bremmer, 2000). In these rituals the death of one or two people as scapegoat was thought to be able to save the community. For instance in Plutarch's time *boulimos*, or famine, represented by a slave, was chased out of a city with rods of agnus castus, a willow like plant (p. 274). The scapegoated person, chosen by an oracle, was often a criminal or a slave (Bremmer, 2000). Originally the scapegoat was both a poison and a *pharmakon* or healing agent (Perera, 1986, p. 8; Dioscorides, 1934/1959). Occasionally a god was sacrificed and Pan performed this duty for his cult (Edmonds, 1912/1977).

Pan's rite of *squilling* is a scapegoat/*pharmakon* ritual and introduced an element, which, if it were to be made conscious, could be helpful. Essentially, by taking on the pain and anguish of his cult, Pan relieved the cult members of stress. The cult's anxieties were projected onto Pan, and so contained in the ritual. The anxieties were transformed through the sacrifice of Pan's aggression.

In other words, a psychological complex can be transformed when the projected aggression, desire, and anxieties are made more conscious through containment by the dominant power, which in this case, was Pan. Squilling's purpose was to restore a balance of order in the cult and promote confidence in the hunters in order to ensure survival. By consciously embodying the suffering of the cult, Pan symbolized the ability of the members to find inspiration and the persistence to carry their own suffering.

But in the US, those caught up in the cultural complex felt compelled to project the cause of their problems, through stereotyping and scapegoating, onto others. The government, as the dominant power in the country in matters of international affairs, failed in any way to inspire the country to consciously carry the suffering caused by the terrible losses on 9/11. Instead the government treated the public more like children.

The fear and panic-driven choices are reflective of Pan's myths. It is difficult to ignore the irony in Bush reading *The Pet Goat* (Engelmann & Bruner, 1995) (which he was inadvertently holding upside down) to kindergartners when the first plane bombed into the first tower.

Pan is an amplification of the paradox of a scapegoat/*pharmakon*, both a monster and a god. Pan as scapegoat embodies the Jungian notion that:

> the living experience of the Self is an aberration, a joining of opposites that appalls the ego and exposes it to anguish, demoralization and violation of all "reasonable" considerations. And yet the same event viewed from above is a coronation, demonstrating once again the reciprocal and compensatory relation between the ego and the unconscious.
> (Edinger, 1987, p. 137)

Today stereotyped and scapegoated immigrants are not seen as healing agents, but as a monstrous apparition that the culture needs to exterminate (Colman, 1995). By allowing more time and space in the culture for reflection on the psychological aspects of modernity, this could change. Pan not only embodied the poison or the monstrous, or in psychological terms, a complex, in which the enterprising spirit of the US finds itself becalmed, but also suggests a possible direction for remedy and renewal.

November 21, 2001

Speaking at a Thanksgiving dinner for troops and their families at Fort Campbell, Kentucky, President Bush stated:

> Afghanistan is just the beginning on the war against terror. . . . There are other terrorists who threaten America and our friends, and there are other nations willing to sponsor them. We will not be secure as a nation until all of these threats are defeated. Across the world, and across the years, we will fight these evil ones, and we will win.
>
> (Bumiller, 2001, para. 2)

Since a principal objective of terrorism is to destroy, this can be achieved more easily psychologically by instilling fear in the imagination of one's enemies and destroying their peace of mind. Thus terrorists have, to an extent, succeeded in seizing power and control because through the media reported goading and threats and with only occasional and unpredictable strikes, terrorism succeeds in making its enemies feel unsafe wherever they are (Glick et al., 2006, p. 364). Once the imagination of the country absorbed that a suicide bomber is more invincible than a tower, an era of uneasiness began (Clarke & Newman, 2006, p. 56).

January 29, 2002

In his State of the Union address, President Bush first used the term "axis of evil" to describe Iraq, Iran, and North Korea (*The Washington Post*, 2002).

> States like these [Iraq, Iran, and North Korea], and their terrorist allies, constitute an axis of evil, arming to threaten the peace of the world. By seeking weapons of mass destruction, these regimes pose a grave and growing danger. They could provide these arms to terrorists, giving them the means to match their hatred. They could attack our allies or attempt to blackmail the United States. In any of these cases, the price of indifference would be catastrophic.
>
> (para. 36)

In the months following 9/11, perceptions in America rapidly compounded to try to relieve the anxiety created by the "monstrous" (Venn, 2002, p. 121) acts by countering them with an overwhelming show of strength and willingness to do violence (p. 124). Bush sought to legitimize the political ideology, known as the Bush Doctrine, that the US has a duty to keep the world free for democracy. American exceptionalism began to be used as justification to, in effect, attempt to create an American empire by spreading democracy (David & Grondin, 2006).

> The Bush administration defends its pursuit of this unlikely goal by means of internationally illegal, unilateralist, and preemptive attacks on other countries, accompanied by arbitrary imprisonments and the practice of torture, and by making the claim that the United States possesses an exceptional status among nations that confers upon it special international responsibilities, and exceptional privileges in meeting those responsibilities.
>
> (Pfaff, 2007)

The Bush Doctrine is a political structure that relies on a continual repetition of belief in American's exceptionalism and the greatness of America, which reinforces the structure of the complex.

March 20, 2003

Projection

Bush advocated for war in Iraq as well as Afghanistan by attempting to justify pre-emptive self-defense as grounds for war in the modern era (World Press Review, 2012, paras. 7–8). He took this argument to the United Nations. When UN General Secretary Kofi Annan was asked if the invasion was legal he stated, "I have indicated it was not in conformity with the UN charter from our point of view, from the charter point of view, it was illegal" (BBC News, 2004, para. 9). Bush charged ahead undeterred.

On March 20, 2003 the US Government led an attack on Iraq using the:

> ad slogan – "shock and awe" – with "fear" as the target emotion, betting that character assassination of those who disagreed with the war and the firepower would spread the right messages at home and abroad. . . . In fear-based decision making, alliances, standards of conduct, and, indeed, common sense go out the window. Whether the opponent is a congressional candidate or an international terrorist, the idea is shoot him before he shoots you.
>
> (Richey & Feldmann, 2003)

This attitude is a mirror image of al Qaeda leader Osama bin Laden's equally inflated attitude. Bin Laden mocked the US in a videotaped message in 2004, it is "easy for us to provoke and bait. . . . All that we have to do is to send two mujahidin . . . to raise a piece of cloth on which is written al Qaeda in order to make the generals race there to cause America to suffer human, economic, and political losses" (as cited in Mueller, 2005).

Bush taunted the enemy, "Bring them on" (as cited in Moore, 2002). "We will make no distinction between the terrorists who committed these acts and those who harbor them" (2001a, para. 9). "I don't care what the international lawyers say, we are going to kick some ass" (as cited in Clarke, 2004, p. 24). Others in the government promoted fear mongering. "It's only a matter of time before they bomb US cities" (Rumsfeld as cited in Moore, 2002). The government used the anxiety in the country in the same way the radical Jihadists used it. Both sides express beliefs to keep the anxiety alive and for both the control of the narrative is a component of the warfare.

One "shocks and awes" while the other "provokes and baits." Apparently the two sides are blind to their similarities. As Jung said, one *meets* one's projections (1951/1959f). "Projections change the world into a replica of one's own unknown face" (p. 9 [*CW* 9, II para. 17]). Projection is driving both sides of the conflicts, while blinding both to their similarities. But "arrogance and stupidity are self-defeating, eventually" (Richey & Feldmann, 2003). America's self-image as protector of the weak has blinded many to the projection of shadow onto other cultures. But the manipulation by both sides in the aftermath of 9/11 aptly fits Henderson's (1984) description of the workings of the cultural unconscious as a place of "mutual projection of unconscious factors" (p. 11).

America's projections onto other peoples and its naïve beliefs about itself are both ripe for analysis. What better time for this work than when the shell has been shattered open as it has been by the continuing attacks on Western nations?

One reason the fall of the buildings at the World Trade Center is iconic is because it symbolizes the postmodern explosion of mythic underpinnings of American beliefs about itself as exceptional (Hodgson, 2009). Its fall has been followed by a consequent depressed paralysis of ideas, which has had the unfortunate consequence of freezing commerce and the progress of government and has not as of yet succeeded in creating stability (Lewis, 2012). Stagnation, recession, and anxiety have increased since 9/11 (Cohen et al., 2006). Economic productivity and growth were adversely affected. A Congressional report from 2002 reported, "Over the longer run 9/11 will adversely affect U.S. productivity growth because resources are being and will be used to ensure the security of production, distribution, finance, and communication" (Makinen, 2002, para. 3).

The strong feelings on both sides of the struggle between radical Islamists and Western cultures are not only birthed out of the anger at past grievances and the fear of annihilation, they are also birthed out of mistaken beliefs in superiority on both sides. The inability to listen to each other and see the complex nature of both sides identities are central to the problem as well as being central to the nature of a complex.

Chapter 9

American apathy toward sexual violence

Rape in the military

The Department of Defense (DoD) estimates that one in three women in the US military have been sexually assaulted by their fellow servicemen (Risen, 2012, para. 7), and the numbers of sexual assaults and rapes are rising (Steinhauer, 2013, p. A1). An overly inflated attitude in the psyche of the American soldier, "The Few, The Proud . . . The Marines" (usmilitary.about.com) shapes an ethos that allows sexual assault to go nearly unnoticed. It is considered here as evidence of an anxiety-based cultural complex in America that is in many ways still completely invisible to much of the public. A symptomatic ethos that has given rise to leniency for rape and sexual assault in the military has been shaped by three attitudes. These are the unquestioned assumption of integrity in the US military leaders' chain of command, an unquestioned belief that justice is best served by the traditional approaches the military uses (usmilitary.about.com), and the lack of concern in the general public about justice for the victims (Dick, 2012).

A closed system like the military provides a prime, target rich environment for sexual predation (Dick, 2012). In the Pentagon's 2012 annual report, 6.1% of the military's women and men came forward in a confidential survey and detailed their experience of sexual assault. In contrast only 0.2% of civilian Americans reported sexual assault in the same year (Steinhauer, 2013, pp. A1, A14). Of course, the #MeToo movement, chronicling the amount of sexual abuse and rape in the general public, has demonstrated how minute the number of reported assaults is in comparison to the number of those that go unreported. The Pentagon's annual report stated "In FY12, there were 3,374 reports of sexual assault involving Service members" (p. 3), which raises the estimated number of annual assaults to 26,000. The discrepancy between estimated number of assaults and the reported numbers exists because it is accepted (even by the DoD) that victims do not speak up for fear of the damage to their reputation, rank, and even survival in the military (Dick, 2012).

Sexual assault and rape are not interchangeable legal terms, as a sexual assault does not necessarily include forcible penetration. However, the effect on the victim is similar in that both stigmatize and are often precursors for serious mental disorders such as Major Depression or Post Traumatic Stress Disorder (APA, 2013).

"Donald Trump stood by his past comment that military sexual assaults should be expected 'when they put men and women together' in the US armed forces" (Diaz, Sept. 8, 2016). No significant effort to improve the situation for the victims has been initiated during his presidency as of this writing. In the recent past, President Barack Obama and Secretary of Defense Chuck Hagel were the two men with the influence to raise public awareness about the widespread sexual assault and rape in the military. Both made speeches in response to the scandals. They voiced their opposition to the assaults but consistently rejected proposals to consider a fundamental policy change for the investigations and trials of accused soldiers (Stan, 2013).

Obama and Hagel were protective of the traditional role of the chain of command as the mediating force within the military (Stan, 2013). On May 7, 2013, Obama spoke strongly about the problem. He said offenders "should be prosecuted, stripped of their positions, court martialed, fired, dishonorably discharged. Period" (Parrish, 2013, para. 10). Paradoxically, the courts subsequently found these comments exerted "apparent unlawful command influence" (Slavin, 2013, para. 4). Military defense attorneys have successfully argued for dismissals in a number of subsequent rape trials, stating that the words of the commander in chief "could be seen as instructions to judges and influence sentencing in military courts" (Hartwell, 2013). Even though Obama attempted to increase protection for the victims, his efforts were used to protect the accused.

American reactions have been apathetic (Steinhauer, 2013) toward what has been described as epidemic levels of rape (Cox, 2013; Dick, 2012). When compared to the dramatic public reactions to the Columbine massacre and the 9/11 terrorist attacks it feels essential to wonder why, rather than a moral panic is the response more a moral torpor? The expression "moral panic" is sometimes used to conceptualize a reaction that is disproportionate to the social problem itself (Rohloff, 2011). This usage has been criticized for being a value judgment and so not provable or disprovable (2011). The term moral panic is used here in the manner described by sociologist Amanda Rohloff (2011) to describe "a heightened sense of concern and a change in the expression of moralizing discourse at a time of perceived crisis" (p. 635). Why is there not a moral panic or at least widespread awareness about epidemic levels of rape and abuse?

Many of the reported sexual assaults took place on US soil and not while the soldiers were in the heat of battle. Not that that would justify the behavior but it would at least make it, on a personal level, more understandable. When a soldier's blood is up after combat some individuals have problems with control. This would imply a few deviant men are the problem, rather than a culture within the military where the pathological behaviors of rape are tacitly accepted.

The problem appears to be rooted in a less obvious source than battle lust. Yet comments such as Republican Senator Saxby Chambliss's remarks to the Senate Armed Services Committee indicate how willing some in power are to condone the behaviors: " 'The young folks that are coming into each of your services are anywhere from 17 to 22, or 23,' the Georgia Republican said. 'Gee whiz, the level – the hormone level created by nature sets in place the possibility for these types of things to occur' " (FoxNews.com, 2013, para. 2). Scandals have erupted at West Point, the prestigious Marine Barracks in Washington DC that forms the Presidential White House guard, the Navy's annual Tail Hook conference, Air Force boot camps, the Aberdeen Proving Ground, and far too many other national bases to name here (Dick, 2012).

Democratic US Representative Jackie Speier of California stated, "If you serve in the US military and you rape or sexually assault a fellow service member, chances are you won't be punished. In fact, you have an estimated 86.5% chance of keeping your crime a secret and a 92% chance of avoiding a court-martial" (2012, para. 1). Out of over 3000 cases that were tried in 2010 only 175 convicted soldiers did any jail time at all (Dick, 2012). The problem within the military does not appear to be indifference, but rather an intensely over protective care of the accused and "it is in the *intensity of affective response* to any given image or situation that we find what is archetypal" (Samuels, 2004, p. xiv).

Besides the passion behind the military's insistence on judging their own alongside the high degree of indifference in the general public can be read as a signal of the intensity of feelings to protect the military as an entity. Though few may share Senator Chambliss's indulgence of individuals who sexually assault, the voices of the few who have spoken out about the selfish underbelly in the disposition of the military are buried beneath the din of other contemporary anxieties. The indifference and indulgence suggest there is unconscious over identification with the military as a source of protection.

The principal characteristic that links the problem to Pan is that the military is one of the last outposts for the prerogatives of dominant males in the US. It is a place where hypermasculine values have been indulged because it was, traditionally, a "male only" society. The rape of US soldiers by US soldiers has been interpreted as a response to the fear of admission of women into the world of soldiering and especially onto the fields of combat (Cox, 2013). This is a role male soldiers in the US have traditionally held (Watson, 2013). Rape, as an expression of dominance, implies an unconscious over identification with the Pan-like elements in the warrior archetype.

The archetype of Pan versus the hero

Cultural complex theory is one way to attempt to make sense of the motivation behind these behaviors. As an expression of a culture's shadow, a cultural complex "consists of unquestioned presumptions, [and] underlying beliefs held to be true by most of the members of the group, certainly by the group's power elite" (Meador, 2004, p. 172).

Proposing Pan, "the rustic and uncouth god of Arcadia" (Farnell, 1909/1971, p. 431), as the archetypal pattern at the core of such a complex in the US is supported by Pan's earliest identifications (Burkert, 1977/1985, p. 172). Pan expressed an instinct for self-preservation; he was the goat-god of fertility, and also a warrior and sexual predator. In the myths, he employed surprise attacks against both his enemies and the nymphs. In many instances he formed alliances with gods and men against outside aggressors (Herodotus, 1921/1960). During periods of unrest in ancient Greece such as the great battle of Marathon, Pan emerged as an avenging protector and persecutor in defense of the collective Athenian spirit (1992).

But Pan is also a mediator between the divine and the monstrous. He exemplified the Greek propensity to contextualize both good and evil in the gods (Hamilton, 1969). Pan can be thought of as a centrifugal force between these two paradoxical threads in human nature. In a way, he is a more complicated figure than the pure-hearted perfection of the hero. The "hero" denotes courage and nobility of purpose ("hero," 2013, OED). Pan is more ambiguous. He is a warrior, hunter, protector of his cult, and sexual predator. In these ways, he more closely resembles modern soldiers than does the hero archetype.

The best and the worst in the tradition of soldiering is amplified in the Greek god Pan. From Oliver Cromwell to George Washington, the soldier with a purpose greater than himself sees his occupation as that of one who must use force to protect his community. This was true for Pan as well. When Pan went to battle it was to aid his fellow leaders (Zeus, Dionysus, etc.) in a greater cause (Kerenyi, 1998; Pausanias, 1959, [xxviii]). He also hunted down nymphs to satisfy his own lustings (Longus, 1916/1978, [III]; Ovid, 1955/1986 [I]; Propertius, 1912 [I. XVIII]). These baser drives are signified by the animal half of his body. Pan is linked to the divine side of the chthonic as well and symbolizes a split in humankind between the divine and the beastly. He also amplifies the possibility that that split can be conjoined.

The victims' stories

Just as the nymph Echo was left in pieces after Pan's angry pursuit, the assaulted victims are reduced to the powerless and isolated position of one with no voice. Echo is doomed to only repeat what others say. "Thus spurned, she [Echo] lurks in the woods, hides her shamed face among the foliage and lives from that time on in lonely caves" (Ovid, 1916/1977, p. 153 [III, 393–395]). Echo personified repetition, cursed by Hera to only repeat what others had said for colluding with Zeus while he "played" with the nymphs (Ovid, 1955/1986, p. 83 [III. 350I *ff*]). Repetition is a curse for the victims as well, as they are left saddled with recurring flashbacks and intrusive memories of their violation. As Jung pointed out, traumas such as these, in and of themselves, are what birth complexes (1948/1960 [*CW* 8]).

The unaddressed conflicting tendencies between the idealism in the mission of the military and the pressure to release aggression in soldiers has led to the command's choice to overlook times when a soldier's baser instincts override more idealistic ones. This tendency naturally births projections to explain the causes as defenses, ("she was drunk and asking for it"), in attempts to protect against further internal conflict. In a cultural complex internal, personal complexes of the soldiers are protected from consequences by prevailing attitudes in the culture. An internal problem has been externalized. In a triggered cultural complex the egocentric tendency of a group is to think it is right because everyone around them agrees with them. This encourages a group to split from its own rejected propensities, and instead of self-reflection and the possibility of redemption, the victim is blamed for the aggression (Singer, 2004).

Even as Echo was fated to live on in a broken state, the victims of rape in the military are left isolated and exposed. At present, not only are approximately 6% of the total numbers of the military subjected to the frenzy of sexual assault, they are also faced with the anxiety of cursory investigations after they report the assault. Subsequent attacks on their credibility are well documented (FoxNews.com, 2013, June 4). A pervasive culture of harassment and danger for the victims has resulted. After the Columbine massacre and the 9/11 terrorist attacks the innocent victims played a role in the search to find meaning in the tragedy. Heroes were found among the fallen. But in this case, rather than shoring up the broken spirits of those who were harmed, the military command and its overseers in the government turn against the victims. The men and women who report sexual assaults by a fellow serviceman are often denied a fair trial, charged with adultery, diagnosed with personality disorders, or discharged from service (Dick, 2012). Their fates have not become a "cause" upon which the general public has focused.

"Today, a female soldier in . . . Afghanistan is more likely to be raped by a fellow soldier than killed by enemy fire" (Futures Without Violence, 2012). Military men and women who are victims of rape have less recourse to justice than the general public because their report of the crime must be given to their superior in the chain of command. This does not operate like the American judicial system. The military gives commanders absolute power in the court martial system. They appoint the defense, the prosecution, and the investigating police force even though most commanders do not have training in this type of work (Dick, 2012). If the victim's claim is found to be unworthy (which most are) they are charged with adultery (if they *or the accused* is married), and suffer a loss of rank (2012). 60% of the men and women who reported abuses were subsequently prosecuted for adultery or for other accusations related to their reporting (FoxNews, 2013).

If a commander is not responsive to a report the only recourse for the victim is to go to the DoD Inspector General. Of 2500 cases that were submitted to the Inspector General in 2010 not one was reviewed and investigated. The DoD cited "other priorities" (Dick, 2012). Even when convicted, at present one in three rapists remain in the military (Steinhauer, 2013, para. 6).

The stories give a face to the complex. In 2006, Marine Lt. Elle Helmer reported to her commander that an officer who was her superior had assaulted and raped her the night before. Her commanding officer told her not to bother with a rape kit but she did anyway (Martin, 2012). Then her rape kit, the nurse examiners report, and pictures of the bruising on her body were lost so her case was closed. She searched on her own and found the rape kit and other evidence at NCIS (Naval Criminal Investigation Service) headquarters but her supervisor refused to reopen the case (Dick, 2012). She was told:

> "You're from Colorado – you're tough. You need to pick yourself up and dust yourself off. . . . I can't babysit you all of the time." Instead of Helmer's attacker being prosecuted, she became the subject of investigation and prosecution. She was ultimately forced to leave the Marine Corps. Her rapist remains a Marine in good standing.
>
> (Martin, 2012)

Attorneys Richard Stevens and Frank Spinner, who defend Marines accused of rape in court martials, suggested that the problem of rape in the military stems from women using what they called the "Rape Card" (Lee, 2012, para. 6). When asked what might motivate a woman to risk her own career in such a way Stevens and Spinner proposed:

> Guilt and confusion after a night of drinking. Avoiding a boyfriend or husband's reaction to unfaithfulness. Shielding oneself from the consequences of one's own misconduct. Protecting one's reputation from the "promiscuous" label. Anger over a sexual encounter not blossoming into a long term relationship as expected.
>
> (Lee, 2012, para. 9)

As predicted by Kimbles, in a cultural complex (2003, p. 219) disowned parts of the soldiers' identities appear to have been cast off onto the victims. This languaging may blunt reactivity in like-minded thinkers, but rather than protecting society the re-imagining of the victim as aggressor protects and serves those in power. Even as racial profiling of Muslims increased after 9/11 (Shahshahani, 2011; Swiney, 2006) the profiling of female victims of rape as the aggressors supports the hypothesis of hypermasculinity in the protector/persecutors and a loss of identity for the naïve victims.

The pattern of blaming the victim has extended to psychiatric diagnosing of disorders that are considered to deem a person unfit for military service. Numerous cases of psychiatric diagnoses applied to victims are documented. Here is Brian Lewis's story. Lewis testified before the US Senate that a superior officer had raped him in 2000. When he told his commander he was ordered not to report the rape. "I was misdiagnosed as having a personality disorder" and discharged (Levs & Fantz, 2013, para. 31). The lack of protection for and blaming of the victims leaves them isolated, fearful, and in reactive states.

A pervasive pattern of predatory behavior and cover up within a patriarchal, old boy's school system have led idealistic recruits who signed up for service following 9/11 to make statements such as BriGette McCoy's, a former Army specialist: "I no longer have any faith or hope that the military chain of command will consistently prosecute, convict, sentence and carry out the sentencing of sexual predators in uniform" (Thistlethwaite, 2013, para. 14). Ms Havialla stated, "'I chose not to do a report of any kind because I had no faith in my chain of command. . . . When she sought help from an Army chaplain, she said, he told her 'the rape was God's will' and urged her to go to church" (Steinhauer, 2013, para. 4).

The threat to personal reputation by those in command has had the unfortunate consequence of immobilizing change. It is much like the school administration's choice at Columbine to underestimate the bully culture (Cullen, 2009; Larkin, 2007). Protector can become persecutor when power is unchecked and put to selfish purpose. Rape is a consequence of the tendency in human nature to take what it wants, especially if it is easy to get and the facts speak to the lack of heroic qualities in the perpetrators and the military chain of command established to contain them. Meanwhile, the country's silence in effect condones the entire affair. The military, as a last bastion of uninhibited hypermasculine expression, demonstrates how the credo of American exceptionalism still permeates the culture.

Not only are the soldier/rapists falling short of a heroic nobility of purpose, their superiors in the chain of command, including their commanders, are complicit in lacking the courage to protect the more vulnerable men and women under their command. For career officers, rape is understood to be a failure to command and to enforce effective discipline. Exposure could hurt an officer's career (Dick, 2012). Often they are friends with the alleged rapists as well. They appear to be frozen in an impassive attitude and protect themselves and their close friends by using the machismo defense of suggesting that anyone who is violated lacks "the right stuff" (Wolfe, 1979) and gets what they deserve.

Supervising officers, senior officers, chaplains, military police, military psychiatrists, and even the Secretary of Defense are, with the soldier/rapists culpable in creating an atmosphere ripe for a rape culture. As Jung said in his concern about the situation in Nazi Germany: "The uprush of mass instincts was symptomatic of a compensatory move of the unconscious. Such a move was possible because the conscious state of the people had become estranged from the natural laws of human existence" (1946/1978b, p. 222 [*CW* 10, para. 453]). The motivations and compulsions in those in the chain of command in the military converge in an unconscious psychic whirlpool.

The high and rising rates of rape in the military signal a pervasive pattern of projection of anxiety and aggression onto the vulnerable in the US. The solution thus far has been to ignore the problem and the rhetoric for "change" has circumvented punishing the perpetrators. The problem is not only that the assaults are the isolated personal misbehaviors of a few atypical soldiers who lack a consistent understanding of common principles of right and wrong. Scapegoating a few high profile offenders would doubtless do no more to stop military rape than executing Timothy McVeigh after the Oklahoma City bombing did to stem domestic terrorism. A systemic problem where unprotected victims are preyed on with virtual impunity indicates a disordered state in the culture: a cultural complex. The cultural complex itself then blocks solutions by channeling consciousness to be selective in its observations of experience. It also tends to focus awareness on what confirms the complexed point of view (Singer & Kimbles, 2004, p. 6).

Legislation introduced to Congress seeks a solution that falls short of limiting the chain of command in their role as prosecutors (O'Keefe, 2013). It specifies, among other reforms, that convicted rapists will be discharged from the service. To scapegoat a few high profile perpetrators suggests that the anxiety of maintaining the defensive shell of the complex unconsciously compels those in power to make a sacrifice in order to retain control. They forfeit what is necessary to keep the systemic nature of the problem hidden. This is why nothing seems to change. A complex remains immune to change and autonomous, as long as it is unconscious.

Containment

Rather than protecting the people, the military and its Congressional overseers are protecting their own unquestioned presumptions. The chain of command fails to contain the soldier/rapists. Instead, the command structure forms a persecutory element within the massive wall of military defense that is intended to protect its people. The intensity of the affective response by the military and the intensity of the moral torpor in the general public point to an underlying complex that is holding the culture in stays and preventing meaningful reforms from taking hold.

In myth, Pan's desire exploded into chase. The autoerotic aspect of Pan's desire leaves the healing nature of a nymph blowing in the wind. The autoerotic side of the patriarchal old boys club within the chain of command in the military exposes a hypermasculine aggression in America. Pan's myths show how this pattern of desire, fear, panic and subsequent torpor continues to percolate in the military and in American reactions to it. This repetitive pattern continually shapes itself in the structure of a cultural complex as defined by Singer and Kimbles (2004).

Though not all the rapes in the military are perpetrated on women, rape itself is a hypermasculine declaration of domination. The raped female soldiers in the US Military are required to speak up for themselves to the officer above them in the chain of command. These officers are mostly male (Speier, 2012). Echoes of Pan's archetypal pattern of desire, anxiety, explosion, and then torpor, that are woven together imaginatively in myth, revolve at the heart of the problems in the military because the military is part of the protective defense of the country. The data bears out that it is not a few atypical soldiers that are the problem, it is the lack of imagination about solutions to contain ambition and aggression in each person, both one at a time and as a group, that threatens the future of the US.

As Jung said, the gods have returned as psychological symptoms (1957/1967a, p. 37 [*CW* 13, para. 34]) and those symptoms are trying to make audible the cries for new understandings of justice. Since the symptoms are heard by some, there is reason to hope the US is capable of responding to its complexes at a systemic level and develop into a less naïve and less aggressive culture.

Chapter 10

Panic stalks America

A hypermasculine archetypal field tends to ignore the needs of the disenfranchised as much as possible. The lack of sensitivity in a culture with an unconscious resonance with this archetype can then cause conflicts with other cultures that mirror that insensitivity. This archetype is currently manifesting in ongoing clashes of cultural complexes spinning each other further and further out of control. We look to rational solutions or *mana* personalities for how to rein in this danger, but perhaps the way out of this is not by using the same sort of thinking that created the problem. Perhaps the compensatory archetype for the hypermasculine dances rather than fights, nurtures rather than wounds, and naturally induces the development of kindness, beauty, and harmony in the human psyche and thus in life. If we look to the immense suffering in the world today and then back to the myths, can we understand these events in terms of re-enactments of mythic patterns? Is there a link that inspires greater security by introducing the balance and harmony expressed in these myths to the modern world? I see the approach the nymphs used toward the Greek god Pan's hypermasculine traits as able to acquaint us with a possible trail to a cultural metamorphosis. Pan's mythic aggression and brutality still exists, present in modernity's agendas though not recognized as such, but where is the archetype of the nymph?

To reiterate, by hypermasculine I mean a propensity to be callous toward the needs of the disenfranchised, routinely emphasizing strength and physical prowess over intelligence or compassion, and addicted to dangerous behaviors for stimulation, such as extreme sports and wars. Hypermasculinity begets social norms that actually support warfare. It thrives in a power system in which men and masculine values control society (Klein, 2012). One way to think about culture from antiquity through modernity is that civilization has been formed out of ongoing colliding, hypermasculine groups. For instance, once Russia subsided as a threat, radical Jihadism and homegrown terrorism emerged from the vacuum, because hypermasculinity seeks high levels of competition.

I see a hypermasculine inflation of the protector/provider archetype as having become triggered in the US around the turn of the millennium. I think this signals the patriarchy needs greater defense, and so suggests a weakening of the patriarchy's hold over civilized behavior. Though the anxious need to defend itself more and more may only be a defense of current patriarchies and not the system itself, since the main adversary, radical Islamists, are even more patriarchal than western governments.

The Greek god Pan holds an archetypal image that reflects this aspect of the psyche. He is remembered for his insensitivity, violence, attempted rapes, and selfish, self-absorbed behaviors. These are all elements of the habitual nature of Pan as relayed to us through the myths and legends of the early Greeks and Romans (Borgeaud, 1979/1988). When unattended, Pan hunted down the nymphs – he would find one alone in the woods and chase her down. But Pan was an ineffective rapist, in myth he never actually consummated a single rape, the climax of the stories are really about the nymphs' metamorphoses. The nymphs always got away by devolving- – they were transformed into beings who either could not move or could not verbally express themselves. They panicked and then lost self-direction. For Pan the chase reflects the desire to feel strength through conquest, a need to feel powerful over another rather than to achieve union or consummation. So these myths are a series of tableaus depicting the instinct to conquer triggering an instinctive response of flight or freeze (Larson, 2001; Longus, 1916/1978; Borgeaud, 1979/1988; Ovid, 1955/1986).

These are characteristics in common with today's terrorists displays of power – Pan's sudden attacks in a bucolic landscape makes us remember them – the assault on the everyday life making it all the more horrible, more theatrical, and more memorable. Pan and both the modern day terrorists and random shooters use sudden, surprise attacks, turn innocents into victims, and create an atmosphere where people feel as if evil may spring out at them at any moment of the day or night. In 9/11, in the Paris shootings, and in Orlando, the list seems to never end, the live news coverage show us the attacks in action, the airplane, the towers, the people hanging out the windows at the Bataclan, the wounded carried off by the less wounded in Orlando. We watch as people go into shock and see pain that is inexpressible: scare tactics by terrorists are designed to cause panic.

Fear then haunts the everyday and the group naturally turns to the leaders for answers, who are all too often responding with the same hypermasculine version of the protector archetype. As then President George W. Bush put it "I don't care what the international lawyers say, we are going to kick some ass" (as cited in Clarke, 2004, p. 24) and as the current leader of the country Donald Trump tweets incendiary remarks at world leaders.

> North Korean Leader Kim Jong Un just stated that the "Nuclear Button is on his desk at all times." Will someone from his depleted and food starved regime please inform him that I too have a Nuclear Button,

but it is a much bigger & more powerful one than his, and my Button works!

(as cited in Rucker, 2018, Jan. 2)

The group gives up its self-direction and is unable to mount a reasonable protest to what the leaders tell them to do. Laws like the US Patriot Act and the demolishment of the DACA (Differed Action for Childhood Arrivals) program are rushed through Congress and the rights of the citizens and refugees are diminished. Like the nymphs there is a devolution among ordinary people caused by these events. The result is a split to either a hypermasculine pushback or the cornered nymphs paralysis and therefore lack of new ideas or solutions.

The patriarchal state capitalizes on the grip of the gut level fear in the culture and rapidly beefs up control – in the first days it must – but fear can be subtly manipulated by the state to create restrictions on freedoms for the citizens, to build up troop and arms levels and to retaliate. In efforts to re-establish power, the state strikes back. This could be plainly seen after 9/11 – and now even though the answer from Bush to start a war spectacularly did not work for the US the similar reaction to strike back at ISIS was immediate after the Paris shootings in 2015 and there is no reason to expect this to change.

Besides the early rape myths Pan figured in battle myths. He was said to have saved the Athenians at the battle of Marathon, who then established him in Athens in 490 BCE (Herodotus, 1921/1960). He was a general in the Athenian's war with the Gauls where he created madness in the minds of the Gallic soldiers – rather than fighting the Athenian army they turned on each other and the Athenians won without even having to fight (Pausanias, 1935/1961). He was also a general in Dionysus' army in India, where he used noise and confusion to invoke panic in the enemy (Polyaenus, 1994). Pan egged his enemies on into battles they could not win, hurting themselves much more than their enemies and then outwitted them. This sort of guerilla warfare is something an established patriarchal state has difficulty outsmarting. The terrorists become crafty, clever, cool, the Che Guevara's of today, baiting the West into battles on their terms – ones that are very hard to defend against.

Pan was the ruling local god of Arcadia; he was an isolated source of power over the land touted as the landscape of a bucolic golden age by the later Roman poets (Virgil, 1916/1999; Ovid, 1955/1986). That fantasy has elements in common with fundamentalist apocalyptic pipedreams of a future return to a time of greatness and perfect peace (Lifton, 2003). Populist Donald Trump's "Make America Great Again" campaign is but one example and there is no reason to think that getting rid of Trump would not bring a new, perhaps even more virulent leader into power since the problem is systemic. Aggression to re-establish sole power and control all resources and fundamentalist calls for an apocalyptic return to a better time all are within archetypal purview of Pan and his land of Arcadia and it is awareness of the archetypal that can alter the direction of the future. Like Syrinx who transformed into a nymph a feminine being able to choose her own sexual partners and ran free in a state of impassioned rapture rather than running in a state of panic, the ending is not a foregone conclusion.

Ecological myopia in America

Pan is a nature god. The motifs in Pan's myths repeat stories landscaped in a bucolic, pastoral world, where sudden dangerous interruptions result in panic. The US, though not alone in this, has risen to power because it holds a dominant position over the natural resources of the world. In general, Americans are sluggish about adapting to energy conservation (Searles, 1972). The US population is too large to remain at the pinnacle of energy consumption given the dwindling resources of the planet (Chen & Chen, 2011).

The United States, with less than 5% of the global population, uses about a quarter of the world's fossil fuel resources – burning up nearly 25% of the coal, 26% of the oil, and 27% of the world's natural gas.

As of 2003, the U.S. had more private cars than licensed drivers, and gas-guzzling sport utility vehicles were among the best-selling vehicles. New houses in the U.S. were 38% bigger in 2002 than in 1975, despite having fewer people per household on average ("The State of Consumption Today," 2013, para. 16).

Energy use in the US is unsustainable. It is the most disproportionate to its population numbers of any world nation (Searles, 1972). Even with overwhelming evidence of the destructive nature of overusing resources, many Americans, including President Trump, refuse to "believe" in global warming (Clark & Stevenson, 2003). Eventually, for survival, less energy will have to be used. Perhaps over-dependency on energy in a culture that has independence as a primary value has led to the apathetic denial of the problem and to an underlying anxiety about the future. The culture appears to be in an inflated energy bubble. The cultural complex has inflated attitude by reinforcing selective thinking toward nature and energy consumption. Nature may be on the brink of a panic like reaction with the super hurricanes and out of control wildfires currently plaguing the country.

A cultural complex could be understood to have constellated in political differences regarding global warming and energy consumption. Projections on to the left leaning, environmentalist "tree huggers" and onto the far right, neoconservative Trumpers are creating an atmosphere where discussion and compromise are not possible. The complex is shored up by arguments to defend the "American lifestyle," as if there is one way Americans choose to live, denying that there is a problem or, at best, denying that there is a problem that is "man-made," and suggesting it is caused by natural forces. Conflict, rage, and distancing has led to political stagnation. America is not leading the planet toward environmental prudence and fortitude and its role as a world leader is becoming increasingly challenged in this arena.

The US has not entirely ignored the energy problem. But when world opinion and treaty makers attempt to move forward more rapidly or in a different direction than US political policies have desired, the US has "broodily" refused to compromise, as witnessed in the withdrawal from the Paris Agreement of 2015. Perhaps the survival instinct in the US has built a psychological wall to protect itself against the fear that the American life style will not survive the energy crisis. Aggressive practices, such as fracking and government confiscation of National Monument lands, are short-sighted answers to caring for the burgeoning masses of humans. Nothing stirs people enough to insist on ending unsustainable harvesting of the Earth's resources. More thought and research would be prudent.

Besides these parallels, since hypermasculinity implies, requires really, being cut off from the sensitivity of the feeling function, it promotes self-centered complexes and behaviors in individuals and cultural complexes in groups. Hypermasculinity connects through competition and thus loneliness and inadequacy underlie it (Klein, 2012). This theme also has roots in Pan's myths.

Pan and his mother

In the Homeric hymn to Pan, his mother bore Hermes a noisy son with goat feet and horns. One look at him and she jumped up and ran off without even nursing him.

Whether women or nymphs, feminine figures continued to run from Pan in the myths. He was repeatedly wounded by their rejection. Pan's loneliness and disconnection from nurturing as well as his need to be recognized for his strength and power were there from the beginning in the Homeric hymns. Pan embodies this one aspect of the archetype of masculine power, though obviously masculine power has other, more positive aspects.

So the origin of this archetype is in a conflicted and panicky relationship with archetypal nurturing in the form of mothers, goddesses, women, and nymphs – and even as Pan lost his mother, the hypermasculine archetype of the protector has lost its relatedness. The paucity of nurturance in the modern hypermasculine system not only seen in the political arena but as entertainment in film and sport as the hero becomes more numbed to pain and more one-sided. Rather than looking at their own and the Others (whoever is seen as the enemy) lack of empathy and compassion, instead many people are becoming more and more hardened, hypermasculine, as they witness the media's reliving of weekly random shootings and massacres and then watch TV shows about the same. But, this inflation of the masculine, the state of increasing hypermasculinity, as we have now in many modern cultures, is in a state of flux, volatile and spreading rapidly and haphazardly like a California wildfire, and so anything could happen, including our being able to influence the outcome as the nymphs did in some of the tales.

But do the myths have any real guidance for us? Pan was rustic and crude but does relate positively to the feminine in some myths. Alone the nymphs were Pan's prey, but when they banded together they could mitigate his aggressions and soothe his hypermasculine spirit. When the nymphs united they were not in danger. In one myth, the nymphs surround Pan while he sleeps away the day after a long night on the hunt. They tie him up and are going to shave off his beard, which he highly values. They get back at him in a playful way rather than countering his knee-jerk, angry reactions with ones of their own (Philostratus, 1931/1960).

The circle dance

In the terra-cotta figurines of Pan and the nymphs discovered at the Corycian cave above Delphi the nymphs surround him and yet are safely distanced by the wheel that unites them. A symmetrical harmony was achieved when the archetype of hypermasculinity was centered within the kind, nurturing presence of the nymphs. Rather than the earlier devolutions of the nymphs, the circle dance suggests the possibility of approaching the opposite without anger, but rather as with music and dance, the nymphs are listening to the music, hearing Pan's feelings in his song, while he is watching the movement, seeing the dancers.

The great god pan

Pan is dead. Now that he is dead, he has been named as great. Alive he was never referred to as *Pan-megas* ("Pan the great"), but in the legend he was (Borgeaud, 1979/1988). Perhaps one meaning of the oracular statement was that *now* he is great. He has certainly continued to be an archetypal influence, even if demonized, in many various cultures descended from the Greeks. Like an echo, he continues, as an elusive, wordless reverberation, a din just outside our hearing. The chthonic side of both our internal divinity and our animal nature is not dead. It is waiting, whispering to be echoed, mirrored, and redeemed. Pan did not die. Pan has stayed alive, slinking about in the collective shadows, at the intersections of the human animal and the divine. Like Christ on the cross, both a human animal and divine, he died, and like Christ, Pan did not die.

> The light of Western metaphysics has obscured darkness; sedimented reason has thrown it to the shadows, naming it only as its inferior counterpart. But darkness is also the Other that likewise shines; it is

> illuminated not by light but by its own intrinsic luminosity. Its glow is that of the *lumen naturae*, the light of nature, whose sun is not the star of heaven but Sol niger, the black sun.
>
> (Stanton, 2005, p. 214)

This is a psychological problem for a modern world currently plagued by hypermasculinity, naiveté, and knee-jerk, fear-based reactions. Today the imagination of a once animated world of nature has succumbed to the enlightenment's vision of a mechanistic set of rules, which have pinned down the fluid truth of the psychological.

It is time to do better.

Panic stalks America

Embedded in the Greek myths of the nature god Pan is one way to understand the value of panic. It was understood by the ancients to be a compulsive, unconscious reaction to the divine. Pan's mother's inability to contain her panic made her irrelevant to the trajectory of the myth. From as early as the mid-sixth century BCE, the ancients handed down Pan's storyline, which conveys the message that when humans are unable to endure anxiety, they panic and disconnect from the divine. They, like the nymphs, devolve and, one could say, become irrelevant, fading away into the background.

As in ancient times, lack of self-reflection still causes humans to split off from their panicky feelings. They project the cause of their anxiety onto others who then become the enemy. This, the ancient myths inform us, causes a split from the divine parts of our nature. It disconnects us from the most terrible and beautiful aspects of the divine, which we, like Pan's mother (a human), are able to naturally birth.

Pan as an embodiment of a conjoined split between the divine and the animal continues to fascinate the modern imagination (Boardman, 1997). His insistence on a connection between the aggressive and sexual drives of humans and their innate divinity mirrors the complexity of being human. A failure to understand this has led to a recurring coil of dread, panic, terror, and subsequently paralysis, which is then followed by further aggression. Internal fears and panics continue to be externalized, and so projected onto others. This pattern has caused cultural complexes to multiply, like cogs in a cogwheel, forcing each other along in a lockstep of what appear to be inevitable, negative outcomes.

This pattern mirrors Pan's myths and channels problems toward certain results. The Native American cultures that were emasculated by the American migration west have stagnated. Scapegoated, bullied school children become school shooters and send others into panics. Radical Jihadists imitate American aggression and dominate using military cunning. Raped service men and women are frozen into submission by an apathetic chain of command. The nymphs Pan lusted after were jailed in natural prisons of bark and branches, while today the men and women who dare to speak up and accuse other service men of rape are arrested for adultery and banished from service.

I am suggesting the United States has been unconsciously organizing its success around this archetypal field and that this has led to the historically successful exploitation of the disenfranchised as well as an inflated sense of self embedded in the country's identity. This has caused an over reliance on its ability to impose its will at will. The expansive impulses once alive in the bold spirit of the European colonists of America have grown rusty and settled into a paralysis of initiative toward contemporary American problems. Currently, socio-cultural problems, such as the need for universal healthcare, respect for the rights of the newer immigrants and for all religious proclivities, conscientious protection of the environment, and peaceful solutions to global conflicts have failed to awaken nurturing, empathic considerations or solutions.

The divine and the beastly

As well as a male god of nature, Pan is represented figuratively as both animal and divine. This is commonly interpreted reductively so that he is called a split god (Farnell, 1909/1971). This projection of splitting onto Pan is informative as it is a modern over simplification of a complex issue. Just because Pan is animal and divine does not mean he represented the dichotomy of a simple duality. He was alive in the imagination of the ancients long before his image as a split god even came into being. "Not until the beginning of the fifth century BCE, and after the introduction of his cult in Athens, does the image of Pan take shape" (Eliade, 1987, p. 160).

Pan, as the Greeks understood him, was a healer, diviner, protector of the wild, provider for his cult, *pharmakos*, scapegoat, trusted ally to his friends, warrior, the instinctive life force, sensitive musician, a lonely figure, and the only god in the Greek myths who is said to have died. "Pan is not only the insistent lover in hot pursuit of the nymphs. He is also their faithful companion (*opados*), their guide (*hegetor*) who leads them in dance on the flowery or wooded meadows, and who accompanies their rounds with his pipes" (Doniger, 1991, p. 505). He was both vulnerable and preyed on the vulnerable in the border regions of his mythic territory. Pan is all, and thus symbolic of how to remain vulnerable to the diversities in ourselves, even the repulsive ones, which most naturally leads to greater tolerance of diversity in others, in the natural world, and in understandings of the divine.

Pan's body, half animal and half divine, reminds that in an animated world, the divine is everywhere. But to the Greeks, even though panic was a facet of the divine, it still was not interpreted as a good omen (Dodds, 1973). Panic threatens survival.

Considering the epidemics of school shootings, terrorist acts, and the eruptions of rape in the military, the election of a leader who disregards the rights of many groups, one could say that Pan stalks America. America is unconsciously identifying itself with an isolating and dominating self-interest; the worst of the Pan archetype underlies an emotional infection within the country. The US appears, just like a person stuck in a complex, to be caught in a cultural complex and is faced with problems that are irresolvable from within this complex.

Final thoughts concerning the great god Pan

"Of all the gods and demigods of classical antiquity, beside perhaps Hercules, his [Pan's] image and reputation are the most readily recognized in the modern world" (Boardman, 1997, p. 7). Pan is not lost in moldering library stacks. His darker sides are known on "the street," leaning against closed doors in the shadows, alive in our sudden urgent outbursts, hidden in melancholy late afternoons and rejected feelings and, most certainly, he is alive in our sexuality. "When we give the name of 'sexuality' to what was once experienced as a chthonic divinity . . . an immense tract of external world has dropped into the human psyche" (Neumann, 1954/1993, p. 339).

Like the other gods who bring madness, Dionysus and Cybele, with whom he is often associated, Pan takes possession of humans through irrational terror (Dodds, 1973). He lives at the edge of the domestic world, guarding the goats. Though Pan is wild, his close relationship with goats suggests the gradual taming of the wild, as domestic goats were one of the first animals tamed by Neolithic peoples (Gimbutas, 1991). He remains, psychologically, the partially tamed animal within the psyche, which, with alarming alacrity can override consciousness when provoked. Panic is antithetical to the Greek and Western ideals of rational thought and heroic action, yet corresponds with the other great Hellenic river of thought that the divine (*theos*) is omniscient and therefore all that will happen is known to the divine and cannot be controlled by humankind's rational mind (Dodds, 1973).

Pan represented an unexpected and frightening side of the divine that can suddenly emerge anywhere – an unknown unknown in Rumsfeld's parlance. The legend of his death created just such an uncanny atmosphere with the startling juxtaposition between the everyday and the invisible world of the soul. In the legend "a good many had not finished their after-dinner wine," when the other-world signaled them (Plutarch, 1936/2003b, p. 401 [419B). "Suddenly from the island of Paxi was heard the voice of someone loudly calling Thamus, so that all were amazed" (p. 401 [419B]). Fear, uncertainty, and amazement awakened respect for the unknown invisibles in the travelers.

Fear, uncertainty, and amazement weave through our modern era as well. The domination of the West and more specifically the US will most surely eventually ebb away. But what will rise in its wake? That uncertainty leads to even more fear. And yet there is also the amazement. Amazement at the landing on the moon, at the American election of a man of color, and that men and women can now marry whom they choose in more and more parts of the world. The point of relating the mythic and archetypal to the everyday is not to come up with a sound bite along the lines of Rodney King's (the African American man viciously beaten by the LA police, which led to the LA riots of 1992) plaintive plea "Can we all just get along?" (1992). These are moving, but do not seem to lead us to change.

> In the face of the collective terror, it is important that analysts too, as individuals and as societies, show ourselves capable of reflecting on our responsibilities and our omissions and of elaborating our guilt. In this effort we have important lessons to learn from the post-modern theorists and artists and their reflections on the social implications and functions of terror.
>
> (Connolly, 2003, p. 428).

By realizing that we are in a profound moment full of the possibility of change, that change is becoming inevitable, and that what we think, say, and do will affect the outcome of that change, leads me to look to the universal patterns the Greeks intuitively tapped into, to leave behind the simplistic good guys and bad guys worldview and adopt a more complex and fluid attitude toward the reshaping of the coming global union in order to circumvent the possibility of a global apocalypse. Perhaps by aiming so high, we can manage to muddle through somewhere between the two poles of reinvention or total destruction.

References

Aaron, D. (2008). *In their own words: Voices of Jihad*. Santa Monica, CA: Rand.

Adams, L., & Russakoff, D. (1999, June 12). Dissecting Columbine's cult of the athlete. *The Washington Post*, A1. Retrieved from http://washingtonpost.com/wp-srv/national/daily/june99/columbine12.htm

Adams, M. V. (1996). *The multicultural imagination: "Race," color, and the unconscious*. London, UK: Routledge.

Adams, M. V. (2006). The Islamic cultural unconscious in the dreams of a contemporary Muslim man. *Journal of Jungian Theory and Practice*, *8*(1), 31–40. Retrieved from http://web.ebscohost.com.pgi.idm.oclc.org/ehost

Agathias. (1975). *Agathias: The histories* (J. D. Frendo, Trans.). Berlin, Germany: Walter De Gruyter.

Aisch, G., & Keller, J. (2016, June). What happens after calls for new gun restrictions? Sales go up. *The New York Times*. Retrieved from www.nytimes.com/interactive/2015/12/10/us/gun-sales-terrorism-obama-restrictions.html?_r=0

Alcock, S. (1993). *Graecia Capta: The landscapes of Roman Greece*. Cambridge, MA: Cambridge University Press.

Alcock, S. (1994). Minding the gap in Hellenistic and Roman Greece. In S. Alcock & R. Osborne (Eds.), *Placing the gods: Sanctuaries and sacred space in ancient Greece* (pp. 247–261). Oxford: Clarendon Press.

American Psychiatric Association. (2013). *Diagnostic and statistical manual of mental disorders* (5th ed.). Washington, DC: Author.

Anxiety Disorders Association of America. (2007). *An audit of healthcare at US colleges and universities: Focus on anxiety disorders*. Retrieved from http://adaa.org/living-with-anxiety/college-students

Apuleius, L. (1958). *The golden ass: Being the metamorphoses of Lucius Apuleius* (W. Adlington, Trans., Revised by S. Gaselee). London, UK: William Heinemann. (Original work published 1915)

Aristophanes. (2000). *Birds – Lysistrata – Women at the Thesmophoria* (J. Henderson, Trans.). Cambridge, MA: Harvard University Press.

Aristotle. (1984). *The complete works of Aristotle* (Vol. I., J. Barnes, Ed. & Trans.). Princeton, NJ: Princeton University Press.

Arndt, J., Solomon, S., Kasser, T., & Sheldon, K. (2004). The urge to splurge: A terror management account of materialism and consumer behavior. *Journal of Consumer Psychology (Lawrence Erlbaum Associates)*, *14*(3), 198–212. doi:10.1207/s15327663jcp1403_2

Aronson, R. (1999, Summer). Hope after hope? *Social Research*, 66(2), 471–494. Retrieved from http:// www.jstor.org/stable/40971333

Ars Industrialis. (2017). Pharmakon. Retrieved from http://arsindustrialis.org/pharmakon

Artemidorus. (1975). *The interpretation of dreams: Oneirocritica* (R. J. White, Trans.). Park Ridge, NJ: Noyes Press.

Athanassakis, A. (Trans.). (1976). *The Homeric hymns*. Baltimore, MD: John Hopkins University Press.

Aune, D. (1983). *Prophesy in early Christianity and the ancient Mediterranean world*. Grand Rapids, MI: William B. Eerdsmans Publishing.

Bair, D. (2003). *Jung: A biography*. New York, NY: Back Bay Books.

Barak, G. (2005). A reciprocal approach to peacemaking criminology: Between adversarialism and mutualism. *American Behavioral Scientist*, 9(2), 131–152. doi:10.1177/1362480605051640

Barnes, T. (2009). Eusebius of Caesarea. *The Expository Times*, *121*(1), 1–14. doi:10.1177/0014524609107031

Barrow, R. H. (1967). *Plutarch and his times*. Bloomington, IN: Indiana University Press.

Bates, K. L., & Ward, S. (2014). *America the beautiful*. [Song lyrics]. Retrieved from www.scoutsongs.com/lyrics/americathebeautiful.html

BBC News. (2004, September 16). Iraq war illegal, says Annan. Retrieved from http://bbc.co.uk/2/hi/3661134.stm

Beardsley, A. (1898). Pan reading to a woman by a brook. Plate taken from *The Studio Magazine*, *13*, 62. London, UK. Retrieved from http://heritage-images.com/Preview/PreviewPage.aspx?id=2325309&licenseType=RM&from=search&back=2325309&orntn=2

Bell, R. E. (1991). *Women of classical mythology: A biographical dictionary*. Santa Barbara, CA: ABC-CLIO.

Bercovitch, S. (1975). *The Puritan origins of the American self*. New Haven, CT: Yale University Press.

Berlin, A. (1999). The archeology of ritual: The sanctuary of Pan at *Banias*/Caesarea Philippi. *Bulletin of the American Schools of Oriental Research*, *315*, 27–45. Retrieved from http://web.ebscohost.com.pgi.idm.oclc.org/ehost/detail

Bernstein, N. (2006, April 3). 9/11 detainees in New Jersey say they were abused with dogs. *The New York Times*. Retrieved from http://nytimes.com/2006/04/03/nyregion/03detain.html?pagewanted=alls

Berry, W. (1993). Foreword. In F. Hull (Ed.), *Earth and spirit: The spiritual dimension of the environmental crisis* (pp. 12–18). New York, NY: Continuum.

Bescoby, D., Cawley, G., & Chroston, P. N. (2004). Enhanced interpretation of magnetic survey data using artificial neural networks: A case study from Butrint, Southern Albania. *Archaeological Prospection*, *11*(4) 189–199. doi:10.1002/arp.236

Blumen, L. (2010). *Bullying epidemic: Not just child's play*. Toronto, Canada: Camberley Press.

Boardman, J. (1997). *The great god Pan: The survival of an image*. New York, NY: Thames and Hudson.

Boer, C. (Trans.). (1970). *The Homeric hymns* (Rev. 2nd Ver.). Woodstock, CT: Spring.

Borgeaud, P. (1983). The death of great Pan: The problem of interpretation. *History of Religions*, 22(3), 254–283.

Borgeaud, P. (1988). *The cult of Pan* (K. Atlass & J. Redfield, Trans.). Chicago, IL: University of Chicago Press. (Original work published 1979)

Bowie, E. L. (1970, February). Greeks and their past in the Second Sophist. *Past and Present*, *46*, 3–41.

Boyle, T. C. (2003). *Drop city*. New York, NY: Penguin.

Bremmer, J. (2000). Scapegoat rituals in ancient Greece. In R. Buxton (Ed.), *Oxford readings in Greek religion* (pp. 271–293). Oxford, UK: Oxford University Press.

Brody, J. (2013, January 7). Keeping children safe, and away, from firearms. *New York Times*, D7.

Broodman, S. (2006, May 16). Gifted and tormented. *The Washington Post*. Retrieved from http://washingtonpost.com/wp-dyn/content/article/2006/05/15/AR2006051501103.html

Brown, D. (2011). The devil in the details: A survey of research on Satan in biblical studies. *Currents in Biblical Research*, *9*(2), 200–227. doi:10.1177/1476993X10363030

Brown, J. E. (1992). *Animals of the soul: Sacred animals of the Oglala Sioux*. Rockport, MA: Element.

Browning, E. B. (1900). *The complete poetical works of Elizabeth Barrett Browning* (H. W. Preston, Ed., Cambridge ed.). Boston, MA: Houghton Mifflin.

Bruckner, M. (2011). The Gulf of Mexico dead zone. Retrieved from http://serc.carleton.edu/microbelife/topics/deadzone/

Bulfinch, T. (1855). *The age of fables or stories of gods and heroes*. Boston, MA: Sanborn, Carter, & Bazin.

Bumiller, E. (2001, November 22). Bush says war may go beyond Afghan border. *The New York Times*. Retrieved from http://nytimes.com/2001/11/22/politics/22BUSH.html

Burkert, W. (1979). *Structure and history in Greek mythology and ritual*. Berkeley, CA: University of California Press.

Burkert, W. (1983). *Homo necans: The anthropology of ancient Greek sacrificial ritual and myth* (Peter Bing, Trans.). Berkeley, CA: University of California Press. (Original work published 1972)

Burkert, W. (1985). *Greek religion: Ancient and classical* (J. Raffan & B. Blackwell, Trans.). Cambridge, MA: Harvard University Press. (Original work published 1977)

Bush, G. (1999, November 19). *A distinctly American internationalism*. Retrieved from www.mtholyoke.edu/acad/intrel/bush/wspeech.htm

Bush, G. (2001a, September 11). *Address to the American public*. Retrieved from http://georgewa-whitehouse.archives.gov/news/releases/2001/09/20010911-16.html

Bush, G. (2001b, September 16). *Bush talks about Crusade on Sept 16–2001*. Retrieved from http://youtube.com/watch?v=NsjgjM56HRw

Bush, G. (2001c, September 21). *At O'Hare, President says "Get on board."* Retrieved from http://georgewbush-whitehouse.archives.gov/news/releases/2001/09/20010927-1.html

Cameron, A. (2000). Justin I and Justinian. In A. Cameron, B. Ward-Perkins, & M. Whitby (Eds.), *The Cambridge ancient history: Late antiquity: Empire and successors, A.D. 425–600* (Vol. XIV, pp. 63–85). Cambridge, MA: Cambridge University Press.

Campbell, J. (1972). *The masks of god: Occidental mythology*. New York, NY: Viking Press.

Casey, E. S. (1993). *Getting back into place: Toward a renewed understanding of the place-world*. Bloomington, IN: Indiana University Press.

Cassaligi, J. (2013). Retrieved from www.youtube.com/watch?v=eSueQsVsk_M

Cattell, P. (1933). Review of *the wild boy of Aveyron*. *Psychological Bulletin*, *30*(5), 367–368. Retrieved from http://web.ebscohost.com.pgi.idm.oclc.org/ehost/detail

Ccrjustice.org. (2009, Nov. 3). Five New York men detained and abused in post-9/11 immigration sweeps settle case for $1.26 million. Retrieved from http://ccrjustice.org/newsroom/press-releases/five-new-york-men-detained-and-abused-post-9/11-immigration-sweeps-settle-ca

Chen, Z. M., & Chen, G. Q. (2011). An overview of energy consumption of the globalized world economy. *Energy Policy*, *39*(10), 5920–5928. doi:10.1016/j.enpol.2011.06.046

Cicero, M. T. (1950). *Brutus, on the nature of the gods, on divination, on duties* (H. B. Poteat, Trans.). Chicago, IL: University of Chicago Press.

Clark, D. E. (Ed.). (1981). *Sunset new western garden book*. Menlo Park, CA: Lane.

Clark, N., & Stevenson, N. (2003, June). Care in the time of catastrophe: Citizenship, community and the ecological imagination. *Journal of Human Rights*, *2*(2), 235–246.

Clarke, R. (2004). *Against all enemies: Inside America's war on terror*. New York, NY: Free Press.

Clarke, R., & Newman, G. (2006). *Outsmarting the terrorists*. Westport CT: Greenwood Publishing Group.

Clay, J. S. (2006). *The politics of Olympus: Form and meaning in the major Homeric hymns*. London, UK: Bristol Classical Press.

Clement. (1960). *Clement of Alexandria* (G. W. Butterworth, Trans.). London, UK: William Heinemann. (Original work published 1919)

Cody, W. F. (2011). *The life of Hon. William F. Cody: Known as Buffalo Bill the famous hunter, scout and guide*. Boston, MA: Indypublish.com. Retrieved from https://archive.org/stream/lifeofhonwilliam00buff#page/n9/mode/2up

Cohen, D. (1998). Culture, social organization, and patterns of violence. *Journal of Personality and Social Psychology*, *75*(2), 408–419. doi.10.1037/0022-3514.75.2.408

Cohen, P., Kasen, S., Chen, H., Gordon, K., Berenson, K., Brook, J., & White, T. (2006). Current affairs and the public psyche: American anxiety in the post 9/11 world. *Social Psychiatry and Psychiatric Epidemiology*, *41*(4), 251–260. doi:10.1007/s00127-006-0033-7

Cole, S. G. (2004). *Landscapes, gender, and ritual space: The ancient Greek experience*. Berkeley, CA: University of California Press.

Colman, A. (1995). *Up from scapegoating: Awakening consciousness in groups*. Wilmette, IL: Chiron.

Colvin, G. (2001). The cost of complacency. *Fortune*, *144*(6), 50. Retrieved from http://web.ebscohost.com.pgi.idm.oclc.org/ehost/detail

Connolly, A. (2003). Psychoanalytic theory in times of terror. *Journal of Analytical Psychology*, *48*(4), 407–431. Retrieved from http://0-web.b.ebscohost.com.serlib0.essex.ac.uk/

Connolly, P. (1981). *Greece and Rome at war*. London, UK: Macdonald Phoebus.

Corbett, L. (2004). *Religious function of the psyche*. [Audiotape]. Chicago, IL: Jung Institute of Chicago.

Cox, A. (2013, June 10). The real roots of the US military's epidemic of sexual assault. *The Guardian*. Retrieved from www.theguardian.com/commentisfree/2013/jun/10/us-military-epidemic-sexual-assaults

Cramer, F. H. (1996). *Astrology in Roman law and politics*. Chicago, IL: Ares Publishers.

Crowder, C. (1999, April 23). Martyr for her faith. *The Rocky Mountain News*. Retrieved from http://m.rockymountainnews.com/news/1999/apr/23/martyr-her-faith/

Cullen, D. (2009). *Columbine*. New York, NY: Grand Central Publishing.

David, C.-G., & Grondin, D. (2006). *Hegemony or empire: The redefinition of US power under George W. Bush*. Hampshire, UK: Ashgate Publishing.

Davies, C. (2006). Two of Elizabeth Barrett Browning's Pan poems and their afterlife in Robert Browning's "Pan and Luna". *Victorian Poetry*, *4*(4), 561–569. doi:10.1353/vp.2007.0003

Davis, W. A. (2006). Bible says: The psychology of Christian fundamentalism. *Psychoanalytic Review*, *93*(2), 267–300. Retrieved from http://web.ebscohost.com.pgi.idm.oclc.org/ehost/detail

de Tocqueville, A. (1840). *Democracy in America: Part second: The social influence of democracy*. New York, NY: J. & H. G. Langley.

De Vries, A. (1984). *Dictionary of symbols and imagery*. Amsterdam, Holland: North-Holland Publishing.

Diaz, D. (2016, Sept. 8). Trump defends tweet on military assault. *CNN*. Retrieved from www.cnn.com/2016/09/08/politics/donald-trump-military-sexual-assault/index.html

Dick, K. (Producer) (2012). *The invisible war*. Los Angeles, CA: Chain Camera Pictures.

Dioscorides. (1959). *The Greek herbal of Dioscorides: Materia medica* (R. T. Gunther, Eds.) J. Goodyer, Trans.). New York, NY: Hafner Publishing. (Original work published 1934)

Dodds, E. R. (1965). *Pagan and Christian in an age of anxiety: Some aspects of religious experience from Marcus Aurelius to Constantine*. Cambridge, MA: Cambridge University Press.

Dodds, E. R. (1973). *The Greeks and the irrational*. Berkeley, CA: University of California Press.

Donen, S., & Holt, D., (Producers) & Donen, S. (Director). (1966). *Arabesque* [Motion Picture]. USA: Universal Studios.

Doniger, W. (1991). *Mythologies* (Vol. 1, G. Honigsblum, Trans.). Chicago, IL: University of Chicago Press.

Dover, K. J. (1978). *Greek homosexuality*. Cambridge, MA: Harvard University Press.

Dunlap, P. (2011). A transformative political psychology begins with Jung. *Jung Journal: Culture & Psyche*, *5*(1), 47–64. doi:org/10.1525/jung.2011.5.1.47

eEdinger, E. (1987). *The Christian archetype: A Jungian commentary on the life of Christ*. Toronto, Canada: Inner City Books.

Edmonds, J. M. (Trans.). (1977). *The Greek bucolic poets*. Cambridge, MA: Harvard University Press. (Original work published 1912)

Eliade, M. (Ed.). (1987). *The encyclopedia of religion* (Vol. 11). New York, NY: Palgrave Macmillan.

Emerson, R. W. (2018). *Pan*. Retrieved from https://quod.lib.umich.edu/a/amverse/BAD1982.0001.001/1:9.2.18?rgn=div3;view=fulltext

Engelmann, S., & Bruner, E. (1995). *Reading Mastery II: Storybook 1* (Rainbow Ed.). Worthington, OH: SRA Macmillan/McGraw-Hill. Retrieved from http://http://dictionary.sensagent.com/Pet%20Goat/en-en/

Epicurus. (1964). *Letters principal doctrines and Vatican sayings* (R. M. Geer, Trans.). Indianapolis, IN: Bobbs-Merrill.

Euripides. (1999). *Ion* (D. Kovacs, Ed. & Trans.). Cambridge, MA: Harvard University Press.

Eusebius. (2011). *Praeparatio Evangelica. V, VXII.* Retrieved from http://ccel.org/ccel/pearse/morefathers/files/eusebius_pe_05_book5.htm

Falzeder, E., Trollope, C., & King, K. M. (Ed.). (2002). *The complete correspondence of Sigmund Freud and Karl Abraham* (C. Schwarzacher, Trans.). London, UK: Karnac.

Farnell, L. R. (1909). *The cults of the Greek states* (Vol. 5). Oxford, UK: Elibron Classics.

Farnell, L. R. (1921). *Greek hero cults and ideas of immortality.* Chicago, IL: Ares Publishers.

Farnell, L. R. (1971). *The cults of the Greek states* (Vol. 5). Chicago, IL: Aegaean Press. (Original work published 1909)

FinCEN. (2012). *USA Patriot Act.* Retrieved from http://fincen.gov/statutes_regs/patriot/index.html

Flaccus, G. V. (1963). *Argonautica* (J. J. Mozley, Trans.). Cambridge, MA: Harvard University Press. (Original publication date 1934)

Fontelieu, S. (2013). *Chthonic deities.* SpringerReference. Retrieved from http://springerreference.com/docs/html/chapterdbid/70288.html

FoxNews.com. (2013, June 4). *GOP Senator suggests "hormones" could be behind military assaults.* Retrieved from http://foxnews.com/politics/2013/06/04/gop-senator-stirs-controversy-by-blaming-hormones-for-military-sexual-assaults/

Frazer, J. (2009). *The golden bough: A study in magic and religion* (R. Fraser, Ed.). Oxford, UK: Oxford University Press.

Freud, S. (1912). Über einige Übereinstimmunungen im Seelenleben der Wilden und der Neurotiker. *Imago, 1*, 17–33.

Freud, S. (1938). Totem and taboo. In A. A. Brill (Ed. & Trans.), *The basic writings of Sigmund Freud* (pp. 807–930). New York, NY: Random House.

Frost, R. (1933). *Collected poems of Robert Frost.* New York, NY: Henry Holt.

Frymer, B. (2009, June). The media spectacle of Columbine: Alienated youth as an object of fear. *American Behavioral Scientist, 52*(10), 1387–1404. doi:10.1177/0002764209332554

Fuchs, E. (2012, December 16). How Congress screwed up and let the assault weapons ban expire. *Business Insider.* Retrieved from http://businessinsider.com/why-did-the-assault-weapons-ban-expire-2012-12

Furedi, F. (2007). *Invitation to terror: The expanding empire of the unknown.* London, UK: Continuum.

Futures without violence. (2012). Retrieved from http://web.ebscohost.com.pgi.idm.oclc.org/ehost/pdfviewer/pdfviewer?vid=17&sid=01241208-939a-426d-8b54-70a317690026%40sessionmgr111&hid=128

Galea, S., Ahern, J., Resnick, H., Kilpatrick, D., Bucuvalas, M., Gold, J., & Vlahov, D. (2002). Psychological sequaelae of the September 11 terrorist attacks in New York City. *New England Journal of Medicine, 346*(13), 982–987. Abstract retrieved from www.ncbi.nlm.nih.gov/pubmed/11919308

Germany, R. (2005). The figure of Echo in the *Homeric hymn to Pan. American Journal of Philology, 126*(2), 187–208.

Geronimo. (1996). *Geronimo: His own story: The autobiography of a great patriot warrior.* New York, NY: Penguin.

Gillespie, M. (1999, April 30). Americans have mixed opinions about blame for Littleton shootings. *Gallup*. Retrieved from http://gallup.com/poll/3889/americans-very-mixed-opinions-about-blame-littleton-shootings.aspx

Gimbutas, M. (1989). *The goddesses and gods of old Europe*. Berkeley, CA: University of California Press.

Gimbutas, M. (1991). *The civilization of the goddess* (J. Marler, Ed.). San Francisco, CA: HarperCollins.

Girard, G. (1989). *The scapegoat* (Y. Freccero, Trans.). Baltimore, MD: John Hopkins University Press. (Original work published 1982)

Gladwell, M. (2015, October 19). Thresholds of violence: How school shootings catch on. *New Yorker*. Retrieved from www.newyorker.com/magazine/2015/10/19/thresholds-of-violence

Glassner, B. (1999). *The culture of fear: Why Americans are afraid of the wrong things*. New York, NY: Basic Books.

Glick, P., Fiske, S., Abrams, D., Dardenne, B., Ferreira, M., Gonzalez, R., . . . Yzerbyt, V. (2006). Anti-American sentiment and America's perceived intent to dominate: An 11-nation study. *Basic and Applied Social Psychology*, *28*(4), 363–373. doi:10.1207/s15324834basp2804_10

Goldstein, L., Cohen, A. (Producer) & Bacon, L. (Director). (1953). *The Great Sioux Uprising*. USA: Universal-International.

Goodman, M., & Sherwood, J. (2002). *The Roman world: 44 BC–AD 180*. London, UK: Routledge.

Goodwin, N. (Producer & Director) (1998). *Geronimo and the Apache resistance* in The American Experience. USA: Peace River Films.

Gozawa, J. (2009). The cultural complex and transformative learning environments. *Journal of Transformative Education*, *7*(2), 114–133. Retrieved from http://web.ebscohost.com.pgi.idm.oclc.org/ehost/detail

Greenberg, A. (2012). *Manifest destiny and American territorial expansion: A brief history with documents*. Boston, MA: Bedford/St. Martins.

Grotstein, J. S. (1997). Internal objects or chimerical monsters? The demonic third forms of the internal world. *Journal of Analytical Psychology*, *42*(1), 47–80. Retrieved from http://web.ebscohost.com.pgi.idm.oclc.org/ehost/detail

Grunewald, T. (2004). *Bandits in the Roman empire: Myth and reality* (J. Drinkwater, Trans.). New York, NY: Routledge. (Original work published in 1999)

Gunpolicy.org. (2013). Facts. Retrieved from http://gunpolicy.org/firearms/compare/194/number_of_privately_owned_firearms/31

Guthrie, W. (2011). *This land is your land*. Retrieved from http://woodyguthrie.org/Lyrics/This_Land.htm

Halford, S. (1993). Pan and nymphs: Violence and transformation in psyche and environment. *Anima*, *20*, 57–65.

Hamilton, E. (1969). *Mythology: Timeless tales of gods and heroes*. New York, NY: Warner Books.

Hankin, C., Skinner, K., Sullivan, L., Miller, D., Frayne, S., & Tripp, T. (1999). Prevalence of depressive and alcohol abuse symptoms among women VA outpatients who report experiencing sexual assault while in the military. *Journal of Traumatic Stress*, *12*(4). Retrieved from http://web.b.ebscohost.com.pgi.idm.oclc.org/ehost

Harris, E. (1998–1999). *Unpublished journal of Eric Harris*. Retrieved from http://acolumbinesite.com/eric/writing/journal/jindex.html

Harris, E., & Klebold, D. (1999, March 15). The basement tapes. Retrieved from http://acolumbinesite.com/quotes1.html

Harris, E., & Klebold, D. (2013). Hitmen for hire. Retrieved from http://acolumbinesite.com/hitmen.html

Harrison, J. E. (1991). *Prolegomena to the study of Greek religion*. Princeton, NJ: Princeton University Press.

Hartwell, M. (2013, July 21). Military sexual assault: Tsongas: Concerns go beyond Obama's stance. *Sentinel & Enterprise News*. Retrieved from www.sentinelandenterprise.com/news/ci_23702649/military-sexual-assault

Hayes, R. B. (1922–1926). *Diary and letters of Rutherford Birchard Hayes: Nineteenth president of the United States*. Ed. C. R. Williams. (Vol. III, Diary, May 25, 1879, p. 554). The Ohio State Archaeological and Historical Society. Retrieved from http://ww2.ohiohistory.org/onlinedoc/hayes/Volume03/Chapter37/May25.txt

Health Information Privacy. (2012). *Health information privacy*. Washington, DC: US Department of Health & Human Services. Retrieved from www.hhs.gov/ocr/privacy

Henderson, J. (1984). *Cultural attitudes in psychological perspectives*. Toronto, Canada: Inner City Books.

Henderson, J. (1990). The cultural unconscious. In *Shadow and self: Selected papers in analytical psychology* (pp. 103–113). Wilmette IL: Chiron.

Hernandez, J. (2010, May 24). Vote endorses Muslim center near ground zero. *The New York Times*. Retrieved from www.nytimes.com/2010/05/26/nyregion/26muslim.html

Hero. (2013). *Oxford English dictionary*. Retrieved from www.oed.com.pgi.idm.oclc.org/view/Entry/86297?rskey=2uXxKU&result=1#eid

Herodotus. (1960). *Herodotus* (Vol 1, A. D. Godley, Trans.). London, UK: William Heinemann. (Original work published 1921)

Herodotus. (1971). *Herodotus* (Vol. III, A. D. Godley, Trans.). Cambridge, MA: Harvard University Press. (Original work published 1922)

Hesiod. (2002). Theogeny. In R. Lattimore (Trans.), *Hesiod* (pp. 123–186). Ann Arbor, MI: Ann Arbor Paperbacks.

Hill, W. (Director). (1993). *Geronimo: An American legend*. [DVD]. USA: Columbia (Producer).

Hillman, J. (1975). *Re-visioning psychology*. New York, NY: Harper and Row.

Hillman, J. (1988). *Pan and the nightmare*. Dallas, TX: Spring.

Hillman, J. (2007). Mythic Figures. In *The uniform edition of the writings of James Hillman*, Vol. 6. Thompson, CT: Spring.

Hippel, von K. (2002, August). The roots of terrorism: Probing the myths. *The Political Quarterly*, *73*(1), 25–39. Retrieved from http://web.ebscohost.com.pgi.idm.oclc.org/ehost/detail

Hodgson, G. (2009). *The myth of American exceptionalism*. New Haven, CT: Yale University Press.

Hoefel, R. (1999). *Zitkala-Sa: A biography*. Ed. G. Carr. In The online archive of nineteenth-Century U.S. women's writings. Retrieved from www.facstaff.bucknell.edu/gcarr/19cUSWW/ZS/rh.html

Hoig, S. (1982). *The Sand Creek massacre*. Norman, OK: University of Oklahoma Press.

Holman, E., & Silver, R. (2011). Health status and health care utilization following collective trauma: A 3-year national study of the 9/11 terrorist attacks in the United States. *Social Science & Medicine*, *73*(4), 483–490.

Holtzman, N., Schott, J., Jones, M., Balota, D., & Yarkoni, T. (2011). Exploring media bias with semantic analysis tools: Validation of the contrast analysis of semantic similarity (CASS). *Behavior Research Methods*, 43(1), 193–200. doi:10.3758/s13428-010-0026-z

Homer. (1996). *The Odyssey* (R. Fagles, Trans.). New York, NY: Penguin.

Howlett, D. R. (Ed.). (2005). *Dictionary of medieval Latin from British sources*. Oxford, UK: Oxford University Press.

Hunley, K., & Long, J. C. (2005, February). Gene flow across linguistic boundaries in native North American populations. *Proceedings of the National Academy of Sciences of the United States of America*, *102*(5), 1312–1317. doi:10.1073/pnas.0409301102

Hutchinson, B. (2010, May 19). Tea party leader Mark Williams says Muslims worship a 'monkey god', blasts ground zero mosque. *NY Daily News*. Retrieved from http://articles.nydailynews.com/2010-05-19/local/27064852_1_muslims-ibrahim-hooper-ground-zero

Hyginus. (2013). *Astronomica, Part 1*. Retrieved from www.theoi.com/Text/HyginusAstronomica.html

Irish, M. (2002). Making us stronger. *Journal of Financial Planning*, *15*(9), 10. Retrieved from http://web.ebscohost.com.pgi.idm.oclc.org/ehost/detail

Jefferson, T. (1805, March 4). *Second inaugural address, Monday, March 4, 1805*. Retrieved from www.let.rug.nl/usa/presidents/thomas-jefferson/second-inaugural-address-1805.php

Johnson, R. (1991). *Owning your own shadow: Understanding the dark side of the psyche*. New York, NY: HarperCollins.

Jones, C. P. (1971). *Plutarch and Rome*. Oxford, UK: Clarendon Press.

Jones, W. H. S. (Trans.). (1954). Introduction. In *Pausanias: Description of Greece* (Vol I). Cambridge, MA: Harvard University Press. (Original work published 1918)

Jost, M. (1994). The distribution of sanctuaries in civic space in Arkadia. In S. Alcock & R. Osborne (Eds. & Trans.), *Placing the gods: Sanctuaries and sacred space in ancient Greece* (pp. 217–230). Oxford, UK: Clarendon Press.

Jung, C. G. (1956). The dual mother. In H. Read et al. (Eds.), *The collected works of C. G. Jung* (R. F. C. Hull, Trans.) (Vol. 5, pp. 306–393). Princeton, NJ: Princeton University Press. (Original work published in 1912)

Jung, C. G. (1959a). Archetypes of the collective unconscious. In H. Read et al. (Eds.), *The collected works of C. G Jung* (R. F. C. Hull, Trans.) (Vol. 9, Pt. 1, pp. 3–41). Princeton, NJ: Princeton University Press. (Original work published 1954)

Jung, C. G. (1959b). The concept of the collective unconscious. In H. Read et al. (Eds.), *The collected works of C. G Jung* (R. F. C. Hull, Trans.) (Vol. 9, Pt. 1, pp. 42–53). Princeton, NJ: Princeton University Press. (Original work published 1936–1937)

Jung, C. G. (1959c). The psychological aspects of the kore. In H. Read et al. (Eds.), *The collected works of C. G. Jung* (R. F. C. Hull, Trans.) (Vol. 9, Pt. 1, pp. 182–203). Princeton, NJ: Princeton University Press. (Original work published 1951)

Jung, C. G. (1959d). The psychology of the child archetype. In H. Read et al. (Eds.), *The collected works of C. G. Jung* (R. F. C. Hull, Trans.) (Vol. 9, Pt. 1, pp. 150–181). Princeton, NJ: Princeton University Press. (Original work published 1951)

Jung, C. G. (1959e). The Self. In H. Read et al. (Eds.), *The collected works of C. G. Jung* (R. F. C. Hull, Trans.) (Vol. 9, Pt. II, pp. 23–35). Princeton, NJ: Princeton University Press. (Original work published 1951)

Jung, C. G. (1959f). The shadow. In H. Read et al. (Eds.), *The collected works of C. G. Jung* (R. F. C. Hull, Trans.) (Vol. 9, Pt. II, pp. 8–10). Princeton, NJ: Princeton University Press. (Original work published 1951)

Jung, C. G. (1959g). The syzygy: Anima and animus. In H. Read et al. (Eds.), *The collected works C. G. Jung* (R. F. C. Hull, Trans.) (Vol. 9, Pt. II, pp. 11–22). Princeton, NJ: Princeton University Press. (Original work published 1951)

Jung, C. G. (1960). A review of the complex theory. In H. Read et al. (Eds.), *The collected works of C. G. Jung* (R. F. C. Hull, Trans.) (Vol. 8, pp. 92–106). Princeton, NJ: Princeton University Press. (Original work published 1948)

Jung, C. G. (1965). *Memories, dreams, reflections* (A. Jaffe, Ed., R. Winston & C. Winston, Trans.). New York, NY: Random House. (Original work published 1961)

Jung, C. G. (1967a). Commentary on "The secret of the golden flower." In H. Read et al. (Eds.), *The collected works of C. G. Jung* (R. F. C. Hull, Trans.) (Vol. 13, pp. 1–56). Princeton, NJ: Princeton University Press. (Original work published 1957)

Jung, C. G. (1967b). The Spirit Mercurius. In H. Read et al. (Eds.) *The collected works of C. G. Jung* (R.F.C. Hull, Trans.) (Vol. 13, pp. 191–250). Princeton, NJ: Princeton University Press. (Original work published 1948)

Jung, C. G. (1970). Mysterium coniunctionis. In H. Read et al. (Eds.), *The collected works of C. G. Jung* (R. F. C. Hull, Trans.) (Vol. 14). Princeton, NJ: Princeton University Press. (Original work published 1963)

Jung, C. G. (1973a). Answer to Job. In H. Read et al. (Eds.), *The collected works of C. G. Jung* (R. F. C. Hull, Trans.) (Vol. 11, pp. 355–470). Princeton, NJ: Princeton University Press. (Original work published 1952)

Jung, C. G. (1973b). *Letters* (G. Adler, Ed.) (R. F. C. Hull, Trans.) (Vol. 2). Princeton, NJ: Princeton University Press. (Original work published 1953)

Jung, C. G. (1977a). Definitions. In H. Read et al. (Eds.), *The collected works of C. G. Jung*. (R. F. C. Hull, Trans.) (Vol. 6, pp. 408–486). Princeton, NJ: Princeton University Press. (Original work published 1921)

Jung, C. G. (1977b). The psychology of the transference. In H. Read et al. (Eds.), *The collected works of C. G. Jung* (R. F. C. Hull, Trans.) (Vol. 16, pp. 163–320). Princeton, NJ: Princeton University Press. (Original work published 1946)

Jung, C. G. (1978a). Mind and earth. In H. Read et al. (Eds.) *The collected works of C. G. Jung* (R. F. C. Hull, Trans.) (Vol. 10, pp. 29–49). Princeton, NJ: Princeton University Press. (Original work published 1931)

Jung, C. G. (1978b). The fight with the shadow. In H. Read et al. (Eds.) *The collected works of C. G. Jung* (R. F. C. Hull, Trans.) (Vol. 10, pp. 218–226). Princeton, NJ: Princeton University Press. (Original work published 1946)

Jung, C. G. (1981). The structure of the psyche. In H. Read et al. (Eds.), *The collected works of C. G. Jung* (R. F. C. Hull, Trans.) (Vol. 8, pp. 139–158). Princeton, NJ: Princeton University Press. (Original work published 1931)

Jung, C. G. (1989a). Marginal notes on Wittels: Die sexuelle not. In H. Read et al. (Eds.), *The collected works of C. G. Jung* (R. F. C. Hull, Trans.) (Vol. 18, pp. 393–396). Princeton, NJ: Princeton University Press. (Original work published 1910)

Jung, C. G. (1989b). On psychological understanding. In H. Read et al. (Eds.), *The collected works of C. G. Jung* (R. F. C. Hull, Trans.) (Vol. 3, pp. 179–193). Princeton, NJ: Princeton University Press. (Original work published 1914)

Jung, C. G. (1998). *Jung's Seminar on Nietzsche's* Zarathustra (J. L. Jarrett, Ed.). Princeton, NJ: Princeton University Press. (Original work published 1988)

Kalsched, D. (1996). *The inner world of trauma: Archetypal defenses of the personal spirit.* London, UK: Routledge.

Kalsched, D. (2013). *Trauma and the soul: A psychosocial approach to human development and its interruption.* London, UK: Routledge.

Kappeler, V. E., & Potter, G. W. (2005). *The mythology of crime and criminal justice.* (4th ed.). Long Grove, IL: Waveland.

Kass, J. (2009). *Columbine: A true crime story.* Denver, CO: Ghost Road Press.

Keats, J. (1935). Ode on a Grecian urn. In C. D. Thorpe (Ed.), *Complete poems and selected letters* (pp. 352–354). Indianapolis, IN: Odyssey Press.

Kerenyi, C. (1998). *The gods of the Greeks.* London, UK: Thames and Hudson.

Khalil, E. (2011). The mirror neuron paradox: How far is understanding from mimicking? *Journal of Economic Behavior & Organization*, 77(1), 86–86. Retrieved from http://web.ebscohost.com.pgi.idm.oclc.org/ehost/detail

Kimbles, S. (2000). The cultural complex and the myth of invisibility. In *The vision thing: Myth, politics and psyche in the world* (pp. 155–169). London, UK: Routledge.

Kimbles, S. (2003). Cultural complexes and the collective shadow process. In J. Beebe (Ed.), *Terror, violence and the impulse to destroy: Perspectives from analytical psychology* (pp. 211–234). Einsiedeln, Switzerland: Daimon Verlag.

Kimbles, S. (2006). Cultural complexes and the transmission of group traumas in everyday life. *Psychological Perspectives: A Quarterly Journal of Jungian Thought*, *49*(1), 96–110. doi.org/10.1080/00332920600733040

King, R. (1992). Retrieved from www.youtube.com/watch?v=mDzvLq4Fiu4

Kirby, D. (Director). (2012). *The invisible war.* [DVD]. Los Angeles, CA: Chain Camera Pictures.

Klebold, D. (1997–1999). *Unpublished journal of Dylan Klebold.* Retrieved from http://acolumbinesite.com/dylan/jindex.html

Klebold, S. (2009, November). I will never know why. O, *The Oprah Magazine.* Retrieved from www.oprah.com/world/Susan-Klebolds-O-Magazine-Essay-I-Will-Never-Know-Why.

Klein, J. (2012). *The bully society: School shootings and the crisis of bullying in America's schools.* New York, NY: New York University Press.

Knickerbocker, B. (2012, September 23). Poll finds high level of distrust in the media. Anybody surprised? Retrieved from www.csmonitor.com/USA/DC-Decoder/2012/0923/Poll-finds-high-level-of-distrust-in-the-media.-Anybody-surprised

Knox, J. (2004). From archetypes to reflective function. *Journal of Analytical Psychology, 49*, 1–19. Retrieved from http://web.b.ebscohost.com.pgi.idm.oclc.org/ehost/

Kroeber, A. L., & Kluckhohn, C. (1952). *Culture: A critical review of concepts and definitions*. Cambridge, MA: Peabody Museum of American archæology and ethnology, Harvard University.

Krugman, P. (2011, January, 10). Climate of hate. *The New York Times*, A19.

Kugler, M. B., & Cooper, J. (2010). Still an American? Mortality salience and treatment of suspected terrorists. *Journal of Applied Social Psychology, 40*(12), 3130–3147. Retrieved from http://web.ebscohost.com.pgi.idm.oclc.org/ehost/resultsadvanced

Kurtis, B. (Director). (2008). *Columbine: Understanding why*. [Documentary Film]. New York, NY: A & E Home Entertainment.

Larkin, R. (2007). *Comprehending Columbine*. Philadelphia, PA: Temple University Press.

Larson, B. J. (2001). *Greek nymphs: Myth, cult, lore*. Oxford, UK: Oxford University Press.

Lawrence, D. H. (1936). Pan in America. In E. McDonald (Ed.). *Phoenix. The posthumous papers of D H. Lawrence* (pp. 22–31). New York, NY: Viking.

Leach, M., & Levy, B. (2014). *Geronimo: Leadership strategies of an American warrior*. New York, NY: Gallery.

Lee, E. (2012, March 12). Marines offer brutally honest insight on military rape culture. *Business Insider*. Retrieved from www.businessinsider.com/marines-discuss-military-rape-allegations-2012-3

Levs, J., & Fantz, A. (2013, March 14). Military rape victims: Stop blaming us. *CNN*. Retrieved from www.cnn.com/2013/03/13/us/military-sexual-assault

Lewis, D. (2012). Exceptionalism's exceptions: The changing American narrative. *Daedalus, 141*(1), 101–117. Retrieved from www.http://0-web.a.ebscohost.com.serlib0.essex.ac.uk/ehost/

Lifton, R. J. (2003). *Super power syndrome: America's apocalyptic confrontation with the world*. New York, NY: Thunder's Mouth Press/ Nation Books.

Lincoln, A. (1862, December 1st). Annual message to congress – concluding remarks. Retrieved from www.abrahamlincolnonline.org/lincoln/speeches/congress.htm

Longus. (1955). *Daphnis and Chloe* (G. Thornley, Trans. and Rev. by J. M. Edmonds.). London, UK: William Heinemann. (Original work published 1916)

Longus. (1978). *Daphnis and Chloe* (G. Thornley, Trans. and Rev. by J. M. Edmonds.). London, UK: William Heinemann. (Original work published 1916)

Lu, K. (2013). Can individual psychology explain social phenomena? An appraisal of the theory of cultural complexes. *Psychoanalysis, Culture & Society, 18*(4), 386–404. doi:10.1057/pcs.2013.18

Lucian. (1961). *Lucian* (M.D. MacLeod, Trans.) (Vol. I). London, UK: William Heinemann. (Original work published 1913)

Lucy, J. (2003, February 1). On the scene at the WTC. *Electrical Wholesaling*. Retrieved from http://ewweb.com/news-watch/scene-wtc

Maddox, G. (2003, September). The "crusade" against evil: Bush's fundamentalism. *Australian Journal of Politics & History, 49*(3), 398–411. doi:10.1111/1467-8497.00294

Maguire, B., Weatherby, G. A., & Mathers, R. A. (2002). Network news coverage of school shootings. *The Social Science Journal, 39*(3), 465–470. Retrieved from www.sciencedirect.com/science/article/pii/S036233190200201X

Main, R. (2004). *The rupture of time: Synchronicity and Jung's critique of modern Western culture*. Hove, UK: Brunner-Routledge.

Makinen, G. (2002). *The economic effects of 9/11: A retrospective assessment: Report for Congress*. Washington, DC: Library of Congress. Retrieved from www.fas.org/irp/crs/RL31617.pdf

Marshall, R. D., & Galea, S. (2004). Science for the community: Assessing mental health after 9/11. *Journal of Clinical Psychiatry*, *65*(Suppl. 1), 37–43. Abstract retrieved from http://psycnet.apa.org.pgi.idm.oclc.org/psycinfo/2004-10639-005

Martin, D. (2012, April 14). Rape victims say military labels them "crazy." *CNNHealth*. Retrieved from www.cnn.com/2012/04/14/health/military-sexual-assaults-personality-disorder

Martin, J. (1880). The birth, life and death of the Devil: An argument, in which the beginning and extinction of evil is biblically demonstrated and the popular personal devil proved to be a pagan myth. *Cowen Tracts*. Retrieved from http://.www.jstor.org.serlib0.essex.ac.uk/stable/60200147

McGuire, W. & Hull, R.F.C. (Eds.). (1977). *CG Jung speaking*. Princeton, NJ: Princeton University Press.

McLuhan, T. C. (1972). *Touch the earth: A self-portrait of Indian existence*. New York, NY: Pocket Books.

Meador, B. (2004). Light seven fires: Seize seven desires. In *The cultural complex: Contemporary Jungian perspectives on psyche and society* (pp. 171–184). Hove, UK: Brunner-Routledge.

Meadows, S. (2003, November 3). Ghosts of Columbine. *Newsweek*, pp. 54–57. Retrieved from www.thedailybeast.com/newsweek/2003/11/02/ghosts-of-columbine.html

Melford, G. (Director). (1921). *The sheik*. Famous Players – Lasky Corp. (Producers). [DVD]. US: Paramount.

Memmott, M. (2011). *Native Americans offended by code name "Geronimo" in Bin Laden mission*. Retrieved from www.npr.org/sections/thetwo-way/2011/05/04/135985017/native-americans-offended-by-codename-geronimo-in-bin-laden-mission

Merivale, P. (1969). *Pan the goat-god: His myth in modern times*. Cambridge, MA: Harvard University Press.

Meyer, R. (Director). (2005). *The great Indian wars*. Centre Communications for BCI, A Navarre Corporation (Producer) (3 DVDs). Minneapolis, MN: Navarre.

Monroe Doctrine. (1823). Retrieved from https://web.archive.org/web/20120108131055/http://eca.state.gov/education/engteaching/pubs/AmLnC/br50.htm

Moore, M. (2002). *Bowling for Columbine*. K. Glynn J. Czarnecki (Producer). [Motion Picture] MGM.

Morales, L. (2012, September 21). *U.S. distrust in media hits new high*. Retrieved from www.gallup.com/poll/157589/distrust-media-hits-new-high.aspx

Moritz, M. (2008). A critical examination of honor cultures and herding societies in Africa. *African Studies Review*, *51*(2), 99–117. Retrieved from http://web.ebscohost.com.pgi.idm.oclc.org/ehost/detail

Morwood, J., & Taylor, J. (2002). *The pocket Oxford classical Greek dictionary*. Oxford, UK: Oxford University Press.

Mueller, J. (2005). Simplicity and spook: Terrorism and the dynamics of threat exaggeration. *International Studies Perspectives*, *6*(2), 208–234.

Mueller, J. (2006, September/October). Is there still a terrorist threat? *Foreign Affairs*, *85*(5), 2–8. Retrieved from http://web.ebscohost.com.pgi.idm.oclc.org/ehost/detail

Mulyran, J. (1980). Literary and philosophical interpretations of the myth of Pan from the classical period through the seventeenth century. *Acta Conventus Neo-Latini Turonensis*. Paris, France: Librairie Philosophique J. Vrin.

Muschert, G. (2007). The Columbine victims and the myth of the juvenile super-predator. *Youth Violence and Juvenile Justice*, 5(4), 351–366. doi:10.1177/1541204006296173

Muschert, G. (2009). Frame changing in the media coverage of a school shooting: The rise of Columbine as a national concern. *The Social Science Journal*, *46*(1), 164–170. Retrieved from www.sciencedirect.com/science/article/pii/S0362331908001328

Nagy, J., & Danitz, T. (2000, April 20). *Parental fears heightened by Columbine, poll shows*. Stateline: The daily news service of the Pew Charitable Trusts. Retrieved from www.pewstates.org/projects/stateline/headlines/parental-fears-heightened-by-columbine-poll-shows-85899392145

Nansel, T., Overpeck, M., Pilla, R., Ruan, J., Simons-Morton, B., & Sheidt, P. (2001, April 25). Bullying behaviors among US youth: Prevalence and association with psychosocial adjustment. *JAMA, 285*(16), 2094–2100. Retrieved from http://0-web.ebscohost.com.serlib0.essex.ac.uk/ehost/detai

National Institute on Drug Addiction. (2017). Retrieved from www.drugabuse.gov/drugs-abuse/opioids/opioid-crisis

Nationmaster. (2018). Retrieved from www.nationmaster.com/country-info/profiles

Neumann, E. (1993). *The origins and history of consciousness* (R. F. C. Hull, Trans.). Princeton, NJ: Princeton University Press. (Original work published 1954)

The New York Times. (2013, September 10). Obama's remarks on Syria. Retrieved from www.nytimes.com/2013/09/11/world/middleeast/obamas-remarks-on-syria.html?pagewanted=3&_r=0

Newman, K., & Fox, C. (2009). Repeat tragedy: Rampage shootings in American high school and college settings. *American Behavioral Scientist, 52*(9), 1286–1308. doi:10.1177/0002764209332546

Nicander. (1953). *The poems and poetical fragments* (A. S. F. Gow & A. F. Scholfield, Eds. & Trans.). Cambridge, MA: Cambridge University Press.

NIMH. (2013). *The numbers count: Mental disorders in America*. Retrieved from www.nimh.nih.gov/health/publications/the-numbers-count-mental-disorders-in-america/index.shtml

Nonnos. (1962a). *Dionysiaca* (Vol. I.) (W. H. Rouse, Trans.). London, UK: William Heinemann. (Original work published 1940)

Nonnos. (1962b). *Dionysiaca* (Vol. II.) (W.H.D. Rouse, Trans.). London, UK: William Heinemann. (Original work published 1940)

Nonnos. (1962c). *Dionysiaca* (Vol. III.) (W. H. Rouse, Trans.). London, UK: William Heinemann. (Original work published 1940)

Nugent, W. (2007). The American habit of empire, and the cases of Polk and Bush. *Western Historical Quarterly*, *38*(1), 5–24. Retrieved from http://web.b.ebscohost.com.pgi.idm.oclc.org/ehost/

Nyhan, B. (2012). Does the US media have a liberal bias? *Perspectives on Politics*, *10*(3), 767–771. Retrieved from http://0-web.ebscohost.com.serlib0.essex.ac.uk/ehost/detai

Obama, B. (2009, April 4). *The President's news conference in Strasbourg*. Retrieved from www.presidency.ucsb.edu/ws/index.php?pid=85959

Office of Homeland Security. (2002). *The national strategy for homeland security*. Washington, DC. Retrieved from www.dhs.gov/xlibrary/assets/nat_strat_hls.pdf

Ogle, J., P., Eckman, M., & Leslie, C. A. (2003). Appearance cues and the shootings at Columbine high: Construction of a social problem in the print media. *Sociological Inquiry*, *73*(1), 1–27. Retrieved from http http://0-web.ebscohost.com.serlib0.essex.ac.uk/ehost/detai

O'Keefe, E. (2013, December 19). Congress approves reforms to address sexual assault, rape in military. *The Washington Post*. Retrieved from www.washingtonpost.com/politics/congress-poised-to-approve-reforms-to-address-sexual-assault-rape-in-military/2013/12/19

Osborn, C., Johnson, B., & Fisher, J. (2006). After 9/11 at ground zero: The anxiety-buffering effects of worldview support on the first anniversary of 9/11. *Basic and Applied Social Psychology*, *28*(4), 303–310. doi:10.1207/s15324834basp2804_3

Ovid. (1959). *Fasti* (J. G. Frazer, Trans.). Cambridge, MA: Harvard University Press. (Original work published 1931)

Ovid. (1976). *Metamorphoses* (Vol. II.) (F. J. Miller, Trans.). Cambridge, MA: Harvard University Press. (Original work published 1916)

Ovid. (1977). *Metamorphoses* (Vol. III.) (F. J. Miller, Trans.). Cambridge, MA: Harvard University Press. (Original work published 1916)

Ovid. (1986). *The metamorphoses of Ovid* (Mary M. Innes, Trans.). Middlesex, UK: Penguin. (Original work published 1955)

Ovid. (1989). *Metamorphoses* (Charles Boer, Trans.). Dallas, TX: Spring.

Palatine Anthology. (2017). *Greek anthology. Vol. 1*. Ed. W.R. Paton. 6.253. Retrieved from www.perseus.tufts.edu/hopper/text?doc=Perseus%3Atext%3A2008.01.0472%3Abook%3D6%3Achapter%3D253

Pan Cult. (2013). *Cult titles of Pan*. Retrieved from http:/www.theoi.com/Cult/PanCult.html#Titles

Parker, R. (1983). *Miasma: Pollution and purification in early Greek religion*. Oxford, UK: Clarendon Press.

Parrish, K. (2013, May 7). Obama to military sexual assault victims: "I've got your backs." *U.S. Department of Defense: American Forces Press Service*. Retrieved from http://www.defense.gov/news/newsarticle.aspx?id=119958

Pasquier, A. (1977). Pan et les Nymphes à l'antre corycien. *Bulletin de correspondance hellénique. Supplément*, *4*(1), 365–387. Retrieved from www.persee.fr/doc/bch_0304-2456_1977_sup_4_1_5131

Patterson, C. (1985). "Not worth the rearing": The causes of infant exposure in ancient Greece. *Transactions of the American Philological Association*, *115*, 103–123. Retrieved from www.jstor.org/stable/284192

Pausanias. (1959). *Pausanias: Description of Greece* (Vol. I.) (W. H. S. Jones, Trans.). Cambridge, MA: Harvard University Press.

Pausanias. (1961). *Pausanias: Description of Greece* (Vol. IV) (W. H. S. Jones, Trans.). Cambridge, MA: Harvard University Press. (Original work published 1935)

Pausanias. (2017). *Pausanias: Description of Greece* (Vol. VIII) (W. H. S. Jones, Trans.). Cambridge, MA: Harvard University Press. (Original work published 1918). Retrieved from www.theoi.com/Text/Pausanias8C.htmlPausanias

Perera, S. B. (1986). *The scapegoat complex: Toward a mythology of shadow and guilt*. Toronto, Canada: Inner City Books.

Perice, G. (2006). The culture of collateral damage: A genealogy. *Journal of Poverty*, *10*(4), 109–123. Retrieved from http://web.ebscohost.com.pgi.idm.oclc.org/ehost/resultsadvanced

Perlman, D. (2002). Intersubjective dimensions of terrorism and transcendence. In C. Stout (Ed.), *The psychology of terrorism* (pp. 17–47). Westport, CT: Praeger.

Perry, J. W. (1970). Emotions and object relations. *Journal of Analytical Psychology*, *15*(1), 1–12. Retrieved from http://0-web.ebscohost.com.serlib0.essex.ac.uk/ehost/resultsadvanced

Pfaff, W. (2007, February 15). Manifest destiny: A new direction for America. *The New York Review of Books*. Retrieved from http://www.nybooks.com/articles/archives/2007/feb/15/manifest-destiny-a-new-direction-for-america/

Philostratus. (1960). *Imagines* (A. Fairbanks, Trans.). London, UK: William Heinemann. (Original work published 1931)

Pindar. (1997a). *Nemian odes, Isthmian odes. Fragments* (Vol II) (W. H. Race, Ed. and Trans.). Cambridge, MA: Harvard University Press.

Pindar. (1997b). *Olympian odes, Pythian odes* (Vol. I) (W. H. Race, Ed. and Trans.) Cambridge, MA: Harvard University Press.

Pindar. (2017). Pindar's. *Pythian 8* (G. Nagy, Trans.). Retrieved from https://chs.harvard.edu/CHS/article/display/5307

Plato. (1917). Cratylus. *Plato* (H. N. Fowler, Trans.) (Vol. VI, pp. 6–191). Cambridge, MA: Harvard University Press.

Plato. (1966). Phaedrus. *Plato* (H. N. Fowler, Trans.) (Vol. I, pp. 405–579). Cambridge, MA: Harvard University Press. (Original work published 1914)

Plato. (1971). *Timaeus and Critias* (H. D. P. Lee, Trans.). London, UK: Penguin. (Original work published 1965)

Plato. (2011). *Theaetetus* (Benjamin Jowett, Trans.). Retrieved from http://classics.mit.edu/Plato/theatu.html

Pliny. (1961). *Natural history* (Vol. II.) (H. Rackam, Trans.). London, UK: William Heinemann (Original work published 1942)

Pliny. (1971). *Natural history* (Vol. V.) (H. Rackam, Trans.). London, UK: William Heinemann. (Original work published 1950)

Plutarch. (1969). On quietude. *Moralia* (F. H. Sandbach, Trans.) (Vol. 15, pp. 267–269). Cambridge, MA: Harvard University Press.

Plutarch. (1972). The Greek questions. *Moralia* (F. C. Babbitt, Trans.) (Vol. 4, pp. 176–249). Cambridge, MA: Harvard University Press. (Original work published 1936)

Plutarch. (2003a). Isis and Osiris. *Moralia* (F. C. Babbitt, Trans.) (Vol. 5, pp. 6–191). Cambridge, MA: Harvard University Press. (Original work published 1936)

Plutarch. (2003b). On the obsolescence of the oracles. *Moralia* (F. C. Babbitt, Trans.) (Vol. 5, pp. 350–501). Cambridge, MA: Harvard University Press. (Original work published 1936)

Polyaenus. (1994). *Stratagems of war* (P. Krentz & E. L. Wheeler, Eds. & Trans.) (Vol. I). Chicago, IL: Ares Publisher.

Propertius. (1912). *Propertius* (H. E. Butler, Trans.). Cambridge, MA: Harvard University Press.

Pyszczynski, T., Solomon, S., & Greenberg, J. (2003). *In the wake of 9/11: The psychology of terror*. Washington, DC: American Psychological Association.

Quigley, K. (2005, September). Bug reactions: Considering US government and UK government Y2K operations in light of media coverage and public opinion polls. *Health, Risk & Society*, *7*(3), 267–291. doi:10.1080/13698570500229770

Qumsiyeh, M. (2013). 100 Years of anti-Arab and anti-Muslim stereotyping. *The Prism*. Retrieved from www.ibiblio.org/prism/jan98/anti_arab.html

Rabelais, F. (1955). *The histories of Gargantua and Pantagruel* (J. M. Cohen, Trans.). Hammondsworth, UK: Penguin.

RealClearPolitics (2017, September 22). *Polls*. Retrieved from www.realclearpolitics.com/epolls/other/direction_of_country-902.html

REB-VoDKA. (n. d.). *Eric & Dylan home video 2*. Retrieved from www.dailymotion.com/video/x9jbbc_eric-dylan-home-video-2_people#.UO8VMInjmxA

Richardson, E. G., & Hemenway, D. (2003). *Homicide, suicide, and unintentional firearm fatality: Comparing the United States with other high-income countries*. Retrieved from www.ncbi.nlm.nih.gov/pubmed/20571454

Richey, W., & Feldmann, L. (2003, September 12). Has post-9/11 dragnet gone too far? *Christian Science Monitor*, *95*(202), 1. Retrieved from http://web.ebscohost.com.pgi.idm.oclc.org/ehost/resultsadvanced

Riley, C. L. (1995). *Rio del Norte: People of Upper Rio Grande from earliest times to Pueblo revolt*. Salt Lake City, UT: University of Utah Press.

Risen, J. (2012, November 2). Military has not solved problem of sexual assault, women say. *The New York Times*. Retrieved from www.nytimes.com/2012/11/02/us/women-in-air-force-say-sexual-misconduct-still-rampant.html?_r=0

Robbins, T. (1984). *Jitterbug perfume*. New York, NY: Bantam.

Rohloff, A. (2011). Extending the concept of moral panic: Elias, climate change and civilization. *Sociology*, *45*(4), 634–649. doi:10.1177/0038511406597

Roscher, W. H. (1988). Ephialtes: A pathological-mythological treatise on the nightmare in classical antiquity. In *Pan and the nightmare* (pp. 68–149). Dallas, TX: Spring. (Original work published 1892)

Rosen, D. A. (2007). Robert J. Miller. Native America, discovered and conquered: Thomas Jefferson, Lewis and Clark, and manifest destiny. *The American Historical Review*, *112*(3), 845–846. Retrieved http://web.ebscohost.com.pgi.idm.oclc.org/ehost/pdfviewer/pdfviewer

Rosivach, V. (1987). Autochthony and the Athenians. *Classical Quarterly*, *37*, 294–306.

Ross, L., & Nisbett, R. (2011). *The person and the situation: Perspectives of social psychology*. London, UK: Pinter & Martin.

Rowland, S. (2002). *Jung: A feminist revision*. New York, NY: Blackwell.

Rucker, P. (2018, January 2). Trump to North Korean leader Kim: My "nuclear button" is "much bigger and more powerful." *The Washington Post*. Retrieved from www.washingtonpost.com/news/post-politics/wp/2018/01/02/trump-to-north-korean-leader-kim-my-nuclear-button-is-much-bigger-more-powerful/?tid=a_mcntx&utm_term=.b19d2f1f31f0

Rudin, S., Schmidt, A., Schroeder, A., Webb, J., & Zanuck, R., (Producers) & Friedkin, W. (Director). (2000). *Rules of engagement* [Motion Picture]. US: Paramount.

Rumsfeld, D. (2006). Retrieved from www.youtube.com/watch?v=_RpSv3HjpEw

Russell, D. (Trans.). (1993). *Plutarch: Selected essays and dialogues.* Oxford, UK: Oxford University Press.

Sailer, H., & Kolb, E. (1995). Influence of craniofacial surgery on the social attitudes toward the malformed and their handling in different cultures and at different times: A contribution to social world history. *The Journal of Craniofacial Surgery*, *6*(4), [Abstract]. Retrieved from http:// http://0-web.ebscohost.com.serlib0.essex.ac.uk/ehost/resultsadvanced

Sallares, R. (1991). *The ecology of the ancient Greek world.* Ithaca, NY: Cornell University Press.

Samuels, A. (1985). *Jung and the post-Jungians.* London, UK: Tavistock/Routledge.

Samuels, A. (1989). *The plural psyche: Personality, morality and the father.* London, UK: Routledge.

Samuels, A. (1991). Foreword. In P. Young-Eisendrath and J. Hall's *Jung's self psychology: A constructivist perspective* (pp. vii–x). New York, NY: Guilford Press.

Samuels, A. (1993a). *The political psyche.* London, UK: Routledge.

Samuels, A. (1993b). The mirror and the hammer: Depth psychology and political transformation. *Free Associations, 3*(4), 545–589. Retrieved from http://web.ebscohost.com.pgi.idm.oclc.org/ehost/resultsadvanced

Samuels, A. (2004). Foreword. In J. S. Baumlin, T. Baumlin, and G.H. Jensen (Eds.) *Post-Jungian criticism: Theory and practice* (pp. vii–xiv). Albany, NY: State University of New York Press.

Samuels, A., Shorter, B., & Plaut, F. (2005). *A critical dictionary of Jungian analysis.* London, UK: Routledge.

Schofield, L. (2005, July/August). The great god Pan in southern Albania. *Minerva*, 16,

Schwartz, J., Beaver, K., & Barnes, J.C. (2015). The association between mental health and violence among a nationally representative sample of college students from the United States. *U.S.: Public Library of Science.* Retrieved from http://web.b.ebscohost.com.pgi.idm.oclc.org/ehost

Schwartz-Salant, N. (1991). *Mythology and clinical practice* [CD]. Evanston, IL: C. G. Jung Institute of Chicago.

Scott, R. (Ed.). (2004). *Eyewitness to the old west: First hand accounts of exploration, adventure, and peril.* Lanham, MD: Robert Rinehart Publishers.

Searles, H. F. (1972). Unconscious processes in relation to the environmental crisis. *Psychoanalytic Review*, *59*(3), 361–374. Retrieved from http://0-www.pep-web.org.serlib0.essex.ac.uk/document.php?id=psar.059.0361a

Segal, C. P. (1969). *Landscape in Ovid's Metamorphoses: A study in the transformations of a literary symbol.* Wiesbaden, Germany: Franz Steiner Verlag GMBH.

Segal, R. (1998a). *Jung on mythology.* Princeton, NJ: Princeton University Press.

Segal, R. (1998b). *Theology as psychology: An approach to the Bible* [CD]. Evanston, IL: C. G. Jung Institute of Chicago.

Segal, R. (2003). Jung's very twentieth-century view of myth. *Journal of Analytical Psychology*, *48*(5), 593–617. Retrieved from http://0-web.ebscohost.com.serlib0.essex.ac.uk/ehost/pdfviewer

Shahshahani, A. (2011). Reflections on the occasion of the tenth anniversary of September 11. *Race/Ethnicity: Multidisciplinary Global Perspectives*, *4*(3), 449–454, Retrieved from http://muse.jhu.edu/results#type=ajax&startYear=&stopYear=&limits=subscription:Y&terms=content:Reflections%20occasion%20tenth%20anniversary%20September

Shamdasani, S. (2005). *Jung and the making of modern psychology: The dream of a science*. Cambridge, MA: Cambridge University Press.

Siegal, P. (2012, December 29). Letter to the editor. *The New York Times*, p. A16.

Simpson, D. P. (Ed.). (1968). *Cassell's Latin dictionary*. New York, NY: Simon & Schuster Macmillan.

Singer, T. (2004). The cultural complex and archetypal defenses of the group spirit: Baby Zeus, Elian Gonzales, Constantine's Sword, and other holy wars (with special attention to the "axis of evil"). In T. Singer & S. Kimbles (Eds.) *The cultural complex: Contemporary Jungian perspectives on psyche and society* (pp. 13–34). Hove, UK: Brunner-Routledge.

Singer, T. (2006). The cultural complex: A statement of the theory and its application. In Panel: The transcendent function in society. *Psychotherapy and Politics International*, *4*(3), 197–212. Retrieved from http://0-web.ebscohost.com.serlib0.essex.ac.uk/ehost

Singer, T. (2010). The transcendent function and cultural complexes: A working hypothesis. In Meador, Singer, and Samuels, Panel: The transcendent function in society. *Journal of Analytical Psychology*, *55*(2), 228–253. doi:10.1111/j.1468-5922.2010.01838_2.x

Singer, T., & Kimbles, S. (2004). Introduction. In T. Singer & S. Kimbles (Eds.), *The cultural complex: Contemporary Jungian perspectives on psyche and society* (pp. 1–9). Hove, UK: Brunner-Routledge.

Sipri. (2014). *SIPRI military expenditure database*. Retrieved from http://milexdata.sipri.org/files/?file=SIPRI+military+expenditure+database+1988-2013.xlsx.

Slattery, D. P. (2012). *Riting myth, mythic writing: Plotting your personal story*. Carmel, CA: Fisher King Press.

Slavin, E. (2013, July 30). USS Germantown chief petty officer sentenced for sexual assault. *Stars and Stripes*. Retrieved from www.stripes.com/news/pacific/uss-germantown-chief-petty-officer-sentenced-for-sexual-assault-1.232848

Slovenko, R. (2005). Euphemisms. *Journal of Psychiatry & Law*, *33*(4), 533–548. Retrieved from http://web.ebscohost.com.pgi.idm.oclc.org/ehost/pdfviewer

Slutkin, G. (2012). *Contagion of violence*. The Contagion of Violence: A Workshop of the Forum on Global Violence Prevention. Retrieved from www.iom.edu/~/media/files/activity%20files/global/violenceforum/2012

Slutkin, G. (2013). *What if we treated violence like a contagious disease?* TEDMED 2013. Retrieved from www.tedmed.com/speakers/show?id=75342

Smith, S. F. (2011). *My country tis of thee*. Retrieved from www.cyberhymnal.org/bio/s/m/i/smith_sf.htm

Sophocles. (1994). *Ajax – Electra – Oedipus tyrannus* (H. Lloyd-Jones, Ed.) (H. Lloyd-Jones, Trans.). Cambridge, MA: Harvard University Press.

Speier, J. (2012, June 21). Why rapists get away with it. *CNNOpinion*. Retrieved from www.cnn.com/2012/06/21/opinion/speier-military-rape

Spencer, J. W., & Muschert, G. (2009). The contested meaning of the crosses at Columbine. *American Behavioral Scientist*, *52*(10), 1371–1386. doi:10.1177/0002764209332553

Spiegel, A. (2005, January 3). The dictionary of disorder: How one man revolutionized psychiatry. *The New Yorker*, pp. 56–63.

Stan, A. (2013, May 30). Obama, Hagel offer lip service on military sexual assault. *RHReality Check: Reproductive Sexual Health and Justice*. Retrieved from http://rhrealitycheck.org/article/2013/05/30/obama-hagel-offer-lip-service-on-military-sexual-assault/

Stanton, M. (2005). *The black sun: The Alchemy and art of darkness*. College Station, TX: Texas A & M University Press.

The State of Consumption Today. (2013). *WorldWatch Institute*. Retrieved from www.worldwatch.org/node/810

Statistics Canada. (2010). *CANSIM*. Retrieved from http://www40.statcan.ca/l01/cst01/legal12a-eng.htm

Strabo. (1949). *The geography of Strabo* (H. L. Jones, Trans.) (Vol. I–XVII). London, UK: William Heinemann. (Original work published 1932) Retrieved from http://penelope.uchicago.edu/Thayer/E/Roman/Texts/Strabo/home.html

Stein, M. (1995). Introduction. In *Jung and evil* (pp. 1–24). Princeton, NJ: Princeton University Press.

Stein, M. (1998). *Jung's map of the soul: An introduction*. Chicago, IL: Open Court.

Stein, M. (2004). On the politics of individuation in the Americas. In T. Singer & S. Kimbles (Eds), *The cultural complex: Contemporary Jungian perspectives on psyche and society* (pp. 292–273). Hove, UK: Brunner-Routledge.

Steinhauer, J. (2013, March 13). *Veterans testify on rapes and scant hope of justice*. Retrieved from www.nytimes.com/2013/03/14/us/politics/veterans-testify-on-rapes-and-scant-hope-of-justice.html?_r=0

Stevens, A. (1998). Response to P. Pietikainen. *Journal of Analytical Psychology*, *43*(3), 345–355. Retrieved from http://web.ebscohost.com.pgi.idm.oclc.org/ehost/detail

Sundaresan, S., & Wang, Z. (2008, March). Y2K options and the liquidity premium in treasury markets. *The Review of Financial Studies*, *22*(3), 1022–1056. Retrieved from http://0-web.ebscohost.com.serlib0.essex.ac.uk/ehost/pdfviewer

Swiney, C. (2006). Racial profiling of Arabs and Muslims in the US: Historical, empirical, and legal analysis applied to the war on terrorism. *Muslim World Journal of Human Rights*, *3*(1), 1053, Retrieved from www.degruyter.com/view/j/mwjhr.2006.3.1/mwjhr.2006.3.1.1053/mwjhr.2006.3.1.1053.xml

Szaluta, J. (1999). *Psychohistory: Theory and practice*. New York, NY: Peter Lang.

Tate, M. E. (1992). Satan in the Old Testament. *Review & Expositor*, *89*(4), 461–474. Retrieved from http://ATLA Religion Database with ATLASerials

Tatius, A. (1969). *Achilles Tatius* (S. Gaselee, Trans.). London, UK: William Heinemann. (Original work published 1917)

Theocritus. (1999). *Theocritus: A Selection: Idylls 1, 3, 6, 7, 10, 11 and 13*. Ed. R. Hunter Cambridge, MA: Cambridge University Press.

Theophrastus. (1977). *Enquiry into plants and other minor works on odours and weather signs*. (Vol II.) (A. Hort, Trans.) Cambridge, MA: Harvard University Press. (Original work published 1926)

Thistlethwaite, S. (2013, May 7). Because they can: Three rapes every hour in the military. *The Washington Post*. Retrieved from www.washingtonpost.com/blogs/on-faith/wp/2013/05/07/because-they-can-three-rapes-every-hour-in-the-military

Tonso, K. L. (2009). Violent masculinities as tropes for school shooters: The Montréal massacre, the Columbine attack, and rethinking schools. *American Behavioral Scientist*, *52*(10), 1266–1285. doi:10.1177/0002764209332545

del Toro, G. (Director) (2001). *The devil's backbone*. [Motion Picture]. Almodóvar, P. & del Toro, G. (Producers). Spain: Warner Sogefilms A. I.E.

del Toro, G. (Director) (2006a). *Pan's labyrinth*. [Motion Picture]. Navarro, B., Cuarón, A., Propertis Torresblanco, F., & Augustin, A. (Producers). Mexico: Picturehouse Films.

del Toro, G. (Director) (2006b). *Pan's labyrinth: Director's analysis*. [DVD]. Navarro, B., Cuarón, A., Torresblanco, F., & Augustin, A. (Producers). Mexico: Picturehouse Films.

Traut, B. (2005). The role of coastal ecotones: A case study of the salt marsh: Upland transition zone in California. *Journal of Ecology 93*(2), 279–290. doi:0.1111/j.1365-2745.2005.00969.x

Trump, D. (2017, January 20). *The inaugural address*. Retrieved from www.whitehouse.gov/briefings-statements/the-inaugural-address/

Twenge, J. M. (2011). Generational differences in mental health: Are children and adolescents suffering more, or less? *American Journal of Orthopsychiatry*, *81*(4), 469–472. doi:10.1111/j.1939-0025.01115x

Tzaferis, V. (1992). Cults and deities worshipped at Caesarea Philippi-Banias. In E. Ulrich, J. W. Wright, R. P. Carroll, & P. R. Davies (Eds.), *Priests, Prophets, and Scribes* (pp. 190–201). Sheffield, UK: Sheffield Academic Press.

US National Churchill Museum. (2017). *Week ahead: Let's hope Churchill was wrong about Americans*. Retrieved from www.nationalchurchillmuseum.org/10-07-13-lets-hope-churchill-was-wrong-about-americans.html

Usmilitary.about.com. (2013). *Careers US Military*. Retrieved from http://usmilitary.about.com/od/marines/l/aamarines.htm

Vanderau, N. (2013). *Columbine: Understanding why*. Retrieved from www.youtube.com/watch?feature=player_detailpage&v=KikvzIlNg9g

Vang, C. T. (2010). *An educational psychology of methods in multicultural education*. New York, NY: Peter Lang.

Vaughan, K. (2001, March 7). *Harris, Klebold have admirers: Columbine killers are honored on web sites: Mimicked by teens who are outcasts*. Retrieved from http://m.rockymountainnews.com/news/2001/mar/07/harris-klebold-have-admirers/

Venn, C. (2002). World dis/order: On some fundamental questions. *Theory, Culture and Society*, *19*(4), 121–136. doi:10.1177/0263276402019004009

Vernant, J.-P., & Vidal-Nauet, P. (1981). *Tragedy and myth in ancient Greece* (J. Lloyd, Trans.). Sussex, UK: Harvester Press. (Original work published 1972)

Virgil. (1999). *Ecologues – Georgics – Aenid I–VI* (H. R. Fairclough, Trans., Revised by G. P. Goold). Cambridge, MA: Harvard University Press. (Original work published 1916)

Virgil. (2011). *Ecologue* X. Retrieved from http://classics.mit.edu/Virgil/eclogue.mb.txt

Volkan, V. (2002). September 11 and societal regression. *Group Analysis*, *35*(406), 456–483. doi:10.1177/0533160260620733

von Franz, M.-L. (1972). *The feminine in fairytales*. Dallas, TX: Spring.

von Franz, M.-L. (1980). *A psychological interpretation of the golden ass of Apuleius*. Irving, TX: Spring.

Wackernage, W., & Vale, J. (1999). Two thousand years of heresy: An essay. *Diogenes*, *47*(187), 134–148. doi:10.1177/039219219904718713

Wanger, W. (Producer) & Ford, J. (Director). (1939). *Stagecoach*. USA: United Artists.

The Washington Post. (2002). Text of President Bush's 2002 state of the union address. Retrieved from www.washingtonpost.com/wp-srv/onpolitics/transcripts/sou012902.htm

Watkins, M., & Shulman, H. (2010). *Toward psychologies of liberation*. New York, NY: Palgrave Macmillan.

Watson, J. (2013, July 4). Marines survey: About 17 percent of male soldiers would leave if women move to combat roles. Retrieved from www.huffingtonpost.com/2013/02/01/marines-survey-women_n_2600382.html

Webster's unabridged dictionary. (1983). (2nd ed.). New York, NY: Simon and Schuster.

Weissman, J., Russell, D., Jay, M., Beasley, J., Malaspina, D., & Pegas, C. (2017). Disparities in health care utilization and functional limitations among adults with serious psychological distress, 2006–2014. *Psychiatric Services*. doi:org/10.1176/appi.ps.201600260. Retrieved from http://ps.psychiatryonline.org/doi/10.1176/appi.ps.201600260

White, J. (Producer) & Witney, W. (Director). (1953). *The old overland trail*. USA: Republic Pictures.

Whitmont, E. C. (1991). *The symbolic quest: Basic concepts of analytical psychology*. Princeton, NJ: Princeton University Press.

Williams, G., & Leavitt, L. (2004, February). How Pan got his tail: The fusion of medicine, art, and myth. *Nisus: Neurology and the Humanities*, *62*(3), 519–522. Retrieved from www.neurology.org/content/62/3/519.full.pdf

Wilson, W. (1917). *Woodrow Wilson, war message to Congress, 1917*. Retrieved from http://wps.prenhall.com/wps/media/objects/107/110495/ch22_a2_d1.pdf

Wolfe, T. (1979). *The right stuff*. New York, NY: Bantam Books.

Wood, G. (2011). *The idea of America: Reflections on the birth of the United States*. New York, NY: Penguin.

Woodward, B. (2004). *Plan of attack*. New York, NY: Simon & Schuster.

Wordsworth, W. (1982). *The poetical works of Wordsworth* (Cambridge Ed.). Boston, MA: Houghton Mifflin.

The World Economic Forum Davos, Switzerland. (2007, January 27). *Rupert Murdock of News Corp/Fox News as aired on CSPAN*. Retrieved from www.youtube.com/watch?v=0K2pLo8JV5Y

World Press Review Online. (2012). *The United Nations, international law, and the war in Iraq*. Retrieved from http://worldpress.org/specials/iraq

Zero Tolerance. (2012). *Information regarding zero tolerance for firearms in schools*. California Department of Education. Retrieved from www.cde.ca.gov/ls/ss/se/zerotolerance.asp

Zimbardo, P. (2007). *The Lucifer effect: Understanding how good people turn evil*. New York, NY: Random House.

Zuckerman, S. (2002, September 8). 9–11–01: Impact on business; American consumers kept economy going. *The San Francisco Chronicle*, G1. Retrieved from www.sfgate.com/cgi-bin/article.cgi?f=/c/a/2002/09/08/BU1537.DTL

Index

9780367466404